全国英语专业博雅系列教材/总主编　丁建新

语　言　学
LINGUISTICS

吴红岩　编著

中山大学出版社
·广州·

版权所有　翻印必究

图书在版编目（CIP）数据

语言学/吴红岩编著 . —广州：中山大学出版社，2013.8
（全国英语专业博雅系列教材/总主编　丁建新）
ISBN 978 - 7 - 306 - 04650 - 5

Ⅰ. ①语…　Ⅱ. ①吴…　Ⅲ. ①语言学—高等学校—教材　Ⅳ. ①H0

中国版本图书馆 CIP 数据核字（2013）第 196420 号

出 版 人：徐　劲
策划编辑：熊锡源
责任编辑：熊锡源
封面设计：曾　斌
责任校对：施兰娟
责任技编：何雅涛
出版发行：中山大学出版社
电　　话：编辑部 020 - 84111996，84113349，84111997，84110779
　　　　　发行部 020 - 84111998，84111981，84111160
地　　址：广州市新港西路 135 号
邮　　编：510275　　传　真：020 - 84036565
网　　址：http://www.zsup.com.cn　E-mail：zdcbs@mail.sysu.edu.cn
印 刷 者：广州中大印刷有限公司
规　　格：787mm×960mm　1/16　15.5 印张　339 千字
版次印次：2013 年 8 月第 1 版　2013 年 8 月第 1 次印刷
印　　数：1 ~ 4000 册　　定　价：36.00 元

如发现本书因印装质量影响阅读，请与出版社发行部联系调换

全国英语专业博雅系列教材编委会

总主编　丁建新（中山大学）

编　委　会

李鸿儒（黑龙江大学）
司显柱（北京交通大学）
赵彦春（天津外国语大学）
田海龙（天津商业大学）
夏慧言（天津科技大学）
李会民（河南科技学院）
刘承宇（西南大学）
施　旭（浙江大学）
辛　斌（南京师范大学）
杨信彰（厦门大学）
徐畅贤（湖南城市学院）
李玉英（江西师范大学）
李发根（江西师范大学）
肖坤学（广州大学）
宫　齐（暨南大学）
张广奎（广东财经大学）
温宾利（广东外语外贸大学）
杜金榜（广东外语外贸大学）
阮　炜（深圳大学）
张晓红（深圳大学）

博雅之辩（代序）

大学精神陷入前所未有的危机，许多人在寻找出路。

我们坚持，提倡博雅教育（Liberal Education）。因为大凡提倡什么，关键在于审视问题的症结何在，对症下药。而当下之困局，根源在于功利，在于忘掉了教育之根本。

博雅教育之理念，可以追溯至古罗马人提倡的"七艺"：文法、修辞、辩证法、音乐、算术、几何、天文学。其目的在于培养人格完美的自由思考者。在中国教育史上，博雅的思想，古已有之。中国儒家教育的传统，强调以培养学生人格为核心。儒家"六艺"，礼、乐、射、御、书、数，体现的正是我们所讲的博雅理念。"学识广博，生活高雅"，在这一点上，中国与西方，现代与传统，并无二致。

在古罗马，博雅教育在于培育自由的人格与社会精英。在启蒙时代，博雅教育意指解放思想，破除成见。"什么都知道一点，有些事情知道得多一点"，这是19世纪英国的思想家约翰·斯图亚特·密尔（John Stuart Mill）对博雅的诠释。同一时期，另外一位思想家，曾任都柏林大学校长的约翰·亨利·纽曼（John Henry Newman）在《大学理念》一书中，也曾这样表述博雅的培养目标："如果必须给大学课程一个实际目标，那么，我说它就是训练社会的良好成员。它的艺术是社会生活的艺术，它的目的是对世界的适应……大学训练旨在提高社会的精神格调，培养公众的智慧，纯洁一个民族的趣味"。

博雅教育包括科学与人文，目标在于培养人的自由和理性的精神，而不是迎合市场与风俗。教育的目标在于让学生学会尊重人类生活固有的内在价值：生命的价值、尊严的价值、求知的价值、爱的价值、相互尊重的价值、自我超越的价值、创新的价值。提倡博雅教育，就是要担当这些价值守护者的角色。博雅教育对于我们来说，是一种素质教育、人文教育。人文教育关心人类的终极目标，不是以"有用"为标准。它不是"万金油"，也无关乎"风花雪月"。

在美国，专注于博雅教育的大学称为"文理学院"，拒绝职业性的教育。在中国香港，以博雅教育为宗旨的就有岭南大学，提倡"全人教育"；在台湾大学，博雅教育是大学教育的基础，课程涉及文学与艺术、历史思维、世界文明、道德与哲学、公民意识与社会分析、量化分析与数学素养、物质科学、生命科学等八大领域。在欧洲，博雅教育历史中的七大范畴被分为"三道"（初级）与"四道"（高级）。前者包括语法、修辞与辩证法，后者包括算术、几何、天文与音乐。在中国大陆的中山大学，许多有识之士也提倡博雅之理念，让最好的教授开设通识课程，涉及现代学科之环境、生物、地理等各门。同时设立"博雅学院"，学拉丁，读古典，开风气之先。

外语作为一门人文性很强的学科，尤其有必要落实博雅之理念。对于我们来说，最好的"应用型"教育在于博雅。早在20世纪20～40年代，在水木清华的外文系，吴宓先生提倡"语""文"并重，"中""西"兼修，教学上提倡自主学习与互动研究。在《西洋文学系学程总则》中，吴宓明确了"博雅之士"的培养目标：

本系课程编写的目的为使学生：（甲）成为博雅之士；（乙）了解西洋文明之精神；（丙）熟读西方文学之名著，谙悉西方思想之潮流，因而在国内教授英、德、法各国语言文字及文学，足以胜任愉快；（丁）创造今日之中国文学；（戊）汇通东西方之精神而互为介绍传布。

博雅之于我们，不仅仅是理念，更重要的是课程体系，是教材，是教法，是实践，是反应试教育，是将通识与专业熔于一炉。基于这样的理念，我们编写了这套丛书。希望通过这样的教育，让我们的学生知道人之为人是有他内在的生活意义，告诉我们的学生去求知，去阅读，去思考，去创造，去理解世界，去适应社会，去爱，去相互尊重，去审美，去找回精神的家园。

无需辩驳，也不怕非议。这是我们的坚守。

中山大学外国语学院　教授、博士生导师
中山大学语言研究所　所长
丁建新
2013年春天

序

吴红岩先生编写的语言学教材就要出版了,邀请我在前面写几句话。

记得徐烈炯学生曾经说过,在一门学科的教材已经较多的情况下,再来编写教材一定要有自己的特色。国内的外语语言学教材已经不少,高校常用的有胡壮麟和戴炜栋的两部教材,还有些学校是直接使用外国的教材如 William O'Grady 等主编的 Contemporary Linguistics 或者 Victoria Fromkin, et al. 的 An Introduction to Language。那么吴红岩先生的教材有什么独特的地方呢?我认为至少有三个方面的特点。

一是适用性。该书编者一直是一线的语言学教师,深知现在普通高校语言学教学现状,如课时限制和学生的兴趣等,因此,该书编者在编写内容上有所舍取,并没有涉及到语言学方方面面,而是将书本内容控制在教师能在有限的授课时间内讲完的范围内,克服了海内外大部头语言学教材动辄三、五百页的缺陷,能够使学生在最短的学时内全面了解语言学的概况。

二是该书的语言通俗易懂,内容清晰新颖。近几十年来,语言学研究方兴未艾,成果斐然。为了更好地帮助学子了解语言学的最新进展,海外的一些语言学教材都会过两三年就适时更新教材内容,国内的教材在内容更新或更新的频度方面却远远滞后,加上有些学校还沿用上个世纪编写的教材,更使得语言学普及现状难以尽如人意。该书弥补了这一缺憾,既适合学生自学,又更新了其他教材没有提及的一些新的内容。比如该书增添了"神经语言学"一章,在介绍句法时,比较详细地介绍了句法学的基本理念,规范了树形图标记,纠正了一些教材中的常识性错误。

三是编者的编写思路有一个明确的主线。教材以 Chomsky 提出的语言学研究的五个基本问题为主线,比较扼要地阐明了对相关问题的解释,如此就会使得学生能够在短时间内比较系统地了解语言学的主流流派。

语言学在国外一直是一门独立的科学,和心理学、数学一样都是一级学科。在欧美国家,好一点的大学都有一个语言学系,和心理学系、生物学系等一样都是独立的系。语言学研究探索的人的大脑和心智,在海外也是一门显学,曾被誉为领先科学(pilot science),对认知科学、心理学、生物学、神经学、言语治疗、教育学等都有理论输出。

但在国内，语言学却按语种被划分成外国语言学、汉语语言学、方言学三个二级学科，各二级学科之间互为樊篱，如此最大程度地限制了对语言普遍性的研究。学语言的大学生多了解海外的主流语言学，有利于我们更好地了解语言共性，从而更好地探索我们的大脑和心智，建构我们自己的语言观，了解作为自然人的我们自己。

是为序。

伍雅清
于科教新村

前　言

　　21世纪的语言学在Chomsky的形式语言学理论的引领下正向着生物语言学领域纵深发展，而国内的英语语言学教材却很难跟上形势的发展，要么过于简洁，缺乏取向，不深不透；要么过于面面俱到，繁杂艰深，让学生望而却步；有些观点和提法存在争议或为大多数语言学家所诟病。由中山大学博士生导师丁建新教授为总主编、中山大学出版社出版的"全国英语专业博雅系列教材"中的这本《语言学》教程将肩负着继往开来的重任，为广大英语专业的本科生提供一本既博且雅，浅显易懂，趣味与知识并重的教材；让他们真正体会 do linguistics 的乐趣。

　　本书主要参考了两本经典的语言学教程：Fromkin, et al. 主编的《语言引论》和Radford等主编的《语言学教程》，并从Chomsky的近期论述中获取灵感和素材。选材和行文中透露出编著者对当代主流语言学发展的把握和学术取向。

　　本书以Chomsky有关语言学研究的五个问题作为主线，试图回答如下问题：语言知识是什么？语言是如何习得的？语言又是如何使用的？语言的神经和生物学基础是什么？对语言本体的研究涉及语言的音（语音学、音位学）、形（词汇学、句法学）、义（语义学），为我们解释第一个问题提供了初步的答案。语用学一章对语言是如何使用的进行了概述，合作原则、礼貌原则、言语行为理论等为语言的使用提供了依据。本书的第八章语言习得涉及母语习得和外语的教和学两方面，我们提供了最基本和最重要的理论和假说，能让学生一窥该领域的全貌。Chomsky的第四和第五个问题至今还处于最初的探索阶段，本书提供了国内语言学教材中最全面的、最新的神经语言学知识，对大脑的语言功能定位及可塑性进行了一定的论述，介绍了三种失语症患者的语言混乱现象，对语言天才、语言基因的发现等进行了描述。本章最后一节对Chomsky的生物语言学视角进行了刻画，材料来自于Chomsky近十年来的著作，包括他的语言进化故事和对存在多种人类语言的原因的解释：作为人类内在的思维语言只有一种，不同的外化方式导致了不同语言的存在，作为思维的人类语言是完美的，作为交际的人类语言是不完美的。

　　作为一直在一线从事语言学教学的老师，编著者使用过国内外各种语言学教材，深知教师在教学中感到为难的地方：一个学期只有三十六节语言学课，大部头的教材存在取舍的问题，简易本信息不够。语言理论枯燥无味，学生缺乏学习兴趣，练习以问答的形式出现，缺乏刺激和挑战性，并且所有教材都没有为练习提供暗示或答案。为了弥补上述不足，本书在编著过程中进行了下列改革：教材内容适量，每两周一章，正符合一个学期的教学任务。本书选取了很多日常生活中有趣的语言现象进行分析，确保学生能在学习中保持浓厚的兴趣；练习具有挑战性，以培养学生 do linguistics 的能力和针对不同语料进行语言学分析的能力，而非单纯地掌握概念和术语。编著者在本书的最后为练习提供了尝试性的解答，以方便教师和学生检验自己的理解和教学成果。当然，我们不希望学生不经过思考而直接找答案，那将对你的学习毫无帮助。

教材中重要的术语用黑体字标示，并能在本书的 Glossary and Index 中找到其翻译和出处，我们应该善加利用。重要的概念和经典的论述在文章中用黑体或斜体突显出来，以利于学生的注意和记忆。每章的结尾都有 Summary 部分，对所学内容进行简单的梳理和总结，方便学生对各章内容的总体把握。总之，我们的编写宗旨是：在有限的时间内提供给学生最新的、主流的、普遍认可的语言学知识，一切为了学生，一切为了教师。

吴红岩

2012 年 10 月

Preface

As an inexperienced foreign teacher of oral English in China I have found myself thinking about language a great deal in the last several months. With each passing week, the challenge of coming up with new and interesting lessons for my classes is renewed. I have tried very hard to find ways of motivating and encouraging my students to use English as much as possible, somehow instinctively knowing that the best way for them to improve their spoken English is to speak it. One of the obstacles that students face is the fear of making mistakes and I can personally relate to this as I feel that same fear when I use my limited knowledge of Chinese to tell a taxi driver where to take me, or when I attempt to order food in a restaurant.

I recount my teaching experiences here because reading this book has confirmed one of the themes I have repeated time and time again in my classroom, that making mistakes is natural and can help the learning process immensely. When I encouraged my students to worry less about making mistakes I was unaware of the *Hypothesis-Testing Hypothesis*, as explained in chapter 8, this is just one example of many interesting topics discussed by the author.

To a novice who has never studied linguistics before, this book is fascinating. It is both easy to understand and detailed enough to also interest more experienced students of the subject. The introduction will spark the readers' interest and provoke thought, there are so many questions raised when you start to think about language and some suggestions in the following pages may allow them to be answered. The 'nuts and bolts' of language are disclosed in the chapters following the introduction, Phonetics and Phonology, Morphology and Syntax, Semantics and Pragmatics to name a few. More terminology than you can throw a book at is contained within these chapters, but it is explained clearly and patiently so that students at any level will find it helpful. The final chapters explain some of the theories associated with linguistics, some fascinating and intriguing ideas that go a long way towards helping to understand the language learning process.

On the whole, I can thoroughly recommend this book as being invaluable to anyone with an interest in language and linguistics. The exercises contained here can help to reinforce and consolidate what you will learn as you read and progress.

Gary Ingyon
May 2013

Contents

Chapter 1　Introduction 1
　1.1　Language: Its Nature and Definitions 1
　　1.1.1　The Traditional View of Language 1
　　1.1.2　The Internalist View of Human Language 2
　　1.1.3　The Designing Features of Human Language 3
　　　1.1.3.1　*Creativity* 4
　　　1.1.3.2　*Discrete Infinity, Recursiveness and Merging Operation* ... 4
　　1.1.4　The Common Features Shared by All Human Languages 5
　1.2　Linguistics 6
　　1.2.1　Linguistics as a Science 6
　　1.2.2　Chomsky's Five Problems for Language Study 8
　　1.2.3　The Study Scope of Linguistic Ontology 9
　　　1.2.3.1　*Competence vs. Performance* 9
　　　1.2.3.2　*The Study Scope of General Linguistics* 9
　1.3　How to Study Linguistics 12
　1.4　Summary 13
　EXERCISES 14

Chapter 2　Phonetics 16
　2.1　The Mechanism of Articulation 17
　　2.1.1　Speech Organs 17
　　2.1.2　The Phonetic Alphabet 18
　2.2　Classification of Speech Sounds 20
　　2.2.1　Consonants 20
　　　2.2.1.1　*Places of Articulation* 20
　　　2.2.1.2　*Manner of Articulation* 21
　　2.2.2　The Articulation of Vowel Sounds 22
　2.3　Phonetic Symbols and Spelling Correspondences 24

2.4 Summary ·· 25
EXERCISES ·· 26

Chapter 3 Phonology: The Sound Patterns of Language ············ 29
3.1 Phonetics and Phonology; Narrow and Broad Transcription ······ 29
   3.1.1 Phonetics or Phonology ··· 29
   3.1.2 Narrow and Broad Transcription ······························ 31
3.2 Some Preliminary Terminologies in Phonological Analysis ········ 32
   3.2.1 Phonemes, Phones and Allophones ···························· 32
   3.2.2 Minimal Pairs, Phonemic Contrast and Complementary Distribution
      ·· 34
3.3 Distinctive Features of Phonemes ··· 35
3.4 The Rules of Phonology ··· 37
   3.4.1 Assimilation Rules ··· 37
   3.4.2 Segment Insertion and Deletion Rules ······················· 38
   3.4.3 Sequential Rules ··· 39
3.5 Syllable Structure and Suprasegmental Features ····················· 40
   3.5.1 Syllable Structure ··· 40
   3.5.2 Stress ··· 42
3.6 Summary ·· 44
EXERCISES ·· 45

Chapter 4 Morphology ·· 48
4.1 Morpheme and Morphology ·· 49
   4.1.1 The Classification of Morphemes ······························ 49
   4.1.2 Inflectional and Derivational Affix ····························· 51
   4.1.3 Root, Stem and Base ··· 52
   4.1.4 Allomorphs ·· 53
4.2 Words ··· 53
   4.2.1 The Definition and Identification of Words ················ 54
   4.2.2 Word-formation ·· 55
      4.2.2.1 *Derivation* ··· 55
      4.2.2.2 *Compounding* ·· 57
      4.2.2.3 *Borrowing* ·· 58
      4.2.2.4 *Coinage* ·· 59
      4.2.2.5 *Conversion* ·· 59
      4.2.2.6 *Back-formation* ·· 60
      4.2.2.7 *Blends* ··· 60
      4.2.2.8 *Reduced Words* ··· 60

4.3　Lexicon ………………………………………………………… 61
4.4　Summary ……………………………………………………… 62
EXERCISES ……………………………………………………… 63

Chapter 5　Syntax ……………………………………………………… 67
5.1　The Study Scope of Syntax ……………………………………… 67
5.2　Basic Terminology ………………………………………………… 68
　　5.2.1　Categories and Functions ………………………………… 68
　　　　5.2.1.1　*Grammatical (or Syntactic) Categories* ………… 69
　　　　5.2.1.2　*Grammatical (or Syntactic) Functions* ………… 70
　　5.2.2　Finiteness vs. Non-finiteness ……………………………… 71
5.3　Sentence Structure ………………………………………………… 72
　　5.3.1　Phrase Structure Rules and Trees ………………………… 73
　　5.3.2　X-bar Theory ………………………………………………… 75
　　5.3.3　Merger ………………………………………………………… 80
5.4　Movement …………………………………………………………… 85
　　5.4.1　Head movement ……………………………………………… 85
　　5.4.2　Wh-movement ………………………………………………… 86
5.5　Structural Ambiguity ……………………………………………… 90
5.6　Summary …………………………………………………………… 93
EXERCISES ……………………………………………………… 94

Chapter 6　Semantics …………………………………………………… 99
6.1　Lexical Semantics—Word Meanings …………………………… 100
　　6.1.1　Reference and Sense ………………………………………… 100
　　6.1.2　Sense Relations ……………………………………………… 101
　　　　6.1.2.1　*Synonymy and Synonyms* ……………………… 101
　　　　6.1.2.2　*Antonymy and Antonyms* ……………………… 102
　　　　6.1.2.3　*Hyponymy: Superordinate or Hyponyms* ……… 103
　　　　6.1.2.4　*Meronymy and Meronyms* ……………………… 103
　　　　6.1.2.5　*Homonymy and Homonyms* …………………… 104
　　　　6.1.2.6　*Polysemy* ………………………………………… 104
　　6.1.3　Semantic Features or Componential Analysis …………… 105
6.2　Sentence Meaning ………………………………………………… 107
　　6.2.1　Sentence Relations—Truth-conditional Semantics ……… 107
　　6.2.2　Sentence Analysis …………………………………………… 109
　　　　6.2.2.1　*Componential Analysis for Sentences* ………… 109
　　　　6.2.2.2　*Predication Analysis* ……………………………… 109
　　　　　　6.2.2.2.1　Argument Structure ……………………… 110

     6.2.2.2.2 Thematic Roles ················· 111
 6.3 Summary ··· 112
 EXERCISES ··· 113

Chapter 7 Pragmatics ··· 118
 7.1 Some Basic Questions in Pragmatic Study ············· 119
  7.1.1 What Is Pragmatics? ························· 119
  7.1.2 Why Do We Call Pragmatics a Wastebasket? ····· 119
  7.1.3 Why Should We Study Pragmatics? ············· 120
  7.1.4 What's the Difference Among Syntax, Semantics and Pragmatics?
    ·· 121
  7.1.5 Meaning: Sentence Meaning or Utterance Meaning ········ 122
  7.1.6 Meaning and Context ························· 124
 7.2 The Coversational Principles and Implicature ·········· 125
  7.2.1 The Cooperative Principle ····················· 125
  7.2.2 Conversational Implicature ···················· 126
  7.2.3 Politeness Principle ·························· 128
 7.3 Speech Act Theory ································· 130
  7.3.1 One Utterance, Three Related Acts ············· 130
  7.3.2 Speech Act Classification ······················ 132
  7.3.3 Direct and Indirect Speech Acts ················ 133
 7.4 Summary ··· 135
 EXERCISES ·· 136

Chapter 8 Language Acquisition ····························· 139
 8.1 First Language Acquisition (FLA) ··················· 140
  8.1.1 The Innateness Hypothesis ···················· 141
  8.1.2 The Logical Problem of Language Acquisition ···· 142
  8.1.3 Poverty of the Stimulus ······················· 143
 8.2 Second Language Acquisition (SLA) ················· 144
  8.2.1 Some Basic Distinctions ······················· 145
  8.2.2 The Study Scope in the Field of SLA ··········· 145
  8.2.3 Contrastive Analysis and Error Analysis ········ 147
   8.2.3.1 *Identification and Classification of Errors* ········ 148
   8.2.3.2 *Contrastive Analysis* ···················· 150
   8.2.3.3 *Error Analysis* ························· 150
  8.2.4 The Major Hypotheses in SLA ················· 152
   8.2.4.1 *Interlanguage Hypothesis* ················ 152
   8.2.4.2 *The Hypothesis-Testing Hypothesis* ········ 153

	8.2.4.3	*Natural Order Hypothesis*	154
	8.2.4.4	*Comprehensible Input Hypothesis*	155
	8.2.4.5	*The Frequency Hypothesis*	156
	8.2.4.6	*The Interaction Hypothesis*	156
	8.2.4.7	*Swain's Comprehensible Output Hypothesis*	157
	8.2.4.8	*The Critical Period Hypothesis*	157

8.3　Four Conditions for Language Learning ············ 158
8.4　Summary ············ 160
EXERCISES ············ 160

Chapter 9　Neurolinguistics ············ 163
9.1　The Brain Structure and Its Lateralization ············ 164
9.2　Brain Plasticity in Early Life ············ 166
9.3　Language Disorder — Aphasia ············ 167
　9.3.1　Broca's Aphasia ············ 167
　9.3.2　Wernicke's Aphasia ············ 170
　9.3.3　Specific Language Impairment (SLI) ············ 171
　9.3.4　The Implications of the Study for the Aphasic Patients ············ 173
9.4　Language Savants ············ 174
9.5　Language Gene ············ 176
9.6　Chomsky's Biolinguistic Perspective ············ 177
　9.6.1　What Is a Biolinguistic Perspective? ············ 178
　9.6.2　The Nature of Language ············ 179
　9.6.3　The Evolution of Language ············ 180
　9.6.4　Internal Thought, Externalization and Communication ············ 181
9.7　Summary ············ 183
EXERCISES ············ 184

Suggested Answers ············ 187
Bibliography ············ 217
Glossary and Index ············ 221

Chapter 1

Introduction

1.1 Language: Its Nature and Definitions

Human beings live in a world of language and hardly a moment of our waking lives is free from language; we even talk in our dreams. The possession of language distinguishes human beings from other animals, i. e. , language makes us human, and only by the act of learning language does the child become a human being.

So, what is a language? There are many different ways to define human languages according to the different perspectives taken by different linguists. Let's try to illustrate the two representative views on human languages: the traditional externalistic view and the internalistic view.

1.1.1 The Traditional View of Language

A commonly accepted traditional definition of language is that **a language is a system of arbitrary, vocal symbols and grammatical signals, by means of which the members of a speech community communicate, interact and transmit their culture.**

In this definition we have two important parts involving the nature and function of human language. As for the nature of language, we know it is a system composed of symbols and signals, and these symbols are arbitrary, which means that the forms of linguistic signs bear no natural relationship to their meaning (**Saussure's arbitrariness**). As Juliet says in Shakespeare's *Romeo and Juliet*:

(1) *What's in a name? That which we call a rose*
    By any other name would smell as sweet.

But we know that at least **syntax** is less arbitrary than words; it is constrained by rules. The following sentences may be used as a good example to show the constraint:

(2) a. The boys are playing basketball.

b. *Basketball playing the are boys the.

(*A star in front of an expression means that it's ungrammatical or ill-formed.*)

On the other hand, these symbols and signals must be vocal (pronounced); but as we know, in **sign languages** this is not the case: even without sounds, the deaf can communicate with each other. Their sign languages are equivalent to our spoken language, which means languages are much more than just speech.

As for the function of language, we say that languages can be used to communicate of course, but we doubt communication is the main function of human languages. As a communicative tool, language is not perfect. It seems that the dislocation and redundant characteristics, and the inflectional system of human language would be unnecessary for a perfect communicative tool. Why should we say "what did you say?" in English while in our common sense we know "what" should be originated from the position after "say" as its object, just like "*ni shuo shenme?*" (you say what?) in Chinese. Why do we need such inflectional endings as "-s", "-ing" or "-ed" in English which make the system so complicated? And other systems like traffic lights or musical tones can also be used as communicative systems. In fact, human language is very well designed for thought and very badly designed for communication according to **Norm Chomsky**.

"*…language is not an instrument of communication. Contrary to what is universally assumed, it's not well designed for communication. But it's well designed—maybe even perfect—for expressing thought.*" (Chomsky 2010: 14)

The analyses above show that the traditional and our common sense definition for human languages may not be so appropriate. The common sense view of language as the reflection of social systems or verbal action may just be an epiphenomenon, and just like any scientific theories, these phenomena or epiphenomena are not the objects for scientific explanation. The reasons underlying these phenomena are the aims for theoretical study.

It seems an external definition for language can not meet the demands for scientific linguistic study; therefore we need turn to an internalist view of human languages.

1.1.2 The Internalist View of Human Language

As we know, five-year-old children are nearly as proficient at speaking and understanding as their parents, even though they don't consciously know the complicated structure underlying their everyday language use. This is just like the situation that a child has the capacity to walk without understanding or being able to explain the principles of balance and support. What we mean here is that the child has internalized a system of rules which allows him to use the language creatively. He has the language **competence** of his native tongue.

When we say Zhang San is a speaker of Chinese, what do we mean? We mean Zhang San owns a certain mental structure which is somehow represented in his brain, or we say that Zhang San has internalized Chinese Grammar in his mind, and his brain is in a certain state. If Li Si can also speak Chinese, then it is reasonable to suppose that Li Si's linguistic system is similar to Zhang San's. By contrast, if John speaks English, then we say John's cognitive system is different from Zhang San's and Li Si's. This perspective of Language as **a cognitive system which is part of any normal human being's mental or psychological structure** was presented by Norm Chomsky (Radford 2000). According to him, Language is "**a natural object, a component of the human mind, physically represented in the brain and part of the biological endowment of the species.**" (Chomsky 2004: 1)

Adopting this view, we can say that the language of human beings is a kind of natural object, a product of hereditary variation. Human language is a biological product and has biological properties, and knowing a language is a biological process rather than a social process; hence the study of language for the purpose of understanding the natural and biological hereditary properties of human language is a kind of natural science.

Human language is extremely intuitive, unconscious and it is highly structured. It is in the minds of the individuals, not collectively made; it can enable users to symbolize objects, events and concepts which are not present (in time and space, in existence or inexistence, concrete or abstract) at the moment of communication. This traditional view of **Displacement of Language** can distinguish human communication from animal communication, the **creativity**, **discrete infinity**, **recursion** (**recursiveness**) **and merging operation** of language are all equally important designing features of human language.

1.1.3 The Designing Features of Human Language

The traditional view on the designing features of human language is **Arbitrariness, Duality, Creativity and Displacement** (Hu 2001); or **Arbitrariness, Productivity, Duality, Displacement and Cultural Transmission** (Dai & He 2002). We have questioned the status of arbitrariness as a designing feature of human language. As for duality, it means that languages consist of two structure sets: the meaningless sound system and the meaningful system of units composed of sounds. If we consider sign languages as natural human languages, then Duality can also be struck off the designing feature list. It is well understood now that sign languages are just like spoken languages, they have similar features. The linear aspect of spoken language is just a kind of reflex of some other system (the **sensory-motor system**) (Chomsky 2010: 7). **Cultural Transmission** means that the details of any language system are not genetically transmitted; it is culturally transmitted from generation to generation through teaching and learning. But that part of property cannot also be regarded as the designing feature of human language. Of course, the lexicon of a language must be learned one by one; how to use language appropriately in a certain situation must also be cultivated; but the computational procedure of a language must be innate. There exists a **Universal Grammar** in the children's minds when they are born. According to Chomsky (2005), human language **grows** in the children's minds as they mature.

1.1.3.1 Creativity

Knowing a language means being able to produce and understand new sentences never spoken or heard before. Language involves "**infinite use of finite means**". A cognitive system (necessarily *finite*, since it is represented within the confines of a brain) can somehow characterize an *infinite* set of objects (the phrases and sentences in a natural language). What all languages have in common is their "creative" aspect, all children come to acquire with ease and complete success a rich and complex body of linguistic knowledge despite both their lack of cognitive sophistication and the **poverty of the stimulus**. Language acquisition is not a purely imitative process, but rather an inherently creative process. Any native speaker is capable of producing and understanding novel sentences, or making judgments about their acceptability, which shows that human languages can't simply be learned by imitation. The novelty of most sentences that we produce or hear provides a strong argument against the claim made by **behavioral psychologists** that language-learning is a purely imitative process which involves the acquisition of a set of linguistic habits.

1.1.3.2 Discrete Infinity, Recursiveness and Merging Operation

One elementary property of Language is that it is a system of "**discrete infinity**". Sentences can be arbitrarily long and go on indefinitely. You could have a five word sentence and a sixty word sentence; but you can't have a five and half word sentence. This characteristic is just like that of numbers; we know that three and a half is out of the natural number system.

In the simplest case, such a system is based on a primitive operation that takes objects already constructed, and constructs from them a new object. We call this operation **Merge**. A merge-based system is the most elementary. With Merge available, we instantly have an unbounded system of hierarchically structured expressions. (Chomsky 2007: 19 – 20)

There must be what's called a **recursive procedure**, or a generative procedure, which forms an infinite number of structured sentences. A recursive operation is one which can be repeated any number of times. For example, the process by which an adjective comes to modify a noun might be said to be recursive in that we can position any number of adjectives in front of a noun (e.g., a tall, dark, handsome stranger).

That natural languages are recursive can also be illustrated by the sentences below:

(3) a. Brown believes that Smith believes that Jack believes that John believes that the earth is flat.

b. This is the dog that worried the cat that killed the rat that ate the milk that lay in the house that Jack built.

1.1.4 The Common Features Shared by All Human Languages

It is necessary to reconsider how much we really understand the nature of language and its role in our life. Language plays a central role in our lives as individuals and social beings. All languages share some features in common, Fromkin, et al. (2007: 28) listed a number of facts belonging to all languages:

1. Wherever humans exist, languages exist.

2. There are no "primitive" languages—all languages are equally complex and equally capable of expressing any idea. The vocabulary of any language can be expanded to include new words for new concepts.

3. All languages change through time.

4. The relationships between the sounds and meanings of spoken languages and between the gestures and meanings of sign languages are for the most part **arbitrary**.

5. All human languages use a finite set of discrete sounds or gestures that are combined to form meaningful elements or words, which may be combined to form an infinite set of possible sentences.

6. All grammars contain rules of a similar kind for the formation of words and sentences.

7. Every spoken language includes discrete sound segments, like /p/, /n/, or /a/, which can all be defined by a finite set of sound properties or **features**. Every spoken language has a class of vowels and a class of consonants.

8. Similar grammatical categories (e.g. noun, verb) are found in all languages.

9. Universal semantic properties like **entailment** (one sentence inferring the truth of another) are found in every language in the world.

10. Every language has a way of negating, forming questions, issuing commands, referring to past or future time, and so on.

11. Speakers of all languages are capable of producing and comprehending an infinite set of sentences. Syntactic universals reveal that every language has a way of forming sentences such as:

Is it a fact that John knows that you know that I know that linguistics is an interesting subject?

12. The ability of human beings to acquire, know, and use language is a biologically based ability rooted in the structure of the human brain and expressed in different modalities (spoken or signed).

13. Any normal child, born anywhere in the world, of any racial, geographical,

social, or economic heritage, is capable of learning any language to which he or she is exposed.

What we should remember is that the above listed language universals are just an observation and description for the shared features of different languages. It is different from the concepts of **Universal Grammar** (UG) presented by Chomsky. According to him,

"*UG may be regarded as a characterization of the genetically-determined language faculty. One may think of this faculty as a 'language acquisition device', an innate component of the human mind that yields a particular language through interaction with presented experience, a device that converts experience into a system of knowledge attained: knowledge of one or other language.*" (Chomsky 1986: 3)

1.2 Linguistics

1.2.1 Linguistics as a Science

Linguistics is generally defined as the scientific study of language; or we may say it is the science of language. In this sense, we say linguistics is more than an informal interest in language, however strong that interest is. People who study difficulties they meet in their everyday life (Sometimes we get tongue-tied; or we can't remember how to spell a word; or we may find it hard to learn a second language. Some people may have hearing difficulties or speech difficulties, or difficulties in learning to read and write, etc.), and try to help others to deal with them, are not necessarily engaged in linguistics: linguistics is not a collection of methods to help people with language problems; and using language is not the same as studying it. Linguistics is not just an informal thinking about language, no matter how intensive and challenging. Linguistics is not a way to solve the problems of language users. It is the study of language, not the use of language. And linguistics is not an interest in language for some other purpose. (Salkie 1990)

Modern linguistics emerged as a distinct field in the 19th and early 20th centuries. Before the 1950s, linguistics was the field which classified (among other things) the pronunciation, grammar, meaning and use of language and hence provided basic terminology (such as *vowel*, *consonant*, *noun*, *participle*, *meaning* etc.) to use when talking about language along with clear criteria for the correct use of each term. It seems that the role of linguistics is purely to serve other fields of knowledge. Many of the major figures from this time studied linguistics alongside other fields: some were also anthropologists like **Edward Sapir**; some were teachers of foreign language and literature, like **Martin Joos**; some were philosophers, like **John Austin**; others were psychologists, mathematicians and sociologists. Many of the other people involved also worked in other areas of study. This kind of linguistics emphasizes differences, rather than similarities, between languages, for very understandable reasons.

Later on, the question of what languages had in common became increasingly important. In the mid-fifties, **Norm Chomsky** initiated a linguistic revolution: he rejected the view that the best way to think of linguistics is as a field which services other fields by providing a classification and a terminology to talk about language. He emphasized similarities between languages, rather than differences. Chomsky often compares the kind of linguistics before 1950s to "natural history" or "butterfly collecting". He claimed that in linguistics, at least, it is possible to go further than this. No matter how diligently people collect specimens, and how painstakingly they classify them, what they are doing is not science. All they are doing is describing the way things are. The point about science is that *it seeks to explain why things are the way they are*.

It is the search for explanations which distinguishes science from other human activities. Science is more than just the collection of facts or specimens: science is about solving puzzles. To solve a puzzle you have to observe the facts closely, classify and describe what you have observed, on the basis of which you decide which facts are relevant and which aren't; you make imaginative guesses or hypotheses, and then check them by logical reasoning. The achievement of a scientist is measured by the importance and complexity of the puzzles he or she sets out to solve, and the degree of success achieved in solving them.

In order to make linguistic study a scientific excercise, we need to meet the following requirements:

1. **Explicitness** (clearly and fully expressed). That is, we need an agreed terminology in the study of linguistics and its definition should be agreed upon by the linguists.

2. **Systematicness**. The structures of a language are so complex, and involve so many variables, that they must be studied in a highly organized way. We need standard procedures to be consistently followed within a reasonably explicit descriptive framework.

3. **Objectivity**. Our research should be based on rigorous empirical tests. It must be verifiable. But according to Chomsky, intuition is also used as data to explain linguistic phenomena.

4. **Economy or Simplicity**. This is a requirement to minimize the theoretical and descriptive apparatus used to describe language.

5. **Exhaustiveness**. The linguist should gather all the materials relevant to his investigation and give them an adequate explanation.

6. **Consistency**. There should be no contradiction between different parts of the total statement.

1.2.2 Chomsky's Five Problems for Language Study

A person who speaks a language has developed a certain system of knowledge, represented somehow in the mind and ultimately, in the brain in some physical configuration. If we take language as such a cognitive system, then we have five classical problems of the study of language (Chomsky 1995: 17; Radford 2000: 1).

(4) a. What does Tom know when he has a particular language? (What is the nature of the cognitive system which we identify with knowing a language?)

b. How does Tom acquire this knowledge? (How do we know such a system?)

c. How does Tom put this knowledge to use? (How is this system used in our production and comprehension of speech?)

d. How did these properties of the mind/brain evolve in the species?

e. How are these properties realized in mechanisms of the brain? (How is this system represented in the brain?)

It is important to be clear that an answer to question (4a) is logically prior to the answers of the other problems. It makes no sense to inquire into its acquisition, its use in production and comprehension and its representation in the brain unless we have a view on the nature of the relevant cognitive system.

The logical priority of problem (4a) should not lead to the conclusion that we must have a complete answer to this question before considering our other problems. Pursuit of problem (4b) will be contributing towards answering problem (4a), and similar possibilities exist for the other problems.

The answers to all these problems or puzzles identify the study scope of different linguistics. **General linguistics** deals with problem (4a), **developmental linguistics** focuses on the acquisition of first language, which is problem (4b). We need to explain the uniformity and rapidity in the pattern of children's linguistic development. **Psycholinguists** address the problem (4c) of how the mentally represented grammar (linguistic competence) is employed in the production and comprehension of speech (linguistic performance). Problems (4d, 4e) are the main concern of **neurolinguists**, or **biolinguistics**. We firmly believe that cognitive capacities are the product of structures in the brain; but ethical considerations forbid intrusive experimentation on human brains; we can only study brain damaged patients who suffer from language disorders to get some understanding of the structure of the brain. (Radford 2000)

Linguistics is also one of the social sciences in that the phenomena forming its subject-matter are part of the behaviour of men and women in society, in interaction with their fellows. The linguist is simultaneously the observer of languages and the producer and evaluator of at least one language, i.e. his own mother tongue. This means that the linguist is free to adopt either the position of the "external" observer of data, supplied by himself or by others in speech or writing, or the position of an "internal" analyst of what is involved in being a speaker-hearer, in knowing a language.

1.2.3 The Study Scope of Linguistic Ontology

1.2.3.1 Competence vs. Performance

Knowing a language means having a mentally represented grammar and this grammar constitutes the native speaker's competence in that language. **Competence** is defined as *the ideal language speaker's knowledge about his native language* by Chomsky; and it is contrasted with **performance**, *the perception and production of speech*, the study of which falls under psycholinguistics. It is important to distinguish these concepts. A speaker of Chinese suffers a blow to the head; consequently, he loses the ability to speak, write, read and understand Chinese. In this case we may say that what he loses is his ability to use language, but what about his knowledge of Chinese, i.e., linguistic competence? If he is lucky enough, such a loss of ability can be temporary. He recovers quickly; he can use his language again. That means his linguistic competence remains intact throughout; otherwise, we would expect to see a longer period for him to regain his language which would correspond to the initial length of time taken in the acquisition of his language.

Linguistic competence is, of course, an abstraction which cannot directly be measured; any techniques that we devise are measures of performance.

"*Linguistic theory is concerned primarily with an ideal speaker-listener, in a completely homogeneous speech-community, who knows its language perfectly and is unaffected by such grammatically irrelevant conditions as memory limitations, distractions, shifts of attention and interest, and errors (random or characteristic) in applying his knowledge of the language in actual performance.*" (Chomsky 1965: 3)

For the most part, linguistic knowledge is not a kind of conscious knowledge. The linguistic system — the sounds, structures, meanings, words, and rules for putting them all together — is acquired with no conscious awareness. Just as we may not be conscious of the principles that allow us to stand or walk, we are unaware of the rules of language. Our ability to speak and understand, and to make judgments about the grammaticality of sentences, reveals our knowledge of the rules of our language. This knowledge represents a complex cognitive system.

1.2.3.2 The Study Scope of General Linguistics

What does a grammar consist of and what do we mean Tom knows English as a native speaker? In fact Tom knows that: (Chomsky 1995: 17)

(5) a. *Pin* rhymes with *bin*.

b. If *Mary is too clever to expect anyone to catch*, then we don't expect anyone to catch Mary.

c. If *Mary is too angry to run the meeting*, then either *Mary is so angry that she can't run the meeting*, or *she is so angry that we can't run the meeting*; in contrast, *which meeting is Mary too angry to run* has only the former interpretation.

d. If *Mary painted the house white*, then its exterior (not necessarily its interior) is white.

From this fact, we can infer that Tom knows the words and its pronunciation in his language; and how to combine the words together correctly (he knows that *The dog chased the cat* is a correct sentence while * *Cat the dog chased the* is a wrong sentence). He can also distinguish the ambiguities of certain sentences; he intuitively knows the exact meaning of the sentence. Tom has this knowledge whether or not he is aware of these facts about himself; it may take some effort to elicit such awareness and it might even be beyond his capacities.

Now we can come to the components of a grammar, which is also the study scope of our general linguistics itself: **Phonetics**, **Phonology**, **Morphology**, **Syntax** and **Semantics**.

That part of linguistics that deals with the materials of speech itself is called **Phonetics**. It is immediately concerned with the organs of speech and the movements of articulation, and more widely, with the physics of sound transmission and the physiology of hearing, and ultimately with the neurological process involved in both speaking and hearing.

When we study how sounds are put together and used to convey meaning in communication in a particular language, or the rules governing the structure, distribution, and sequencing of speech sounds and the shape of syllables, we come to the study scope of **Phonology**. Phonology deals with the sound system of a particular language.

Grammar is traditionally subdivided into two different but inter-related areas of study—**Morphology** and **Syntax**. Morphology is mainly concerned with the internal organization of words; it studies how words are formed out of smaller units (the minimal units of meaning—**morphemes**), and the rules of word formation. In morphological study we often have the questions such as:

What are the various component parts (= morphemes) of a word like *antidisestablishmentarianism*?

What kinds of principles determine the ways in which the parts are combined together to form the whole?

The combination of words to form grammatical sentences is governed by rules, and the study of how words are combined together to form phrases and sentences is called Syntax. In syntactic study, the following questions are often presented:

Why is it OK in English to say *who did you see Mary with*, but not OK to say * *who did you see Mary and*?

What kind of principles determine the ways in which we can and cannot combine words together to form phrases and sentences?

A grammar can be said to **generate** (i. e. specify how to form) a set of phrases and sentences, and the task of the linguists is to develop a theory of **Generative Grammar** (i. e. a theory about how phrases and sentences are formed).

However, grammar is traditionally concerned not only with the principles which determine the formation of words, phrases and sentences, but also with the principles which govern their interpretation — i. e. with the principles which tell us how to interpret (= assign meaning to) words, phrases and sentences. The meaning aspect is said to be part of the domain of grammar. **Semantics** is such a field to examine how meaning is encoded in a language. It is the study of the relationships between linguistic forms and entities in the world; in simple terms, how words literally connect to things. Of course the study of meaning includes the meaning of morphemes, words, phrases and sentences exclusively.

In this sense, we can define grammar as *"the study of the principles which govern the formation and interpretation of words, phrases and sentences"* (Radford 2002: 2). The first five chapters (Chapter 2 – 6) of this book seek to provide some basic answers to Chomsky's problem (4a): what is the system of language knowledge? i. e., what is in the mind/brain of the speaker of English or Chinese or Japanese?

So far we have described the five basic study scopes of linguistics itself; these sub-subjects will be the main topics in this book. As we know, languages are used in context; the meaning of a sentence may be decided by the context and the speaker. **Pragmatics** is the study of speaker meaning, contextual meaning; it is the study of how more gets communicated than is said and the study of the expression of relative distance (the closeness of the speaker and the listener) (George Yule 2000: 1). A brief introduction to Pragmatics is available in chapter 7, which serves as some certain answer to Chomsky's problem (4c), though it would be unreasonable to pose the problem of how Tom decides to say what he does, or how he interprets what he hears in particular circumstances.

According to Radford (2000), **Language Acquisition** belongs to the study scope of developmental linguistics. Some answers to Chomsky's problem (4b) will be given in chapter 8 of this book. There exists an important convergence of the interests of the linguists and the developmental linguists. The linguists seek to find and formulate universal principles of human languages on the basis of detailed study of the grammars of adult languages, while the developmental linguists aim to uncover such principles by examining children's grammars and the conditions under which they emerge.

The problem (4d-e) is a relative new one, in fact one that is still on the horizon and as such is beyond serious inquiry for the time being. However, we firmly believe that cognitive capacities are the product of structures in the brain. The neurolinguists have achieved some encouraging results in this area, which will be discussed in chapter 9: **Neurolinguistics**.

There are different schools in the study of linguistics. Because we take a cognitive perspective for the language in this book, and based our discussion of linguistics on Chomsky's **Transformational — Generative Grammar**, we have no space to give an introduction to other influential schools of modern linguistics, including **Cognitive Linguistics**, **Functional Linguistics**, and **American Structuralism**. Readers may refer to some other materials to gain a detailed understanding.

Language is not an isolated phenomenon; the study of language has established close links with other academic branches, resulting in some interdisciplinary branches of linguistic study. Among them we have **Sociolinguistics**, **Historical Linguistics**, **Applied Linguistics**, **Computer Linguistics**, **Corpus Linguistics**, etc. Due to the limited space, the social nature of language, the relationship between social structure and different dialects or varieties of a language, the historical change of particular languages, etc., cannot be discussed in this book; those who are interested in all these areas may refer to the related books in such specific fields.

1.3 How to Study Linguistics

In the last two sections, we have introduced some basic concepts about human language and linguistics. A few words on how to study linguistics may be necessary for beginners in linguistics. We should develop the correct mental attitude towards the subject, seeing it as an open-ended and participatory pursuit. As native language speakers, we know the rules of our language, but **we don't know that we know them**; in studying linguistics we are trying to discover what we already know; we are, in a sense, studying ourselves: the grammatical rule book exists inside us. *Linguistics then is about discovery; we try to observe, describe and explain our language intuition.*

The second piece of advice we wish to give is this: learn to think linguistically. The whole notion of **correctness** is too prescriptive to be of any use linguistically. Linguists prefer to use **well-formed** or **ill-formed** in linguistic judgments: a particular usage is ill-formed if it is not generated by a grammatical rule. Norm Chomsky introduced another set of terms for social judgments: **acceptable** vs. **unacceptable**. The notion of "acceptability" offers a much better way of coping with variant forms than that of "correctness". Some sentences may be correct grammatically but in a certain situation they are unacceptable; any usage which is ill-formed must necessarily be unacceptable whereas the reverse is not the case. The concepts of well-formedness and acceptability are descriptive in character; they seek to establish rules, whether of the social or linguistic kind from actual language use.

Terminology is a stumbling block for many people when studying linguistics. As a consequence, they think that the only way to understand the subject is to decode the terms; but there is a sense in which a new term will only have any meaning for you at the point at which you need to use it. These terminologies used by linguists are **metalanguages**, which are languages about languages; it consists of words, usually of a technical variety, which enable us to comment on, and describe more accurately, our everyday use of words.

In fact, terminologies are not being used by linguists simply to put obstacles in your path, or to make a simple point seem more complicated than it is. Don't stop reading at every unfamiliar term you come across and start consulting dictionaries or glossaries; you will find it frustrating and lose thread of what you are reading. What you can do is to make a note of all terms which are unfamiliar to you and then at a later point look them up.

We begin our linguistic study by considering human languages as an intrinsic and essential ingredient of our everyday lives, and from that develop a way of describing the kinds of knowledge which linguists seek to explore. It is a good idea to reflect on how much you already know about some of the linguistic processes involved.

1.4 Summary

In this introduction, we have been concerned with the different perspectives on human language: external vs. internal view, and have illustrated the **designing features** of human languages, arguing that **creativity**, **displacement**, **discrete infinity**, **recursion** and **the merging operation** are the most important properties; while **arbitrariness**, **duality** and **cultural transmission** as the designing features of human languages may be inappropriate in some aspects. Human languages share much more similarities than differences. Fromkin, et al. 's listing may be a good evidence to prove that.

A grammar of a language is a model of the **grammatical competence** of the fluent native speaker of that language, and that grammatical competence is reflected in native speakers' intuitions about grammaticality and interpretation. In the second section we have explained why linguistics is a natural science, and described the study scope of the linguistic ontology. We quoted Chomsky's 5 problems or puzzles for linguistic study and aimed to answer those questions to some extent in this book. Some suggestions for beginners of linguistic study have been provided with the hope of helping students to think linguistically.

The Chomskyan approach to linguistics maintains that *we can formulate and evaluate proposals about the nature of the human mind by doing linguistics*. In order to do linguistics, we usually rely on native speakers of a language who act as informants and provide us with data, and it is with respect to such data that we test our hypotheses about native speakers' linguistic cognitive systems. The data supplied by native speakers usually has very clear properties; we hope in your linguistic study, you will make full use of your **intuition** about your native language.

EXERCISES

Exercise I

For the following English sentences, please judge whether they are acceptable or unacceptable, well-formed or ill-formed. How do you know how to judge each case?

a. Tom seems asleep.
b. Tom seems sleeping.
c. John wants Bill to go.
d. John wants Bill go.
e. Colorless green ideas sleep furiously.
f. Colorless sleep green furiously ideas.
g. 地球围着太阳转。
h. 太阳围着地球转。
i. 太阳转围地球着。
j. I knew that she was ill, but I was wrong.
k. My goldfish thinks that I'm a very bad cook.
l. My wife is not my wife.
m. My toothbrush is pregnant again.

Exercise II

The following statements about human language may be appropriate or inappropriate. Please give your judgments according to what we have explained in the text.

a. Language is a symbolic system for communication.
b. Language is mainly for thinking, not necessarily for communication.
c. Language is also a biological product and has biological properties.
d. Language is outside (external to) the human body.
e. There are constraints on what can be a language. It is not true that any symbolic system can serve as a human language.
f. Language is a social product.
g. Language is inside the human body.
h. Knowing a language undergoes a biological process. Knowing a language is a biological process rather than a social process.

Exercise III

Discuss the following sentences, some of them may have two different interpretations. Please give an appropriate paraphrase for each interpretation.
 a. He loves me more than you.
 b. Who do you want to / wanna help?
 c. Visiting relatives can be a nuisance.
 d. The president is eager/easy to please.
 e. They are hunting dogs.
 f. Who would you like to visit?
 g. Do Americans call cushions what the British call pillows?

Exercise IV

Are the following sentences grammatical? If they are, how should they be interpreted? What kinds of reasons make them difficult to understand?
 a. The milk that the rat that the cat killed ate lay in the house.
 b. The rapidity that the motion that the wing that the bird has has has is remarkable.

Exercise V

Are the following sentences well-formed? If they are, please paraphrase them. Do you have any difficulties in interpreting them? What reasons make you feel that they are difficult to interpret?
 a. The horse raced past the barn fell.
 b. The cotton clothing is usually made of grows in Mississippi.
 c. The glass shattered into pieces was useless.
 d. The soldiers marched across the parade ground are a disgrace.

Exercise VI

Why should linguists distinguish between the concepts of Competence and Performance in their language study? What's the main study scope for theoretical linguists: Competence or Performance?

Exercise VII

Define the following terminologies:
language	merging operation
creativity	discrete infinity
well-formed	competence
grammar	metalanguage

Chapter 2

Phonetics

Human beings can produce all kinds of sounds because of the special structure of their articulation system, but only some sounds can be used as units in the language system. Throat-clearing, coughing and snoring sounds can't be sounds of human language because they can't be **segmented**. When we know a language we know its sounds; we know how to combine those sounds into words; we can segment that word into parts. For example, if we know English we know the sounds represented by the letters *s*, *u*, *b*, and we can combine them to form the words *sub* or *bus*. We have intuitions about what are possible and impossible sound sequences among native words in English. We would probably all agree that *blick* is a possible, but non-occurring English word; whereas *bnick* by contrast is not a possible native English word; such a word could only occur in English as a foreign borrowing. When we know the language we hear the individual sounds in our "mind's ear", and we have no difficulties in segmenting the continuous sounds. We can segment sentences into words and words into sounds.

The sounds of all the languages of the world together constitute a class of sounds that the human vocal tract is designed to make; they are called **speech sounds**; and the study of all these speech sounds is called **Phonetics**. *The science of phonetics attempts to describe all of the sounds used in all languages of the world.* Our knowledge of a language determines when we judge physically different sounds to be the same. We know which aspects of pronunciation are linguistically important and which are not. It is possible for human beings to ignore nonlinguistic differences in speech and we are capable of making sounds that we know are not speech sounds in our language. For example, if someone coughs in the middle of saying "How old (cough) are you?" a listener will ignore the cough and interpret this simply as "How old are you?" Our knowledge of a language determines when we judge physically different sounds to be the same, and we are able to understand the individual words in an utterance given the continuity of the speech signals.

In general, languages differ to a greater or lesser degree in the list of speech sounds out of which words are built. This chapter will discuss these speech sounds. We'll specifically focus on the speech sounds used in English. In our discussion of Phonetics, we will be mainly concerned with the study of how the vocal tract produces the sounds of language; that is **Articulatory Phonetics**. Of course we can also study the physical properties of sounds produced in speech (**Acoustic Phonetics**), or approach it from the perspective of the listeners; that is, how the listeners perceive these sounds (**Auditory Phonetics**); but these two sub-fields will be left for the reader to study in details after class if they are interested in the transmission and perception of speech sounds.

2.1 The Mechanism of Articulation

2.1.1 Speech Organs

We will begin by describing how speech sounds are made. In pronouncing the speech sounds, the basic source of power is the respiratory system pushing air out of the **lung**. The air from the lung goes up the **windpipe** and into the **larynx**, at which point it must pass between two small muscular folds called the **vocal cords**. If the vocal cords are apart, as they normally are when breathing out, the air from the lung will have a relatively free passage into the **pharynx** and the **mouth**. But if the vocal cords are adjusted so that there is only a narrow passage between them, the pressure of the airstream will cause them to vibrate. Sounds produced when the vocal cords are vibrating are said to be **voiced**, as opposed to those in which the vocal cords are apart, which are said to be **voiceless**. The difference between voiced and voiceless sounds is important in distinguishing sounds. In each of the pairs of words *fat/vat*, *thigh/thy*, *sue/zoo*, the first consonant in the first word of each pair is voiceless whereas in the second word, it is voiced. *Voiced and voiceless may be the first distinctive feature for every speech sound in human languages.*

The air passages above the larynx are known as the **vocal tract**. Its shape is a very important factor in the production of speech. The air passages that make up the vocal tract may be divided into the **oral tract** within the mouth and pharynx, and the **nasal tract** within the nose. The parts of the vocal tract that can be used to form sounds are called **articulators**. The articulators that form the lower surface of the vocal tract often move toward those that form the upper surface. In the mouth, we have **lips**, **teeth**, and the **alveolar ridge**; the front part of the roof of the mouth is formed by a bony structure, which is called the **hard palate**; if you curl the tongue up far enough to touch the upper part at the back of the mouth, you are touching the **soft palate**, or **velum**. The soft palate is a muscular flap that can be raised to press against the back wall of the pharynx and shut off the nasal tract, preventing air from going out through the **nose**. This action separates the nasal tract from the oral tract so that the air can go out only through the mouth. If the air is stopped in the oral tract but the soft palate is down so that it can go through the nasal tract, you get a nasal stop. At the lower end of the soft palate there is a **uvula**; the part of the vocal tract between the uvula and the larynx is the pharynx.

The most important articulator in the lower surface of the vocal tract is certainly the **tongue**. In the articulation of speech sounds, different parts of the tongue may be involved, thus we have **tongue tip** and the **blade** of the tongue, which are the most mobile parts. Behind the blade is the front of the tongue; it is actually the forward part of the tongue body, and lies underneath the hard palate when the tongue is at rest. The remainder of the tongue body may be divided into the center and the back part of the tongue. Of course, we have the **tongue root**, which is opposite to the back wall of the pharynx; the **epiglottis** is attached to the lower part of the root of the tongue. Figure 1 shows a detailed description for the speech organs of the vocal tract.

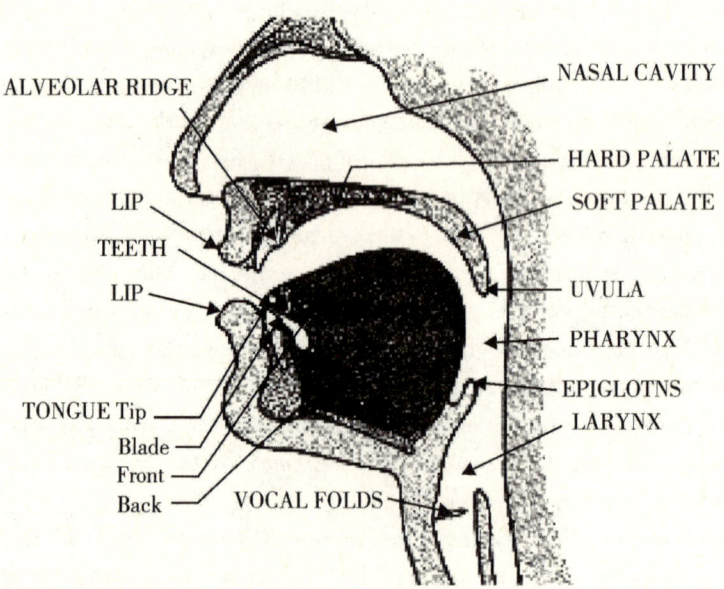

Figure 2.1　Speech Organs

2.1.2　The Phonetic Alphabet

Orthography, or alphabetic spelling, does not represent the sounds of a language in a consistent way. To be scientific — and phonetics is a science — we must devise a way for the same sound to be spelled with the same letter every time, and for any letter to stand for the same sound every time.

Pay attention to the sound represented by different black letters in the following sentence:

(1) Did h**e** bel**ie**ve that C**ae**sar could s**ee** the p**eo**ple s**ei**ze the s**ea**s?

The same sound [i:] is represented variously by **e**, **ie**, **ae**, **ee**, **eo**, **ei**, and **ea**. On the other hand, consider the following sentence:

(2) My f**a**ther w**a**nted m**a**ny **a** vill**a**ge d**a**me b**a**dly.

Here the letter **a** represents the various sounds in different words. In some other cases, a combination of letters may represent a single sound (s**h**oot, **th**eater) and some letters have no sound in certain words (so-called silent letters: autum**n**, **gh**ost, resi**g**n, lam**b**, etc.); or there may be no letter to represent sounds that occur (in many words, the letter *u* represents a [j] sound followed by a [u] sound: c**u**te, f**u**me, **u**se, etc.).

George Bernard Shaw complained that in English spelling was so inconsistent that *fish* could be spelled as *ghoti* — *gh* [f] as in tou*gh*, *o* [i] as in w*o*men, and *ti* [ʃ] as in na*ti*on. In order to guarantee a one sound-one symbol correspondence, the phoneticians invented a phonetic alphabet system to symbolize the sounds of all languages. They used both ordinary letters and invented symbols, each character of the alphabet had exactly one value across all of the world's languages. The main principles were that **there should be a separate letter for each distinctive sound, and that the same symbol should be used for that sound in any language in which it appears**. In this way, someone who knows this alphabet would know how to pronounce a word written in it, and upon hearing a word pronounced he would know how to write it by using the alphabetic symbols. We call this system **International Phonetic Alphabet**, or **IPA**. At the end of this chapter, we have a detailed description of the phonetic alphabet symbols in English.

With IPA symbols, we can now unambiguously represent the pronunciation of words. For example, in the six words below, ou represents six distinct vowel sounds. The phonetic transcription gives us the actual pronunciation.

Spelling	Pronunciation
though	[ðəu]
thought	[θɔːt]
tough	[tʌf]
bough	[bau]
through	[θruː]
would	[wud]

Square brackets around phonetic transcriptions are used to distinguish them from ordinary spelling.

2.2 Classification of Speech Sounds

2.2.1 Consonants

The production of any sound involves the movement of the air. *Most speech sounds are produced by pushing lung air through the vocal cords up the throat, and into the mouth or nose, and finally out of the body.* The sounds of all languages fall into two classes: consonants and vowels. **Consonants are produced with some restriction or closure in the vocal tract that obstructs the flow of air from the lung. While vowels are pronounced with no significant blockage of the air as it is pushed out of the lung.** Consonants can be classified according to the places of articulation; that is, where in the vocal tract the airflow restriction occurs, or the manners of articulation, i. e. , the articulators may completely close off the oral tract for an instant or a relatively long period; they may narrow the space considerably, or they may simply modify the shape of the tract by approaching each other. Of course, the consonants can also be classified according to whether the vocal cords are apart (not vibrating, air flows freely through the glottis into the oral cavity) or close together (the airstream forces its way through and causes them to vibrate); thus we have voiceless consonants and voiced consonants.

2.2.1.1 Places of Articulation

As we know, movement of the tongue and lips creates the constriction, reshaping the oral cavity in assorted ways to produce the various sounds. According to the different articulators involved in the pronunciation of consonants, we can classify the consonants in English as **bilabials, labiodentals, (inter) dentals, alveolars, palatals, velars and glottal.**

Bilabials [p] [b] [m]. When we produce these sounds, we bring both lips together to create an obstruction.

Labiodentals [f] [v]. We articulate these sounds by touching the bottom lip to the upper teeth.

(Inter)dentals [θ] [ð]. The two sounds are both spelled as th. They are produced by inserting the tip of the tongue between the teeth, but for some speakers, the tongue merely touches behind the teeth, making a sound more correctly called dental.

Alveolars [t] [d] [n] [s] [z] [l] [r]. These seven sounds are produced with the tongue raised in various ways to the alveolar ridge.

Palatals [ʃ] [ʒ] [tʃ] [dʒ] [j]. For these sounds, the obstruction occurs by raising the front part of the tongue to the hard palate.

Velars [k] [g] [ŋ]. In producing these sounds, the back of the tongue is raised to the soft palate or velum.

Glottal [h]. When producing this sound, the vocal cords are brought momentarily together to create the obstruction.

2.2.1.2 Manner of Articulation

Speech sounds also vary in the way the airstream is affected as it flows from the lung up and out of the mouth and nose. It may be blocked or partially blocked. In terms of manner of articulation, English consonants may be classified into **stops, fricatives, affricates, liquids (lateral and retroflex), nasals and glides (semivowels)**.

Stops [p] [b] [t] [d] [k] [g]. The airstream is completely blocked in the oral cavity for a short period, and then the air passes out again with the obstruction audibly released. The articulators involved have a complete or total closure. For example, in producing [p] and [b], the airstream stopped at the mouth by the complete closure of the lips.

Fricatives [f] [v] [s] [z] [θ] [ð] [ʃ] [ʒ]. In the production of these **hissing sounds**, the airflow is so severely obstructed that it causes friction, and the sounds are therefore called fricatives. Although the airstream is obstructed as it passes through the oral cavity, it is not completely stopped; a narrow passage in the mouth will permit the air to escape.

Affricates [tʃ] [dʒ]. They are produced by a stop closure followed immediately by a gradual release of the closure that produces an effect characteristic of a fricative. That is, the obstruction is, complete firstly, and then released slowly with the friction resulting from partial obstruction.

Liquids [l] [r]. When we produce such sounds, there is some obstruction of the airstream in the mouth, but not enough to cause any real constriction or friction. [l] is also called a **Lateral**. Because in the production of [l] we have an incomplete closure between one or both sides of the tongue with the roof of the mouth. [r] is also called a **Retroflex** because the tip of the tongue is curled back and the air passes over it in its production.

Nasals [m] [n] [ŋ]. Sounds produced with the velum up, blocking the air from escaping through the nose, are **oral sounds**. When the velum is not in its raised position, that is, when the nasal passage is opened by lowering the soft palate at the back of the mouth and the air escapes through both the nose and the mouth. Sounds produced in this way are **nasal sounds**.

Glides [j] [w]. Glides are transitional sounds (halfway between consonants and vowels). They are also called **Semivowels**; they are produced with little obstruction of the airstream, always followed directly by a vowel. After articulating [j] [w], the tongue glides quickly into the place for pronouncing the next vowel, hence the term

glide. They are consonants because they never form the nucleus of a syllable as vowels do.

We now have three ways of classifying consonants: by *voicing*, by *place of articulation*, and by *manner of articulation*. For example, [f] is a voiceless, labiodental fricative sound; [n] is a voiced, alveolar, nasal stop. All sounds are oral unless nasal is specifically mentioned, and all nasals are voiced stops in English.

Table 2.1 lists the consonants by their phonetic features. The rows stand for manner of articulation and the columns for place of articulation. The entries are sufficient to distinguish all consonants in English from one another.

Table 2.1　The Phonetic Symbols for English Consonants

Manner of articulation		Place of articulation						
	VL or VD	Bilabial	Labiodental	Interdental	Alveolar	Palatal	Velar	Glottal
Stops(oral)	VL	p(pie)			t(tie)		k(kite)	
	VD	b(buy)			d(die)		g(guy)	
Fricatives	VL		f(fire)	θ(thin)	s(sue)	ʃ(mission)		h(high)
	VD		v(view)	ð(thy)	z(zoo)	ʒ(measure)		
Affricates	VL					tʃ(china)		
	VD					dʒ(jar)		
Nasal	VD	m(my)			n(no)		ŋ(sing)	
Liquids lateral retroflex	VD				l(lie) r(row)			
Glides	VD	w(we)				j(you)		

(Adapted from Fromkin, et al. (2007: 235), with some modifications)

2.2.2　The Articulation of Vowel Sounds

In the production of vowel sounds, the passage of the airstream is relatively unobstructed; we have no blockage of the air as it is pushed out of the lung. Vowel sounds may be specified in terms of the position of the highest point of the tongue and the position of the lips. We classify vowels according to three questions:

　1. How high or low in the mouth is the tongue?
　2. How forward or backward in the mouth is the tongue?

3. Are the lips rounded or spread?

Of course, English vowels can also be classified according to the length of the sound. Long vowels are all **tense vowels** and short vowels are **lax vowels**. When we pronounce a long vowel, the larynx is in a state of tension; while pronouncing a short vowel, the larynx is quite relaxed.

Table 2.2 Part of the Tongue Involved

Tongue Height	FRONT SPREAD	CENTRAL	BACK ROUNDED
HIGH (CLOSE)	iː beet i bit		boot uː put u
MID	e bet	əː bird ə Rosa ʌ but	bore ɔː
LOW (OPEN)	æ bat		bomb ɔ bar ɑː

(Adapted from Fromkin, et al. (2007: 239), with some modifications)

Vowels can be described in terms of different factors such as (1) the height of the body of the tongue, (2) the front-back position of the tongue, (3) the degree of lip rounding and (4) the length of the vowels (that is, tense vowels or lax vowels as illustrated above). In this way, [iː] can be described as a high, front, spread, long (tense) vowel; while [u] can be described as a high, back, rounded short (lax) vowel.

In all these vowels the tongue tip is down behind the lower front teeth, and the body of the tongue is domed upward. When you are pronouncing the vowels [iː], [i], [e] and [æ], the highest point of the tongue is in the front of the mouth; they are front vowels. The mouth becomes progressively more open while the tongue remains in the front of the mouth.

In pronouncing the vowels [uː] [u] [ɔː] [ɔ] and [ɑː], the tongue is close to the upper or back surface of the vocal tract; they are back vowels.

The position of the lips varies considerably in different vowels. In English, all the front vowels and the central vowels are unrounded vowels, and all the back vowels, with the exception of [ɑː], are rounded.

A **diphthong** is a sequence of two sounds: a vowel plus a glide. The vowel sound in the word *bite* [bajt] is the [a] vowel sound followed by the glide [j], resulting in the diphthong [aj]; similarly, the vowel in *bout* [bawt] is [a] followed by the glide [w], resulting in [aw]. *Boy* can also be pronounced as [bɔj]. (Fromkin, et al.

2007: 239) Traditionally we transcribe them as [ai], [au], and [ɔi]. The diphthongs in English include [ei], [ai], [ɔi], [au], [əu], [iə], [eə], [uə].

2.3 Phonetic Symbols and Spelling Correspondences

Generally speaking, we have 44 phonetic symbols in English. Phoneticians don't treat the four symbols [tr], [dr], [ts], [dz] as isolated sounds; they are treated as combinations of different sounds. Table 2.3 shows sound / spelling correspondences for English consonants and vowels. The symbol [ə] in *sofa* is called a **schwa**; we use it only to represent vowels in syllables that are not emphasized in speaking and whose duration is very short. It is reserved for the vowel sounds in all reduced syllables. All other vowel symbols in the table occur in syllables that receive at least some emphasis.

We hope the examples in the table will help you relate English orthography to the English sound system. Some of these pronunciations may differ from your own, and there may be other differences, too, because English is a worldwide language and is spoken in many forms. The English examples used in this book are a compromise; our purpose is to teach phonetics in general, and to show you how phoneticians might describe the speech sounds of the world's languages with the proper symbols. We only use the traditional phonetic transcription in our textbook for illustration, with the hope of showing you how such symbols may be used to describe the phonetics of the world's languages.

The following table is revised from Fromkin, et al. (2007: 246 – 247).

Table 2.3 Phonetic Symbol / English Spelling Correspondences

	Consonants (24)
p	**sp**it ti**p** **app**le am**p**le **p**it **p**rick **app**ear
b	**b**it ta**b** **b**u**bb**le
m	**m**ite ta**m** s**m**ack ca**mp** co**mb**
t	s**t**ick pi**t** kiss**ed** wri**t**e **t**ick in**t**end a**tt**ack
d	**D**ick ca**d** **d**rip love**d** ri**d**e
n	**n**ick ki**n** **sn**ow **gn**ostic p**n**eumatic **kn**ow **mn**emonic
k	s**k**in sti**ck** s**c**at **c**ritique el**k** **c**url **k**in **c**riti**c** me**ch**ani**c** **c**lose
g	**g**irl bur**g** lon**g**er Pittsbur**gh**
ŋ	si**ng** thi**n**k fi**n**ger
f	**f**at **ph**ilosophy **f**lat **ph**logiston co**ff**ee ree**f** cou**gh**
v	**v**at do**v**e gra**v**el
s	**s**ip **s**kip **ps**ychology pa**ss** pat**s** democra**c**y **sc**issors de**c**eive
z	**z**ip ja**zz** ra**z**or pad**s** ki**ss**es **X**erox de**s**ign la**z**y **sc**i**ss**ors
θ	**th**igh **th**rough **th**ink **th**in wra**th** e**th**er Ma**tth**ew
ð	**th**y **th**eir wea**th**er la**th**e ei**th**er **th**ose

ʃ	**sh**oe mu**sh** mi**ss**ion na**ti**on fi**sh** gla**ci**al **s**ure
ʒ	mea**s**ure vi**s**ion a**z**ure ca**s**ual deci**s**ion rou**g**e
tʃ	**ch**oke ma**tch** fea**t**ure ri**ch** righ**te**ous
dʒ	**j**u**dge** mi**dg**et **G**eor**g**e ma**g**istrate resi**d**ual
l	**l**eaf fee**l** ca**ll** sing**l**e
r	**r**eef Pa**r**is
j	**y**ou **y**es f**eu**d **u**se
w	**w**itch s**w**im **qu**een **wh**ich **wh**ere **wh**ale
h	**h**at **wh**o **wh**ole re**h**ash
Vowels (20)	
iː	b**ee**t b**ea**t b**e** rec**ei**ve k**e**y bel**ie**ve am**oe**ba C**ae**sar ser**e**ne
i	b**i**t cons**i**st **i**njury b**i**n
e	b**e**t ser**e**nity s**a**ys g**ue**st d**ea**d s**ai**d
æ	p**a**n **a**ct f**a**t c**a**t
uː	b**oo**t l**u**te wh**o** s**e**wer thr**ough** t**oo** tw**o** m**o**ve
u	p**u**t f**oo**t b**u**tcher c**ou**ld
ʌ	c**u**t t**ou**gh am**o**ng **o**ven d**oe**s c**o**ver fl**oo**d
ɔː	c**augh**t st**a**lk c**o**re s**a**w b**a**ll **a**we
ɔ	c**o**t c**o**ck g**o**d
ɑː	f**a**ther p**a**lm f**a**r
ə	s**o**fa **a**lone s**y**mphony s**u**ppose mel**o**dy th**e**
ɜː	f**u**r b**i**rthday b**i**rd v**e**rb
ei	g**a**te b**ai**t r**a**y gr**ea**t **eigh**t g**au**ge r**eig**n th**ey**
ai	b**i**te s**igh**t b**y** d**ie** d**ye** St**ei**n **ai**sle l**ia**r **i**sland h**eigh**t s**ig**n
ɔi	b**oy** d**oi**ly j**oy**
au	**a**b**ou**t br**ow**n d**ou**bt c**ow**ard
əu	c**oa**t g**o** b**eau** gr**ow** th**ough** t**oe** **ow**n **o**ver
eə	f**ear** b**ear** c**are** p**air**
uə	s**ure** l**ure**
iə	b**eer** m**ere** n**ear**

2.4 Summary

Phonetics is a science of speech sounds. It tries to provide the set of properties necessary to describe and distinguish all the sounds in human languages.

When we speak, the physical sounds we produce are continuous stretches of sounds, which are the representations of strings of discrete linguistic **segments**. Knowledge of a language permits us to separate continuous speech into individual sounds and words.

One letter corresponding to one sound is a principle in the design of the

International Phonetic Alphabet (**IPA**), by means of which the sounds of all human languages can be represented.

Speech sounds come from the movement of lung air through the **vocal tract**. The air passes through the **glottis** up the **pharynx**, through the **oral** (and possibly the **nasal**) **cavity**, and out the mouth or nose. All speech sounds are either **consonants** or **vowels** according to whether the airstream is obstructed in the vocal tract or not.

Consonants may be further classified according to their manner of articulation (thus we have **stops**, **fricatives**, **affricates**, **liquids**, **or glides**), place of articulation (**bilabials**, **labiodentals**, **alveolars**, **palatals**, **velars**, **and glottals**), **voiced** or **voiceless**, oral or nasal.

Vowels may be classified according to the position of the tongue and lips: high, mid, or low tongue; front, central, or back of the tongue, round or spread lips. Vowels in English may be **tense** or **lax**; tense vowels are slightly longer in duration than lax vowels. All the unstressed vowels in English may be pronounced as the **schwa** [ə].

Suprasegmental features like **length**, **pitch**, **loudness and stress** are not mentioned in this book due to the limitation of space. They are imposed over and above the segmental values of the sounds in a **syllable**. Stress can be used to distinguish meaning in English. For example, the different stress in the pronunciation of the words as *content*, *rebel*, *progress*, etc. can be used to distinguish whether it is a verb or a noun. **Tone languages** such as Chinese may use pitch to distinguish meaning; readers interested in this part may refer to other books dealing with Phonetics specially.

EXERCISES

Exercises I

Describe the consonants in the word "skinflint" using the chart below.

	1. voiced or voiceless	2. place of articulation	3. manner of articulation	4. oral or nasal
[s]	*voiceless*	*alveolar*	*fricative*	*oral*
[k]				
[n]				
[f]				
[l]				
[t]				

Exercises II

Studying a new subject often involves learning a large number of technical terms.

Phonetics is particularly difficult in this respect. Read over the definitions of the terms in this chapter, and do the exercises below.
1. Circle the words that begin with a **bilabial** consonant:
    mat gnat sat bat rat pat
2. Circle the words that begin with a **velar** consonant:
    knot got lot cot hot pot
3. Circle the words that begin with a **labiodental** consonant:
    fat cat that mat chat vat
4. Circle the words that begin with an **alveolar** consonant:
    zip nip lip sip tip dip
5. Circle the words that end with a **fricative**:
    race wreath bush bring breathe bang rave rose rough
6. Circle the words in which the consonant in the middle is **voiced**:
    tracking mother robber leisure massive stomach razor
7. Circle the words that contain a **high** vowel:
    sat suit got meet mud
8. Circle the words that contain a **low** vowel:
    weed wad load lad rude
9. Circle the words that contain a **front** vowel:
    gate caught cat kit put
10. Circle the words that contain a **rounded** vowel:
    who me us but him

Exercise III

Write the phonemic symbols for the described sounds and specify the distinctive features of the following phonemic symbols.
  a. voiced velar nasal stop _____
  b. voiceless glottal fricative _____
  c. voiced bilabial glide _____
  d. mid back rounded long vowel _____
  e. high tense front spread vowel _____
  f. /j/_____
  g. /ð/_____
  h. /d/_____
  i. /r/_____
  j. /æ/_____

Exercise IV

Read the following passage in phonetic transcription, try to pronounce it as indicated, take care to put the stresses on the correct syllables, and say the unstressed syllables with the vowels as shown, and then transform them into English with normal spelling [a revised exercise from Ladefoged (1982: 43)].

it iz ˈpɔsəbl tə trænˈskraib fəˈnetikli ˈeni ˈʌtrəns, in ˈeni læŋgwidʒ, in ˈsevrəl ˈdifrənt ˈweiz ˈɔl əv ðəm ˈjuziŋ ði ˈælfəbet ənd kənˈvenʃnz əv ði ˈai piˈei. (ðə ˈseim ˈθiŋ iz ˈpɔsəbl wið ˈməust ˈʌðə intəˈnæʃənl fəˈnetik ˈælfəbets.) ə trænˈskripʃn witʃ iz meid bai ˈjuziŋ ˈletəz əv ðə ˈsimpləst ˈpɔsəbl ˈʃeips, ənd in ðə ˈsimpləst ˈpɔsibl nʌmbə, iz ˈkɔːld ə ˈsimpl fəuˈniːmik trænˈskripʃn.

Exercise V

Transcribe the following phrases as you would say them yourself.
1. Please come home.
2. He is going by train.
3. The angry American.
4. His knowledge of the truth.
5. I prefer sugar and cream.
6. Norm Chomsky is a linguist who teaches at MIT.
7. Phonetics is the study of speech sounds.
8. Some people think Phonetics is very interesting.

Exercise VI

For each group of sounds listed, state the phonetic feature(s) they all share.
Example: [p] [b] [m] Features: bilabial, stop, consonant.
1. [g] [p] [t] [d] [k] [b]
2. [uː] [u] [ɔ] [əu]
3. [iː] [i] [e] [æ]
4. [t] [s] [ʃ] [p] [k] [tʃ] [f] [h]
5. [v] [z] [ʒ] [dʒ] [n] [g] [d] [b] [l] [r] [w] [j]
6. [t] [d] [s] [l] [n] [r] [z]

Chapter 3

Phonology: The Sound Patterns of Language

As we all know, there are thousands of languages in the world, but there are only hundreds of speech sounds and each language may just use dozens of them to represent the sound system of that language. Even more remarkable, only a few dozen features, such as *voicing*, or *stop*, or *alveolar*, or *rounded*, are needed to describe every speech sound that occurs in every human language.

In this case, you may wonder why the multitudinous languages of the world may all sound so diverse. The most important reason is that *the sounds form different patterns in different languages*. In fact, there is no general notion of "difficulty of articulation" that can explain all of the sound patterns of particular languages; the ease or difficulty of certain sounds and sound combinations depend on a speaker's unconscious knowledge of the sound patterns of his/her language. This chapter will deal with the native speakers' subconscious knowledge of the sound patterns contained within their language.

3.1 Phonetics and Phonology; Narrow and Broad Transcription

3.1.1 Phonetics or Phonology

Different languages make use of different selections from the speech sounds that the human vocal tract can produce, and may be shown to organize these sounds differently. As a result, two separate ways of studying speech sounds are recognized in linguistics: **phonetics**, the study and analysis of the sounds of languages or of a particular language, in respect of their articulation, transmission, and perception; **phonology**, the study and analysis of the sound system of a language. It is the component of a grammar that includes the inventory of sounds (phonetic and phonemic units) and rules for their combination and pronunciation, and it is the study of the sound systems of all languages.

As we have illustrated in the last chapter, a **phonetician** is a person who can describe speech, who understands the mechanisms of speech production and speech perception, and who knows how languages use these mechanisms. **Phonetics** is *general* (That is, it deals with all the speech sounds used in all human languages; it studies speech sounds without reference to their function in a particular language), *descriptive* (It tries to describe the detailed features of each speech sound, to study how the speech sounds differ from each other), and *classificatory* (How can the speech sounds be classified? For example: consonants vs. vowels; voiced sounds vs. voiceless sounds; different consonants classified in terms of the place of articulation or manner of articulation, etc.).

When phoneticians transcribe an utterance, they usually do so by noting how the sounds convey differences in meaning. In this sense, they are dealing with the sound patterns of that particular language; they have become phonologists and are doing a phonological study. Thus, **phonology** is the study of the way speech sounds form patterns. It refers both to the linguistic knowledge that speakers have about the sound patterns of their language and to the description of that knowledge that linguists try to produce. That is just like the definition of *grammar*; it may refer to your mental knowledge of your language, or a linguist's description of that knowledge.

In order to understand how phonetic transcription works, it is necessary to understand the basic principles of phonology. **Phonology** is the description of the systems and patterns of sounds that occur in a particular language. It involves studying a language to determine its distinctive sounds and to establish a set of rules that describe the set of changes that take place in these sounds when they occur in different relationships with other sounds.

Phonology is *particular* (about a particular language or languages), and *functional* (i.e., it is concerned with the working or functioning of speech sounds in a language or languages). It deals with the functioning of speech sounds in the phonological systems of various languages, with the analysis of such systems, and with the phonological possibilities of languages.

Phonology tells you what sounds are in your language and which ones are foreign, what combinations of sounds are legal, whether they make an actual word (*black*) or not (*blick*), and which ones are illegal (*lbick*). Phonology can also explain why certain features are important to the meaning of a word. For example, voicing in English as in *pat* versus *bat* will determine the different meanings of the two words; while the other feature, such as **aspiration** in English, are not crucial to meaning. In the word *speak*, whether the sound [p] is aspirated or not, it is the same word.

If you are a native English speaker, you know that [ŋ] cannot begin a syllable or a word in English. You also know that [g] in *sign* is silent; while in *signature*, it is pronounced. You have known such kinds of **phonological processes** since you were a child, and you don't feel it is unreasonably complex. Linguists are only making explicit what the native speakers already know. As English learners, this kind of knowledge will certainly help us to have a good understanding of the sound pattern of English.

3.1.2 Narrow and Broad Transcription

In the last chapter (2.2), we have described the basic principles in the designing of **the International Phonetic Alphabet (IPA)**. We know that it was devised to provide a precise and universal means of writing down the spoken forms of utterances as they are spoken without reference to their orthographic representation, grammatical status, or meaning. This is an essential part of phonetic analysis and of the phonetic study of the sounds of languages. What we have provided is the broad transcription of English speech sounds. These transcriptional systems of far fewer symbols and **diacritical signs** are devised for each language separately, to serve the purpose of representing the pronounced forms. They are known as **broad transcriptions**, and there are clearly a minimal number of distinct symbols required for the unambiguous indication of the pronunciation, as opposed to the potentially infinite number needed to symbolize separately each difference of actual sound.

Phoneticians and phonologists also need some means to transcribe the minute differences between variations of the same sound in actual language environments or by different speakers. They use a set of **diacritics** which are added to the normal IPA symbols representing the special pronunciation of that particular sound; this kind of transcription is called a "**narrow**" **transcription**, which uses more specific symbols to show more phonetic details in our pronunciation.

For example, vowels could be nasalized in front of a nasal sound; thus, the [e] sound in *bed* may be a little bit different from the [e] in *ten*. In order to distinguish this difference, the phoneticians may add a curved line to the top of the symbol [e] in the pronunciation of *ten*, as [ẽ]. In the same way, they can distinguish the [p] sound in the words *peak* and *speak*; the [p] sound in the word *peak* may be **aspirated**; thus it is transcribed as [pʰ]; whereas the **unaspirated** sound [p] in *speak* could be transcribed as [p⁼]. The symbols as ʰ, ⁼, are called diacritics.

Distinguishing these two types of transcription will be helpful for the phoneticians and phonologists. Firstly, with these diacritics, many of the differences among sounds in a language may be shown to be conditioned by the phonetic environment of each sound, i.e., the other sounds near it in the uttered form, and therefore do not need separate symbolization in the transcription of the languages. Secondly, a narrow transcription can be indifferently used of the material of any language, so that linguists can use them conveniently in some special circumstances.

A **Broad Transcription** uses a simple set of symbols; conversely, a **Narrow Transcription** shows more phonetic details, either just by using more specific symbols or by also representing some allophonic differences. **The use of diacritics (small marks that can be added to a symbol to modify its value), is a means of increasing precision.** Of course, a symbol could only be regarded as an approximate specification of the articulations involved; in practice it is difficult to make a transcription so narrow that it shows every detail of the sounds involved.

The following diacritics are commonly used in the transcription of the sounds by phoneticians and phonologists. Of course, we have some other diacritics which are not indicated here.

t^h, d^h: aspirated; $p^=$: unaspirated; $\tilde{e}$, $\tilde{z}$: nasalized; $ɚ$, $ɜ˞$: retroflexion;

ɹ̩, n̩: syllabic; e̯, ʊ̯: unsyllabic; s̬, t̬: voiced; n̥, d̥: voiceless;

t̪, d̪: dental; $t^ɣ$, $d^ɣ$, . ɫ . : velarization; t^w, d^w: transitional labialization;

t^j, d^j: transitional palatalization.

3.2 Some Preliminary Terminologies in Phonological Analysis

The phonology of a language is the set of rules that describe the changes in the underlying sounds when they occur in speech. The majority of linguists base their phonological analysis and derive their principles of phonology from the theory of the phoneme. In the theory of phonology, there are some preliminary terminologies involved in the analysis of phonological process; anyone entering on the study of linguistics must be sure to master these essentials. These basic terms include **Phoneme**, **Phone**, **Allophone**, **Minimal Pair**, **Phonemic Contrast and Complementary Distribution**, etc. Let's look at a general introduction to them.

3.2.1 Phonemes, Phones and Allophones

In the phonological analysis, the most important concept is **Phoneme**. In fact, the number of the phonemes in any language is relatively small. We say, in English there are 44 phonemes; that is, the 44 IPA symbols we used in transcribing the pronunciation of English words in the last chapter. But we also need to realize that those phonemes can be pronounced differently in different environments (thus, the vowels can be pronounced nasalized in front of a nasal; the /p/ phoneme can be pronounced aspirated (as in *peak*) or unaspirated (as in *speak*), and by different people (we are sure to say that in all the world, there are no two people who can pronounce the same sound with the same phonetic value). In this sense, we can say that *phonemes are abstract mental representations of the phonological units of a language.* They are not physical sounds or any particular sounds but rather represented or realized by some certain phones in some certain phonetic contexts. These units are used by linguists to form the basis for writing down a language systematically and unambiguously. In a word, phonemes are a class of phonetically similar sounds, contrasting and mutually exclusive with all similar classes in the language. All the segmental sounds used in each language can be classified into a limited number of phonemes.

A phoneme should be distinct or differentiable; that means it is of distinctive value. To differ distinctively, two sounds must be able to occur in the same position and in the same environment as far as other distinctive sound units are concerned. Thus, in English, /p/ and /b/ can each occur in the environment [-æn], in [pæn] *pan*, and in [bæn] *ban*; they are two different phonemes in English.

A particular realization (pronunciation) of a phoneme is called a **phone**. It is a phonetic unit; the speech sounds we hear or produce in speaking are all phones. A phone does not necessarily distinguish meaning. Each phoneme has associated with it one or more sounds, the collection of phones that are the realizations of the same phoneme are called the **allophones**, which represent the actual sound corresponding to the phoneme in various environments. We can use the following examples to show the differences among these terminologies.

In English, we have the phonemes /p/, /t/, /k/, because they can be used to distinguish meaning, as in /pen/ *pen*, /ten/ *ten* and /ken/ *Ken*. When pronounced in initial positions they are aspirated ([p^h], [t^h], [k^h]), as in the last three words: [p^hen], [t^hen] and [k^hen]. But if they immediately follow an initial /s/ in a consonant cluster they are pronounced without aspiration, as in *steam* /sti:m/, [st⁼i:m]. The **phonological rule** may state that **the aspirated [p^h] occurs before a stressed vowel, the unaspirated [p⁼] occurs directly after /s/.**

Of course, such a difference is not necessarily noticed by a native speaker of standard English, but a little attention and phonetic training make these differences apparent. As aspirated [t^h] and unaspirated [t⁼] cannot replace one another in the same environment in English, they cannot contrast or distinguish one utterance from another. That is, [st^{h}i:m] or [st⁼i:m] may be the pronunciation of the same word *steam*. We therefore group these two sounds: [t^h] and [t⁼], phonetically different as they are, into one phonologically distinctive unit, or phoneme, symbolized by /t/. The phoneme /t/, therefore, consists of several phonetically different sounds (phones), or "members" and may be regarded logically as a class; similarly, we have [p^h] and [p⁼] of *pan* and *span*, [k^h] and [k⁼] of *can* and *scan*. These sounds (or phones) are the **allophones** of the same phoneme. They are variants of the same phoneme that occur in detailed phonetic transcriptions.

Some other well-known examples of allophonic differences in English may include *clear* [l] and *dark* [ɫ]. They are the allophones of the same phoneme /l/: *clear* [l] can be pronounced with the front of the tongue raised toward the hard palate as in *lip* [lip]; *dark* [ɫ] is pronounced with the back of the tongue raised toward the soft palate as in *pill* [pi. ɫ.].

How about the vowel /e/ in the words *bed* [bed] and *ten* [ten]? In fact, the vowel /e/ in the word *ten* [tẽn] may be nasalized in actual pronunciation; they may belong to two different allophones of the same phoneme /e/. There is a phonological rule in English that states: **a vowel becomes nasalized before a nasal segment** (**within the same syllable**). But we know that the [e] in *bed* and the nasalized [ẽ] in *ten* do not make a difference in meaning. Similarly, the [iː] sound in *beep* and *beam* will be phonetically different.

What we should pay attention to is that the phonemic segments are usually placed between slanting lines; thus we may say that the underlying phonemic segments in *cat* and *catty* are /kæt/ and /kæti/. But the phonetic segments that are actually pronounced are usually [kæt] and [kæti]. The pronunciations are indicated by phonetic transcriptions, and written between square brackets.

3.2.2 Minimal Pairs, Phonemic Contrast and Complementary Distribution

Linguists use minimal pairs to discover the phonemes of a particular language. A **minimal pair** is two words with different meanings that are identical except for one sound segment that occurs in the same place in each word. For example, *cab* [kæb] and *cad* [kæd] are a minimal pair that differ only in their final segments; whereas *cat* [kæt] and *mat* [mæt] are another minimal pair that differ only in their initial segments. In this sense, minimal pairs refer to pairs of words differing by one phoneme.

The process of substituting one sound for another in a word to see if it makes a difference is a good way to identify the phonemes of a language. Here are some words differing only in their vowels:

(1)
beat	[biːt]	[iː]	boot	[buːt]	[uː]
bit	[bit]	[i]	but	[bʌt]	[ʌ]
bait	[beit]	[ei]	boat	[bəut]	[əu]
bet	[bet]	[e]	bought	[bɔːt]	[ɔː]
bat	[bet]	[e]	bout	[baut]	[au]
bite	[bait]	[ai]	bot	[bɔt]	[ɔ]
Bart	[bɑːt]	[ɑː]	book	[buk]	[u]

Similarly, we can substitute the first consonant of the following words to get some of the consonant phonemes in English: **t**ake, **m**ake, **l**ake, **f**ake, **s**ake, **c**ake, **b**ake, **sh**ake, **w**ake, **r**ake, or the sets **p**ick, **V**ic, **th**ick, **ch**ick. Any two of these words in the same set may form a minimal pair: *two different words that differ in one sound*. The two sounds that cause the word difference belong to different phonemes. Thus we have the phonemes /t/, /m/, /l/, /f/, /s/, /k/, /b/, /ʃ/, /w/, /r/, or /p/, /v/, /θ/, /tʃ/. By finding other minimal pairs and sets, we could discover the other consonant phonemes in English. We can say these sounds form a **phonemic contrast**, because they are different phonemes in a language and capable of distinguishing the meaning of the words in that language.

Minimal pairs illustrate that some speech sounds are contrastive in a language, and these contrastive sounds represent the set of phonemes of that language. But we also know that some sounds are not distinct; they do not contrast meanings; the substitution of one for the other does not create a minimal pair. For example, the vowel [e] and its nasalized allophone [ẽ] in *ten*, or the aspirated [p^h] and unaspirated [$p^=$] in *pit* or *spit*.

Oral and nasal vowels in English are non-distinct sounds; what's more, the oral and nasal allophones of each vowel phoneme never occur in the same phonological context. That is, where oral vowels occur, nasal vowels do not occur, and vice versa. For the aspirated consonant [p^h] and unaspirated [$p^=$], it's the same case. In this sense, the sounds (or phones) are said to complement each other or to be in **complementary distribution**. The allophones of a phoneme are in complementary distribution—*never occurring in identical environments*. When sounds are in complementary distribution, they do not contrast with each other; they cannot distinguish one word from another. Of course, the choice of the allophone is not random or haphazard; it is rule-governed, which is illustrated in the fourth section in this chapter. The phonological rules of the language apply to phonemes to determine the pronunciation of words.

3.3 Distinctive Features of Phonemes

One way of describing the sounds of English is by specifying the features of which they are composed; we may regard a **feature** as *a phonetic property that can be used to classify sounds*. In the last chapter, we have classified consonants in English according to their place and manner of articulation, and the vowels in terms of tongue height and lip rounding. In fact, we have **binary features** such as Voice, Nasal, Lateral, Sibilant, Back, and Syllabic. Thus, all English segments may be classified as being [+ voice] or [− voice]; i.e., we have two possibilities in terms of this feature. We also have **multi-valued features** as Place, Stop, and Height; thus, in English, for the feature Place, we have four classificatory possibilities: [labial, denti-alveolar, palatal, velar]. In this description, we do not distinguish between bilabial and labiodental sounds; they can all be regarded simply as [labial]. Similarly, there are no oppositions between dental and alveolar sounds; they are classified as [denti-alveolar].

Table 3.1 Some of the Features Required for Classifying English Sounds

Feature name	Classificatory possibilities	English segments
Voice	[+ voice]	b, d, g, m, n, v, ʒ, dʒ, ŋ, ð, z, w, r, l, j (and all vowels)
	[− voice]	p, t, k, f, s, θ, ʃ
Place	[labial]	p, b, m, f, v
	[denti-alveolar]	θ, ð, t, d, n, s, z, l, r
	[palatal]	ʃ, ʒ, j (and front vowels)
	[velar]	k, g, w (and back vowels)
Stop	[stop]	p, t, k, b, d, g, m, n
	[fricative]	f, s, v, z, ʃ, ʒ, θ, ð
	[approximant]	w, r, l, j (and all vowels)
Nasal	[+ nasal]	m, n, ŋ
	[− nasal]	(all other speech sounds)
Lateral	[+ lateral]	l
	[− lateral]	(all other speech sounds)
Sibilant	[+ sibilant]	s, z, ʃ, ʒ, tʃ, dʒ
	[− sibilant]	(all other speech sounds)
Height	[maximum]	(all consonants except w, j)
	[4 height]	iː, uː, w, j
	[3 height]	ei, i, əu, u
	[2 height]	e, ɔ
	[1 height]	æ, ɑː
Back	[+ back]	uː, u, ɔː, ɔ, əu, ɑː, w, k, g
	[− back]	i, iː, ei, e, æ (and all other consonants)
Syllabic	[+ syllabic]	all vowels and some consonants as m, n, ŋ, l, r
	[− syllabic]	all other consonants, including w, j

(Taken from Ladefoged, P. 1982: 39 with some minute revision)

In the last table, the feature **Sibilant** refers to an acoustic property of the sounds being classified; it specifies the amount of hissing noise in a sound. And the feature **Approximants** refer to all other sounds that have a lesser degree of approximation of two articulators except for the stops and fricatives.

In a language, each phoneme differs from all the other phonemes by at least one distinctive feature or a feature value difference.

We have seen that **nasality** is a distinctive feature of English consonants, but it is a **nondistinctive feature** for English vowels. That is, whether you pronounce the word *ten* as [ten] or [tẽn], they are the same word; similarly, you could say *spit* [spˉiːt] if you pleased with an aspirated [pʰ], as [spʰit], and it would be understood as *spit*, but listeners would probably think it is a little bit strange. That means aspiration is a nondistinctive feature in English. But this is not the case in all languages. In French, nasality is a distinctive feature for vowels and consonants (Fromkin, et al. 2007: 268); and in Chinese, aspiration may be used to distinguish meaning; thus we have 拼 [pʰ in] and 宾 [p⁼ in] (Hu 2001: 57). In a word, different languages may use different phonemic systems to transcribe that particular language.

The examples above illustrate why we refer to the phoneme as an abstract unit or as a mental unit. We do not utter phonemes; we produce phones, the allophones of the phonemes of the language. In English /p/ is a phoneme that is pronounced as both [pʰ] and [p⁼], depending on the context. The phones or sounds [pʰ] and [p⁼] are allophones of the same phoneme /p/.

3.4 The Rules of Phonology

The relationship between the phonemic representations of words and the phonetic representations that reflect the pronunciation of those words is rule-governed. Phonological rules exist to ensure that the surface or phonetic forms of words do not violate phonotactic constraints.

In the discussion of allophones and nondistinctive features above, we show what speakers know about the predictable aspects of speech through phonological rules: the nasality feature value of the vowels in *bean*, *ten*, *mean*, *comb*, and *sing* is **predictable** because they occur before nasal consonants, and the aspiration rule in English applies to the class of [-voiced] non-continuant sounds in word-initial position. As in the vowel nasality rule, we do not need to consider individual sound segments; the rule automatically applies to initial /p/, /t/, /k/. In fact, the phonological rules that relate the phonemic representation to the phonetic representations are part of a speaker's knowledge of the language. In this section, we'll illustrate several well-known phonological rules.

3.4.1 Assimilation Rules

The **assimilation rule** assimilates one sound to another by "copying" a feature of a sequential phoneme, thus, making the two phones similar (Dai & He 2002). It is a process by which one sound takes on some or all the characteristics of a neighboring sound (Hu 2001); it makes two neighboring segments more similar by duplicating a phonetic property of the other segment.

When we speak, there is a tendency to increase the ease of articulation, that is, to articulate efficiently. It is easier to lower the velum while a vowel is being pronounced before a nasal stop than to wait for the completion of the vowel and then force the velum to move suddenly. In this sense, the **vowel nasalization rule** is an assimilation rule. It can be described as: **Nasalize vowels when they occur before nasal consonants**

(**within the same syllable**). In a formulaic way, it is:
(2) **V** (owel) → [+nasal] / ＿＿ [+nasal] $

This rule can be explained in the following way piece by piece:

V	→	[+nasal]	/	＿＿	[+nasal]	$
Vowels	become nasalized		in the environment	before	nasal segments	within a syllable

The knowledge of phonology also determines how we pronounce words and the parts of words we call morphemes. For example, the pronunciation of different plural forms. There is a **voicing assimilation rule** in English: **Change the plural morpheme /z/ to a voiceless [s] when preceded by a voiceless sound.**

In English, the voiced /z/ of the regular plural suffix (here we assume that the basic or underlying form of the plural morpheme is /z/) is changed to [s] after a voiceless sound; thus, we have the above rule.

These rules will derive the phonetic forms — that is, the pronunciations — of plurals for all regular nouns. Thus we have the following derivation of *cats* and *buses*:

/kæt + z/ → [kæts]
/bʌs + z/ → [bʌsəz]

Similarly, the voiced /d/ of the English regular past-tense suffix is changed to [t] after a voiceless sound. Readers can make the rule by themselves.

In these cases, the value of the voicing feature goes from [+voice] to [−voice] because of assimilation to the [−voice] feature of the final consonant of the stem.

We have some other assimilation phenomena in English; for example, the negative morpheme prefix spelled as *in-* or *im-* agrees in place of articulation with the word to which it is prefixed:

(3) in + correct [in + kərekt] → incorrect [iŋkə′rekt].
    [n] has become a velar nasal [ŋ] before a velar consonant [k].
    in + possible [in + pɔsəbl] → impossible [im′pɔsəbl].
    [n] has become a bilabial nasal [m] before a bilabial stop [p].
    in + legal [in + liːgl] → illegal [i′liːgl].
    [n] has become a lateral [l] before the lateral [l].
    in + regular [in + regjuːlə] → irregular [i′regjuːlə]
    [n] has become a retroflex [r] before the retroflex [r].

In effect, the rule makes two consonants that appear next to each other more similar.

3.4.2 Segment Insertion and Deletion Rules

Phonological rules may add or delete entire segments. The process of inserting a consonant or vowel is called **epenthesis**. The rules for forming regular plurals, possessive forms, and third-person singular verb agreement in English all require an epenthesis rule. For example:

(4) Insert a [ə] before the plural morpheme /z/ when a regular noun ends in a sibilant, giving [əz].

e. g. bus + plural form : /bʌs + z/ → [bʌsəz].

(5) Insert a [ə] before the past-tense morpheme when a regular verb ends in a non-nasal alveolar stop, giving [əd].

e. g. , gloat + past tense: /gləut + d/ → [gləutəd].

Segment deletion rules are commonly found in many languages. For example, we often delete the unstressed vowels that are shown in bold type in words like the following examples:

myst**e**ry gen**e**ral mem**o**ry fun**e**ral vig**o**rous Barb**a**ra

The silent g in such words as *sign* and *design* is actually an indication of a deletion rule.

(6)   A   B

sign [sain]   signature ['signətʃə]
design [də'zain]   designation [dəzig'neʃən]
paradigm ['pærədaim]   paradigmatic [pærədig'mætək]

In column A there is not a phonetic [g], but in each corresponding word in column B a [g] occurs. Our knowledge of English phonology accounts for these phonetic differences. The " [g] —no [g]" alternation is regular, and we even apply it to words that we never have heard. The rule can be described as : Delete a /g/ when it occurs before a final nasal consonant.

3. 4. 3 Sequential Rules

Your knowledge of English phonology includes information about what sequences or phonemes are permissible, and what sequences are not. There are many **sequential rules** in English. There are rules that govern the combination of sounds in English. Given four sounds: [k], [b], [l], [i], we can pronounce them as [blik], [klib], [bilk], [kilb]; but we cannot pronounce them as * [lbki], * [ilbk], * [bkil], * [ilkb], etc. Similarly, if we want to combine three consonants together (in English, no more than three sequential consonants can occur at the beginning of a word), the combination should obey the following three rules; they are called **consonant cluster rules**:

(7) a. The first phoneme must be /s/;
    b. The second must be /p/, or /t/, or /k/;
    c. The third must be /l/ or /r/ or /w/ or /j/.

Thus we have words such as *spring* [spriŋ], *strict* [strikt], *square* [skweə], *splendid* [splendid], *scream* [skri:m], *spew* [spju:]. And there are even restrictions if this condition is met; for example, /stl/ is not a permitted sequence, so *stlick* is not a possible word in English.

The phonological rules illustrated above are just some well-known rules explained in most linguistic textbooks. Of course, there are many other phonological rules which we cannot explain here due to the limitation of space. The last rule I'd like to mention is that in English, we can **change a vowel to a [ə] when the stress rules mark it as reduced**. That means [ə] is an allophone of all English vowel phonemes. Thus, we have *compete* [i] —*competition* [ə], *maintain* [ei] —*maintenance* [ə], *analysis* [æ] —*analytic* [ə] and so on. At least, this rule can help us to pronounce the vowels in English words correctly if we are clear about the stressed syllable of the word.

3.5 Syllable Structure and Suprasegmental Features

3.5.1 Syllable Structure

Words are composed of one or more syllables. Although there is no agreed phonetic definition of a syllable for linguists and there are different theories dealing with syllable structure, a common accepted definition is that a **syllable** is a phonological unit composed of one or more phonemes. In this sense, a syllable is a unit in speech which is often longer than one sound and smaller than a whole word. In fact, every syllable has a **nucleus**, which is usually a vowel [but which may be a syllabic liquid (/l/, or /r/) or nasal (/m/, /n/, /ŋ/)]. The nucleus may be preceded by one or more phonemes called the syllable **onset** and followed by one or more segments called the **coda**. Generally speaking, the onset and coda of a syllable may be composed of consonants, and in English, the onset and coda of a syllable may be consonant clusters. The onset is no more than three consonants; and the coda is no more than five consonants; and these kinds of consonants clusters must be arranged in a certain order, which is illustrated in the last section. The structure of a syllable may be described in (8):

(8) The syllable structure for the words with one syllable:

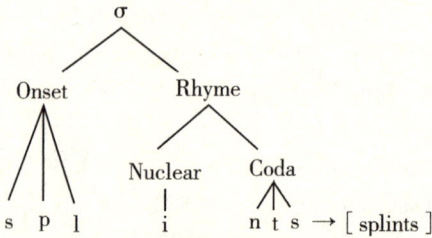

From the above description, we know that the nucleus + coda constitute the sub-syllabic unit **rhyme** (or **rime**), and onset + rhyme constitute a syllable represented by a Greek letter sigma σ. The hierarchical structure of the monosyllabic word has been shown for us.

As for the rhyme, from a very early age, children learn that certain words rhyme. In rhyme words, the nucleus and the coda of the final syllable of both words are identical, as in the poem *Thinking of You* by Joanna Fuchs.

(9)   I'm thinking of you
With joy and pl**easure**,
Remembering times
I'll always tr**easure**.

When I think of you,
My heart is **light**;
You're a special person,
A sheer del**ight**.

Thoughts of you cheer me up,
Whenever I'm bl**ue**;

I'm always happy
When I think of y**ou**.

I think of you often
In the fondest w**ay**;
I cherish you more
Than I ever could s**ay**.

(10) The syllable structure for words with more than one syllable:

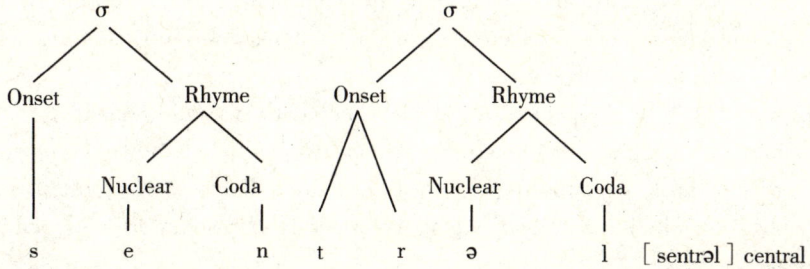

The common syllabic structure in English are V, VC, CV, CVC and the biggest structure in English is CCCVCCCCC according to Roach (2000); here, V represent a vowel, and C represent a consonant. The following examples may be a good illustration for all these structures.

(11) Some examples for the words with one syllable.

Front onset	onset	back onset	vowel	front coda	coda	back coda (1)	back coda (2)	back coda (3)
		onset	nuclear (peak)			coda		

	Front onset	onset	back onset	vowel	front coda	coda	back coda (1)	back coda (2)	back coda (3)	
e.g.: eye				ai						[ai]
it				i	t					[it]
me	m			iː						[miː]
bit	b			i	t					[bit]
scrimps	s	k	r	i	m	p	s			[skrimps]
screen	s	k	r	iː	n					[skriːn]
twelfths	t	w		e	l	f	θ	s		[twelfəs]

One way of determining the number of syllables in a word is to try singing it; each syllable is sung on a separate note. If we want to distinguish the syllables of a word, we distinguish it according to its phonetic transcription, not the spelling of the word, but in some dictionaries we may show the syllables of the word by a hyphen (-) or a dot (.) among the syllables. For example, the word *terminology* may be written in the following ways in the dictionary: *ter-mi-no-logy* or *ter. mi. no. logy*.

There is a **Maximal Onset Principle** in the distinction of the syllables of a word in case you don't know how to classify the consonants of a syllable. They may be stated as 1. *Maximal onset*, and 2. *No coda or minimal coda or maximal open syllable*. In the case of the word *extra* [ekstrə], we have two syllables, but where we divide the consonants between the two vowels is a problem. In order to meet the demands of the two rules, we'd better divide it as [ˈek. strə]. The first syllable has no onset consonant, but a syllable must consist of two **moras** (A single sound is a mora, but the long vowel and the diphthongs are two moras; that's the reason why a diphthong or a long vowel can be syllables themselves). In this case, the first consonant [k] may belong to the first syllable, and the other consonants belong to the second syllable; it meets the demands of part 1. Of course, in the dictionary we still use the spelling to indicate the syllable structure *ex. tra*.

The vowels can be the peak of a syllable, but what we should remember is that the nasal sounds and the glides could also form a peak of a syllable. They are generally considered as **syllabic consonants**; thus we have two syllable words *bottom* [bɔt**m**], *table* [teib**l**], in which the second syllable is formed by a nasal or a liquid, without the vowel peak.

3.5.2 Stress

So far in this chapter we have examined segments, that is, individual sounds and their pronunciations. However, pronunciation involves far more than just stringing together individual sounds. Those aspects of speech that involve more than single consonants or vowels are called **suprasegmental features**. They are **stress**, length, tone, and **intonation**. **Stress** applies not to individual vowels and consonants but to whole syllables. A stressed syllable [which can be marked by an acute accent (')], is pronounced with a greater amount of energy than an unstressed syllable. The following examples show that stress can be contrastive in English; in these cases it distinguishes between nouns and verbs: 'pervert / per'vert, 'subject / sub'ject, 'import / im'port, 'rebel / re'bel, 'insult / in'sult, 'progress / pro'gress, 'increase /in'crease, etc.

Some syllables have a degree of stress intermediate between full stress and no stress. For the word *photographic*, the main stress falls on the third syllable, while the second and fourth syllable are unstressed; the first syllable has some stress, though not as much as the third; this is called **secondary stress**. Thus we have [fəutə'græfik]. Generally, speakers of a language know which syllable receives **primary stress**, which ones receive secondary stress, and which ones are reduced (unstressed); it is part of their knowledge of the language. It's easy to distinguish between stressed and reduced syllables, because the vowel in reduced syllables is pronounced as a schwa [ə] or deleted, except at the ends of certain words such as *confetti* or *laboratory*.

As for the stressed syllable of a compound noun in English, we place primary stress on the adjectival part; thus we have 'blackbird, 'greenhouse, 'hot-dog, 'dining-room, 'sewing machine, 'redcoat, 'White House, etc. But when the words are a noun phrase consisting of an adjective followed by a noun, we place the stress on the noun; of course, the meaning may be totally different from that of the corresponding compounding noun. You can find the differences by consulting the dictionary: black 'bird, green'house, hot'dog, dining 'room, sewing 'machine, red'coat, White 'House.

Stress is a property of the syllable rather than a segment. To produce a stressed syllable, one may change the pitch (usually by raising it), make the syllable louder, or make it longer. We often use all three of these phonetic means to stress a syllable. When words are combined into phrases and sentences, one syllable receives greater stress than all others; that is, only one of the vowels in a phrase or sentence receives primary stress; all of the other stressed vowels are reduced to secondary stress. This kind of knowledge may be predictable from the morphology and syntax.

For the other suprasegmental features as **length**, **pitch** and **intonation**, we have not space to give a detailed description, but we must remember that some languages use them to distinguish the meaning of the word. For example, Korean uses *vowel length* to distinguish the meaning (such as [il] (day), and [iːl] (work) (Ladefoged 1982: 225); while Chinese uses **tone** to distinguish the meaning of the word (The classic example is yī (一, one), yí (遺, lose), yǐ (已, already), yì (意, idea). All spoken languages make use of **intonation**, and knowing intonation patterns is an important though often neglected part of speaking a foreign language. English use intonation to change the attitude the speaker is expressing. The following different intonations may express different attitudes of the speaker in a certain situation, but we should notice that unlike in Chinese, these tones cannot be regarded as an inherent part of a single word. If it is a phrase or a sentence, the tone is spread over the whole of that utterance.

(12) Different intonations representing different attitudes of the speaker (Radford 2000: 48).

a.	b.	c.	d.	e.
me	me?	me!	me	me?!
eat peas	eat peas?	eat peas!	eat peas	eat peas?!
↓	↗	↘	╱	↘↗
A simple statement,	a question,	a strong assertion,	a matter of fact assertion,	disbelief

3.6 Summary

Part of one's knowledge of a language is knowledge of the **phonology** or sound system of that language. It includes the phonetic sounds that occur in the language (**phones**) and the ways in which they pattern. This patterning determines the inventory of **phonemes** (the abstract basic units that differentiate words).

Phonetic **segments** are enclosed in square brackets [ ], and phonemes between slashes / /. When similar phones occur in **complementary distribution**, they are **allophones**—predictable phonetic variants—of phonemes. On the other hand, phones in the same environment that differentiate words, like the [b] and [m] in *boat* [bəut] and *moat* [məut], represent two distinct phonemes, /b/ and /m/. Linguists use **minimal pairs** (two distinct words are distinguished by a single phone occurring in the same position) to discover the different phonemes in a language; these phonemes form a **phonemic contrast** in a language.

Phonemes are composed of **distinctive features**; some phonemes contrast by means of a single distinctive feature, such as /b/ and /m/; [± nasal] may be used to distinguish them, where /b/ is [− nasal], /m/ is [+ nasal]. Others may be contrasted by more than one feature: /d/ is a voiced alveolar stop; /s/ is a voiceless alveolar fricative in *dip* and *sip*. Phonetic features that are predictable are nondistinctive; the nasality of vowels in English is a **non-distinctive feature** because all vowels are nasalized before nasal consonants; similarly, aspiration of the consonant stops may be nondistinctive because whether you pronounce the phoneme /p/ aspirated or not does not change the meaning of the word *speak* [sp^{h}i:k] / [sp⁼i:k].

The relationship between the **phonemic representation** of words and sentences and the **phonetic representation** (the pronunciation of them) is determined by phonological rules, which apply to phonemic strings and change them in various ways to derive their actual phonetic pronunciation. We have discussed three kinds of phonological rules in this chapter; they are **assimilation rules**, **segment insertion** and

deletion rules and **sequential rules**. They can be used to explain many phenomena in the actual pronunciation of the words in a certain context.

A word can be segmented into several **syllables**. A syllable typically contains a consonant (or set of consonants) followed by a vowel which is followed by another consonant (or set of consonants). Although there are some disagreements in the definition or analysis of the syllable structures, we have provided some principles to distinguish the syllables of a word.

Suprasegmental features may be used to distinguish the meaning of the words or utterances. We have a detailed description of the **stress**; as for the **length** of the sounds, the **tones** and **intonation**, readers may refer to some books of phonetics and phonology to gain a good understanding.

EXERCISES

Exercises I, II, III are adapted from the exercises 299 – 310 in Fromkin, et al. (2007); Exercises IV, V are revised according to those provided in Radford (2000): 101 – 102.

Exercises I

Minimal pairs can be used to find the phonemes of the particular language. Find the sets of minimal pairs for each pair of English consonants given below:
/k/—/g/, /b/—/m/, /l/—/r/, /p/—/f/, /s/—/ʃ/,
/tʃ/—/dʒ/, /e/—/æ/, /n/—/ŋ/, /θ/—/ð/, /i/—/iː/.

Exercises II

In some dialects of English, the following words have different vowels, as is shown by the phonetic transcriptions (in American transcription [ai] is transcribed as [aj]):

A	B	C
bite [bʌjt]	bide [bajd]	die [daj]
rice [rʌjs]	rise [rajz]	by [baj]
ripe [rʌjp]	bribe [brajb]	sigh [saj]
wife [wʌjf]	wives [wajvz]	rye [raj]
dike [dʌjk]	dime [dajm]	guy [gaj]

a. How may the classes of sounds that end the words in columns **A** and **B** be characterized? That is, what feature specifies all the final segments in **A** and all the final segments in **B**?

b. How do the words in column **C** differ from those in columns **A** and **B**?

c. Are [ʌj] and [aj] in complementary distribution? Give your reasons.

d. Give the phonetic representations of the following words as they would be spoken in the dialect described here:

life [ ], lives [ ], lie [ ], file [ ], bike [ ], lice [ ]

e. Formulate a rule that will relate the phonemic representations to the phonetic representations of the words given above.

Exercises III

Consider the following English verbs. Those in column **A** have stress on next-to-last syllable, whereas the verbs in column **B** and **C** have their last syllable stressed.

A	B	C
astonish	collapse	amaze
exit	exist	improve
imagine	resent	surprise
cancel	revolt	combine
elicit	adopt	believe
practice	insist	atone

a. Transcribe the words under columns **A**, **B**, and **C** phonemically. (Use a schwa for the unstressed vowels.)

b. Consider the phonemic structure of the stressed syllables in these verbs. What is the difference between the final syllables of the verbs in columns **A** and **B**? Formulate a rule that predicts where stress occurs in the verbs in columns **A** and **B**.

c. In the verbs in column **C**, stress also occurs on the final syllable. What must you add to the rule to account for this fact? (Hint: for the forms in columns **A** and **B**, the final consonants have to be considered; for the forms in column **C**, consider the vowels.)

Exercises IV

Recall that the symbol ⁼ means an unaspirated consonant and the symbol ʰ means aspiration. Show how the pattern of data below can be explained by the Maximal Onset Principle. Assume that separate words are syllablified separately.

1. a. stub [st⁼ʌb]　　2. a. spare [sp⁼eə]　　3. a. scar [sk⁼ɑː]
　　b. this tub [ðis tʰʌb]　　b. this pear [ðis pʰea]　　b. this car [ðis kʰɑː]
　　c. disturb [dist⁼əːb]　　c. despair [disp⁼eə]　　c. discard [disk⁼ɑːd]

Exercises V

Break the following words into syllables, and applying the Maximal Onset Principle, identify the onsets, nuclei and codas by providing a diagram such as that in (10).

a. comfortable   b. secretary   c. cooperation   d. confessional

Exercises VI

In the discussion of the phonological rules, we have a deletion rule stated as: **Delete a /g/ when it occurs before a final nasal consonant**. Thus, in the pairs like *sign/signature*, *design/designation*, *paradigm/paradigmatic*, there is not a phonetic [g] in the first word, but in the pairs like *gnosis/agnostic*, the pronunciation of the first word is also lacking a phonetic [g]. Can you give a more general rule describing these data?

Exercises VII

Suppose /d/ is the basic form of the pronunciation of the past-tense morpheme -ed; given the following data, please form some rules to explain the past-tense formation of regular verbs as those in section 3.

Set A: grab [græb], grabbed [græbd]; hug [hʌg], hugged [hʌgd]; faze [feiz], fazed [feizd]; roam [rəum], roamed [rəumd]

Set B: reap [riːp], reaped [riːpt]; poke [pəuk], poked [pəukt]; kiss [kis], kissed [kist]; patch [pætʃ], patched [pætʃt]

Set C: fight [fait], fighted [faitəd]; load [ləud], loaded [ləudəd]

Exercises VIII

In the pronunciation of the word *speak* [spʰiːk], *bean* [biːn], the phonemes /p/, /iː/ may be described according to its phonetic features as the following:

/p/: [voiceless, labial, stop, unaspirated], /iː/: [voiced, high, front, spread, nasalized].

Among these features, which ones may be distinctive, which are nondistinctive features? Give the reasons to support your argument.

Chapter 4

Morphology

Any native speaker knows a huge amount of words in his language, and words are an important part of linguistic knowledge and constitute a component of our mental grammars. If you don't know English, then you wouldn't know where one word begins or ends in an utterance like *Thecatsatonthemat*. Knowing a word means knowing that a particular sequence of sounds is associated with a particular meaning. A speaker of English has no difficulty in segmenting the above stream of sounds into six individual words: *the*, *cat*, *sat*, *on*, *the*, and *mat* because each of these words is listed in his mental dictionary, or **lexicon** (the Greek word for dictionary), which is part of a speaker's linguistic knowledge.

As we all know, in English, many words can easily be split into smaller component; words like *reader*, *printer* are nouns related to the verbs *read*, and *print*; they all mean roughly "person or instrument that Verb-s". Clearly, it is the ending *-er* which conveys this new aspect of meaning and we can say that *-er* creates a new noun from a verb. Sometimes, a complex word consists of a number of components, each with its own meaning.

On the other hand, some languages (**Agglutinative Languages**) have no word-like unit. They are mainly composed of strings of units, none of which have any independent, word-like status. For example, in an eastern African language, we have sentences like this:

Ninakupenda: Ni   na   ku   pend   a.
                I   (*pres. tense*)   *you*   *love*   (*end*).
Nisikupendi: Ni   si   ku   pend   i.
                I   not   *you*   *love*   (*end*).

(Here verb ending indicating present tense and negation.)

And in Japanese we also have the unit smaller than a word like masu (. ま. す.) ; that's the reason why we need morpheme instead of word as the base of grammatical analysis.

From the discussion above, we know that word is the most important physical object in our minds, and there are internal structures for complex words, which may be composed of smaller units, each with its own meaning. This field of linguistics which examines the internal structure of word and processes of word formation is known as **morphology**. In this chapter, we will explain the concepts of morpheme, how morphemes are combined to form words, and how words are formed by compounding and other methods.

4.1 Morpheme and Morphology

Generally speaking, we think of **words** as being the most basic, the most fundamental units through which meaning is represented in language. But actually there are even smaller units that carry the fundamental meanings of a language. Words are made up of these units. For example, *undesirable* is composed of *un* + *desire* + *able*; for each part, we have a certain meaning contributing to the whole meaning of the word. **Morphology** is such a science dealing with the composition of words; it is the study of the semantic and grammatical structure of words, which is part of our grammatical knowledge of that language; and generally this kind of knowledge is unconscious. In this section, we manage to illustrate this knowledge explicitly.

4.1.1 The Classification of Morphemes

In the study of morphology, we have the smallest unit of grammatical analysis, **morpheme**, which can be split as *morph-* and *-eme*, meaning "*shape*, *form*" and "*meaningful*" respectively in Greek. A morpheme is the basic element of meaning in a word; i. e. , it is the smallest component of a word which contributes to its meaning—a minimal linguistic sign.

Morpheme is an arbitrary union of a sound and a meaning that cannot be further analyzed. It is the smallest meaningful unit of a language, not divisible or analyzable into smaller forms. And the decomposition of words into morphemes illustrates one of features of human language — **discreteness**, one of the properties that distinguish human languages from the communication systems of other species.

A word can be composed of one or more different morphemes. For example, the words *ungentlemanliness* and *indecipherability* can be formed in the following way:
gentle—gentleman—gentlemanly—gentlemanliness—ungentlemanliness,
cipher—decipher—decipherable—indecipherable—indecipherability.
Structurally represented, we have the following tree diagrams for the two words:

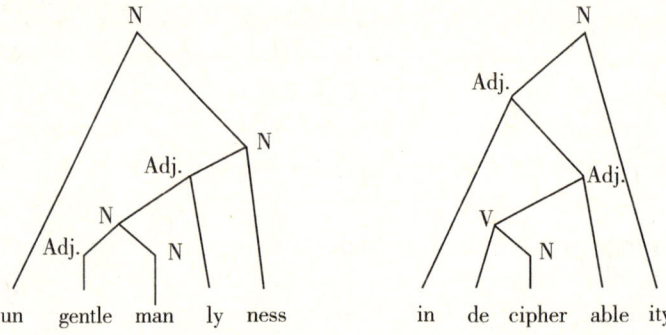

Our morphological knowledge has two components: knowledge of the individual morphemes and knowledge of the rules that combine them. Morphemes convey semantic and syntactic information. Not all morphemes are equally central to the formation of a word. One of the things we know about particular morphemes is whether they can stand alone or whether they must be attached to a base morpheme. According to this feature, a morpheme can be classified as a free or a bound morpheme: a morpheme which can stand as a word is called a **free morpheme**; by contrast, those morphemes which are unable to function as free standing words are called **bound morphemes**; they occur only as part of a word which could not stand on its own (*un-*, *pre-*, *bi-*, *-s*, *-ed*, *-er*...). Thus, for the word *reader*, read is a free morpheme, while *-er* is a bound morpheme. Of course, bound morphemes can be further classified; the classification of morphemes can be exemplified in the following way:

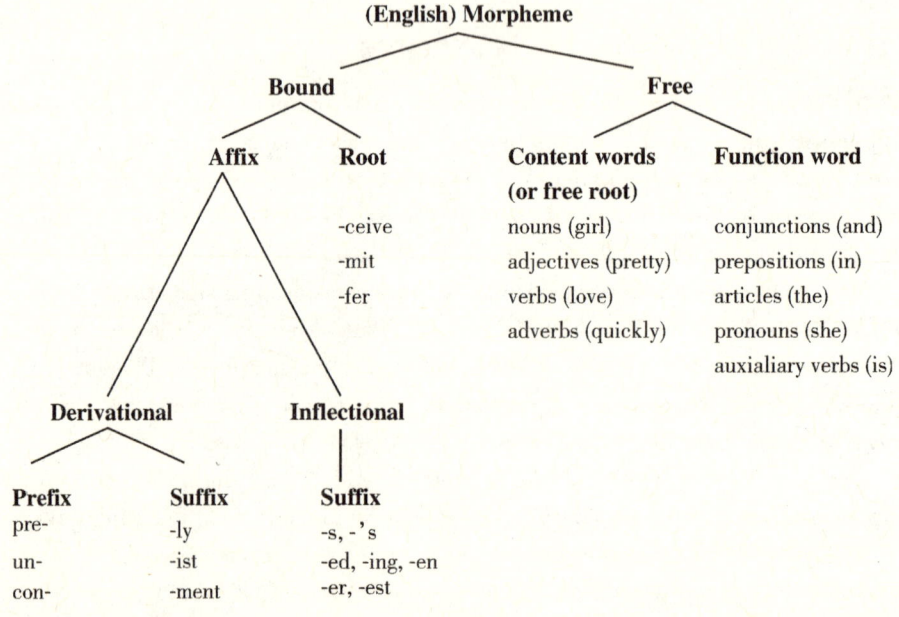

[Classification of English Morphemes (adapted from Fromkin, et al. 2004: 103)]

4.1.2 Inflectional and Derivational Affix

Among bound morphemes, we have two classes: one is called **inflectional affixes** (affixes that do not participate in word formation at all); the other is **derivational affixes** (affixes that have the function of deriving new words).

Inflectional affixes are for the most part purely grammatical markers, representing such kind of grammatical meaning as agreement, tense and aspect for the verb; person, number and case for the noun; and comparative and superlative degree for the adjectives. It is the manifestation of grammatical relationships through the addition of inflectional morphemes. An inflectional affix in English does not form a new word with new lexical meaning when it is added to another word. Nor does it change the word-class of the word to which it is affixed. In English, we have the following inflectional morphemes:

Verb endings: -(e)s, indicating third person singular present tense —reads
-(e)d, indicating past tense —talked
-ing, indicating progressive aspect —doing
-en, indicating past participle —eaten
Noun endings: -(e)s, indicating plurality of nouns —boys
-'s, indicating the possessive case of nouns —girl's
Adjective endings: -er, indicating comparative degree —easier
-est, indicating superlative degree —finest

Derivational morphemes are those morphemes which change the syntactic categories or the lexical meaning of words. When they are added to a base, a new word with a new (grammatical or lexical) meaning is derived. The word that results from the addition of a derivational morpheme is called a **derived word**.

An **affix** is the collective term for the type of bound morphemes that can be added to the beginning, or ending of another morpheme; thus we have the familiar affixes as prefix and suffix in English. Of course, there are **infixes**; they are those morphemes that are inserted into other morphemes, such as:

fucking → *fuckin*: unbelievable — un-*fuckin*-believable, or

bloody → bloomin: absolutely—abso-*bloomin*-lutely.

We also have the so-called **circumfixes**, which are morphemes that are attached to a base morpheme both initially and finally. In German, the past participle of regular verbs is formed by adding the prefix *ge-* and the suffix *-t* to the verb root, thus we have *lieb* (love) —*geliebt* (loved). English infixing has been the subject of the linguists; we don't discuss it here, please see Fromkin, et al. (2004: 80 – 81).

Prefixes are added to the beginning of another morpheme, they can be used to change the lexical meaning of that morpheme, e.g., mini-, un-, in- and so on.

Suffixes are added to the ending of another morpheme to change its grammatical class or adding its grammatical meaning (in such cases, they are called inflectional suffixes: e. g. , -ed, -s, -er). In English, we have such suffixes as -er, -ise, -tion and so on.

4.1.3 Root, Stem and Base

For the morphemes to which the affixes are added, we have different terms for them: **root**, **stem**, and **base**. They are used in linguistics to designate that part of a word that remains when all the affixes have been removed. We need pay attention to their differences.

Firstly, morphologically complex words consist of a root and one or more affixes. A **root** is the basic unchangeable part of a word. It cannot be analyzed into smaller parts; it conveys the main lexical meaning of the word; and it is the ultimate starting point for deriving a word (Radford 2000). Roots are at the center of word-derivational processes. For example, in English, for the words *painter*, *reread*, and *conceive*, the roots are *paint*, *read* and *ceive* respectively. In fact, many roots are free morphemes: *paint*, *read*, *man*, *sun*, *run*, *milk*. And **free roots** provide the English language with a basis for the formation of new words. On the other hand, there are many **bound roots** in English; and most bound roots found in English today are of classical origin; i. e. , they were borrowed into English from Latin and Greek during the Renaissance, or through French. For example, *tain* (means to *hold*) is from Latin (thus we have *contain*, *detain*, *retain*), and *ceive* (means to *take*) is also from Latin (thus we have *conceive*, *deceive*, *receive*. To be completed, bound roots require that another morpheme be attached to them.

A **stem** is of concern only when dealing with inflectional morphology. It is the part of the word-form which remains *when all inflectional affixes have been removed* (Bauer 1983). All the inflectional affixes are added to a stem; thus we have stems as *greenhouse*, *read*, and *fine* from the words *greenhouses*, *reads* and *finer* respectively.

Linguists sometimes use the word **base** to mean any root or stem to which an affix is attached. It is *a form to which a rule of word-formation is applied.*

Thus, for the words *unbelievable*, *unsystematically* and *painters*, we can analyze them as:

```
Word: (unbelievable)    un     +   believe   +   able
                        prefix     verb          suffix
Base: (believable)                 believe   +   able
Base and root: (believe)           believe

Word: (unsystematically)   un + system + atic + al + ly
Base: (unsystematical)     un + system + atic + al
Base: (unsystematic)       un + system + atic
```

Base: (systematic)   system + atic
Base and root: (system)   system

Word: (painters) paint + er + s
Stem and base: (painter) paint + er
Base and root: (paint)   paint

4.1.4 Allomorphs

Just as a phoneme may have different allophones, one morpheme may have alternate shapes or phonetic forms. We say the shapes of morphemes as they are actually pronounced in a word are referred to as **morphs**, and where two morphs are variants of one morpheme we say they are **allomorphs** of that morpheme. For example, the morpheme expressing plurality in English (so morpheme is an abstract concept as phoneme) can be:

[s] (maps), [z] (dogs), [iz] (watches), [ai] (mice), [iː] (teeth), [n] (oxen) ...

An allomorph is any of the variant forms of a morpheme as conditioned by position or adjoining sounds. For example, we have the positional variants: *-ion*, *-tion*, *-sion*, *-ation* as in the words *invention*, *description*, *justification*, *expansion*; and the adjoining sounds may lead to different allomorphs for the same morpheme: *im-*, *in-*, *ir-*, *il-* as in the words *imperfect*, *incorrect*, *irrelevant*, *illegal* (Stockwell 2001: 58 – 61).

On the other hand, certain morphemic shapes represent different morphemes and thus have different meanings, or we say two different morphemes may have the same shape. For example, the morpheme -s in English may represent the plural form, the third singular form of the verb and the possessive case as in the words *tables*, *talks*, and *boy's* respectively.

The last point about morphemes is that morphemes must not be confused with syllables. Syllables have nothing to do with meaning, while a morpheme possesses both sound and meaning. It may be represented by any number of syllables, though typically only one or two, sometimes three or four.

4.2 Words

In the last section, we have discussed the smallest meaningful unit for grammatical analysis — morpheme. We know the reasons why we need such a linguistic unit. But we cannot avoid discussing the familiar unit — word, because most languages have words and in those languages some words, at least, have an internal structure, and consist of one or more morphemes.

Words can be classified in different ways. On the morphemic level, according to the number and type of morphemes they contain, words can be classified into simple words (words consisting of a single morpheme: *man*, *work*, *kind*), derived words (words which are the result of a derivational process: *fruitless*, *fruitful*, *unfruitful*, *unfruitfulness*), and compound words (words which are composed of two or more free morphemes: *forget-me-not*, *spacesuit*).

In fact, in the study of words, the most important problem is how to define words; there is no consensus of opinion on this issue among linguists.

4.2.1 The Definition and Identification of Words

A natural first step in a scientific approach to words is to give a working definition, but as we know, this defining can be difficult. Linguists try to define words in various ways, but each of these ways has its own problems. Anyway let's review those definitions given by linguists, which will help us to acquire a good understanding of the properties of words.

A practical common-sense definition of words is that a word is *any sequence of letters bounded on either side by a space or punctuation mark* (Carter 1998). The definition is used as the basis of such activities as counting the number of words needed for an essay. But this orthographic definition is problematic. Firstly, **orthography** refers to a medium of written language. Even in writing, there are potential and theoretical problems. For example, we are not sure that pairs like *bring*, *brings*, *brought*, *bringing*; or *cat*, *cats*; or *postbox*, *post box*, *post-box*; or *can't*, *cannot* belong to one word or several words. Secondly, spoken discourse does not generally allow for such a clear perception of a word. Even if you use the criterion of "potential pause" for the spoken languages, sometimes it won't work.

Another suggested procedure is that words are *the smallest units in a language that can be used alone as a sentence* or *a minimum free form* in Bloomfield's sense. We can say *Go*, *Here*, *Possibly*, *Wonderful* alone, but we can't use the bits of words as sentences, as with *un-*, *-ize*, *-ing*. But here too there are problems, the articles *a* and *the* in English could not stand by themselves.

Yet another criterion for word identification is in terms of *minimal unit of positional mobility*; that is, the word is the smallest unit which can be moved from one position to another in a sentence, while bits of words cannot be so moved.

A more reliable way of trying to discover words in a language is to view them as units which have a *fixed internal structure*. We say a word has "*internal stability*". If we want to insert fresh information into a sentence, then it is between the words that this information goes and not within them; words are not interruptible. But this definition cannot explain those words with infixes, such as the words *kangabloodyroo* (*kangaroo* + *bloody*), *unfuckinbelievable* (*unbelievable* + *fuckin*), *absobloominlutely* (*absolutlely* + *bloomin*) (the infixes here are used for emphasis).

Sometimes words are defined as *the minimum meaningful unit of language*, but a unit of meaning may consist of more than one word (e. g. idioms and phrasal verbs: kick the bucket, spick and span, give in). And those function words like *if*, *but*, *because*, *could*, *them* may be without any lexical meaning. On the contrary, a unit of meaning may also consist of less than one word (morphemes: *un*healthy). We say it is no good simply using a semantic definition as a basis, since across languages speakers package meaning into words in very different ways.

If we say *a word will not have more than one stressed syllable* (Lyons 1995: 52), then how to explain those two-word orthographic units such as *bus conductor*? They would be defined as single words according to this definition. And some of the forms do not normally receive stress (*if*, *but*, *by*, *them*).

According to the discussion above, we can say that intuitively, orthographic, free-form or stress-based definitions of a word make sense, but there are many words which do not fit these categories. Words have different forms, but the different forms do not necessarily count as different words. On the other hand, words can have the same forms but different and, in some cases completely unrelated meanings. The existence of idioms seems to upset attempts to define words in any reasonably formal way.

4.2.2 Word-formation

In the study of morphology, we mainly focus on the internal structure of the words and the word-formation process by **derivation**; that is, how affixes are added to the roots to form new words. In fact, English has many other ways to form new words. Let's begin with derivation.

4.2.2.1 *Derivation*

Derivation is a morphological process where, by adding affixes to the roots, we can form a huge amount of new words. We know the rules that enable us to create and understand new words, and to recognize possible and impossible words. Generally speaking, we have two main processes to derive a new word; they are prefixation and suffixation.

1. Prefixation

Prefixes modify the lexical meaning of the base; they do not generally change the word-class of the base. But we have exceptions. For example:

  be + *adj.* ⇒ *v.* *becalm*, *belittle* ... (to cause/make ...)

  de + *n.* / en + *n.* / un + *n.* ⇒ *v.* *deform*, *enslave*, *unearth*...

  anti + *n.* / inter + *n.* / post + *n.* / pre + *n.* ⇒ *adj.* *anti-war*, *inter-state*, *postwar*, *pre-calculus*...

We can classify the prefixes according to their meanings (Quirk et al. 1972):

  a. "Negative" prefixes (*un-*, *non-*, *in-*, *dis-*, *a-*...).

   e.g. *uncertain*, *nonprofit*, *incompetent*, *disadvantage*, *anonymous*...

b. "Reversative" or "privative" prefixes (*un-*, *de-*, *dis-*...).
   e. g. *unpack*, *decode*, *disappear*...
c. "Pejorative" prefixes (*mis-*, *mal-*, *pseudo-*...).
   e. g. *misfortune*, *maltreatment*, *pseudoscientific*...
d. Prefixes of degree or size (*arch-*, *super-*, *out-*, *sub-*, *over-*, *under-*, *hyper-*, *ultra-*, *mini-*...).
   e. g. *archbishop*, *superbug*, *outrank*, *subdivision*, *overreact*, *underestimate*, *hypersensitivity*, *ultraviolet*, *ultramodern*, *miniseries*...
e. Prefixes of attitude (*co-*, *counter-*, *anti-*, *pro-*...).
   e. g. *coexist*, *counterproductive*, *anti-social*, *pro-choice*...
f. "Locative" prefixes (*super-*, *sub-*, *inter-*, *trans-*...).
   e. g. *superstructure*, *submarine*, *interaction*, *transmit*...
g. Prefixes of time and order (*fore-*, *pre-*, *post-*, *ex-*, *re-*...).
   e. g. *foreword*, *predict*, *postpone*, *ex-president*, *regroup*...
h. "Number" prefixes (*uni-*, *mono-*, *bi-*, *di-*, *tri-*, *multi-*, *poly-*...).
   e. g. *uniform*, *monologue*, *bilingual*, *dialogue*, *triangular*, *multinational*...

2. Suffixation

Since suffixes usually change the word from one part of speech to another. It is convenient to classify them not only according to the word-class of the word they form [As verb-forming suffixes (*simplify*), adjective-forming suffixes (*useful*), noun-forming suffixes (*friendship*) and adverb-forming suffixes (*clockwise*)], but also according to the kind of base to which they are typically added [As de-verbal adjectives (*washable*), de-verbal nouns (*worker*) and de-adjectival verbs (*modernize*)].

a. Noun-to-noun suffixes.
   Occupational suffixes: *-er*, *-eer*, *-ster*... (*New Yorker*, *engineer*, *gangster*...)
   Diminutive or feminine endings: *-let*, *-ette*, *-ess*, *-y*, *-ie*... (*piglet*, *cigarette*, *waitress*, *cookie*...)
   Suffixes having to do with status and domain: *-hood*, *-dom*, *-ship*... (*boyhood*, *kingdom*, *friendship*...)
   Count noun to mass noun: *-ful*... (*cupful*, *mouthful*...)
b. Noun-to-*adj.* suffixes:
   -ite, *-ian*, *-ese*... (*socialite*, *Republican*, *Chinese*...)
c. Verb-to-noun suffixes:
   -er, *-or*, *-ant*, *-ee*, *-ation*, *-ment*, *-al* (*refusal*) *-ing*, *-age* (*drainage*)...
d. Adjectives:
   adj.-to-noun suffixes: *-ness*, *-ity*...
   adj.-to-verb suffixes: *-ify*, *-ize*, *-en*...
   verb-to-*adj.* suffixes: *-able*, *-ible*...
   noun-to-*adj.* suffixes: *-ly*...

e. Adverbs:
   adj. -to-adverb suffixes: *-ly*, *-ward* ...
   noun-to-adverb suffixes: *-wise*, *-ize*, *-en* ...

4.2.2.2 Compounding

Compounding is a common and frequent process for enlarging the vocabulary of all languages. In English, compounding is perhaps the most powerful word building process; it consists of joining two or more old words to form a new unit— a compound word. What we should remember is that the meaning of a compound is not always the sum of the meanings of its parts: a *blackbird* may be green, brown or white; the person who wears a red coat may be not a *Redcoat* (slang for a British soldier during the American Revolutionary War). Many compounds do not seem to relate to the meanings of the individual parts at all; for example, a *highbrow* does not necessarily have a high brow, nor does a *bigwig* have a big wig.

Like certain words with the prefix *un-*, the meaning of many compounds must be learned as if they were individual words. Some of the meanings may be figured out, but not all. The pronunciation of English compounds differs from the way we pronounce the sequence of two words that are not compounded. In an actual compound, the first word is usually stressed, and in a noncompound phrase, the second word is stressed.

Generally speaking, in English, the rightmost word in a compound is the head of the compound, which is the part of a word or phrase that determines its broad meaning and grammatical category. On the other hand, compounds formed with a preposition are in the category of the non-prepositional part of the compound; hence we have the words like *overtake*, *sundown*, *afterbirth*, *downfall*, *uplift*, etc.; the parts of speech of these words are very obvious to us.

Linguists have provided some relative criteria of judging a compound word. They are **orthographic criterion**, **phonological criterion**, and **semantic criterion**.

Orthographically, compounds can be written in various ways. They can be joined together (*airmail*), or hyphenated (*air-conditioning*), or open (*air force*). But sometimes, the same compound may appear in different forms. It is difficult to decide which form should be used as the correct form (e.g., *flowerpot*, *flower-pot*, *flower pot*). There are no principled criteria that would tell us whether *windmill* has to be written as one word, as two words (*wind mill*) or as a hyphenated word (*wind-mill*).

Phonologically, many compounds have a so-called **compound accent** (i.e., a single stress on the first element), or a main stress on the first element and a secondary stress on the second element (*'space rocket*, *'black-list*). There is usually no difficulty in distinguishing a compound from a phrase by phonological criterion. You are sure to know the difference between *'bluebird* and *blue 'bird*, or between *'blackboard* and *black 'board*.

Semantically, just as described above, the meaning of some compounds is derived from the combined lexical meanings of their component (*picture book*, *chocolate cake*, *backdoor*, *sunset* ...). But one cannot always tell what the compound means by the sum of the meanings of its components (*dog days*, *flatfoot*, *green-hand* ...).

Bauer (1998) described the meaning relationships between the two parts in compounds as follows:

A causes B: *heat rash*, *shell shock* ...
A is caused by B: *flu virus* ...
A is prevented by B: *tetanus jab* ...
B resembles A: *frogman*, *hairpin bend* ...
A is at place B: *ant heap*, *bookshop* ...
A is at time B: *night worker* ...
B is made of A: *rye bread*, *soap suds* ...
B is made with A: *needlework* ...
B is part of A: *eardrum*, *shirtsleeve* ...

Compounds can be classified according to parts of speech of the compounds. Thus we have noun compounds which are the commonest, most productive type, adjective compounds, verb compounds and preposition compounds (such as *into*, *throughout*, but compounding is limited to only lexical category words). The following compounds may be formed by the combination of different parts of speech with different meaning relationships, different syntactic relationships; you can analyze them in the following way:

Ashtray: a noun compound, noun + noun (*ash* + *tray*), *ash* is at the place of *tray*, a restrictive relation.

The syntactic relation of compounding elements may be: subject + verb, verb + object, verb + adverbial, subject + object, restrictive relation, appositive relation and so on.

a. Noun compounds: *headache*, *pickpocket*, *swimming pool*, *steamboat*, *moonwalk*, *girlfriend*, *breakdown* ...

b. Adjective compounds: *thunder-struck*, *peace-loving*, *hardworking*, *seasick*, *knee-deep*, *bittersweet*, *never-to-be-too-old-to-learn* (spirit), (the) *do-what-you-can-and-take-what-you-need* (policy) ...

c. Verb compounds: *housekeep*, *machine-gun*, *baby-sit* ...

Compounds are useful ways of condensing information. They add variation to the way we refer to concepts in discourse because of their brevity and vividness; thus we have the expressions like: **up-to-the-minute** *information*, or other such kinds of sentences: *The old man would sit for hours, thinking sadly of all* **the might-have-beens**.

4.2.2.3 Borrowing

All languages borrow words from other languages. Borrowing words refers to those words which originated in one language (or dialect), but which have come to be used in another, even by people who don't speak the "lending" language.

Language speakers borrow words from other languages because they need to develop words for new and unfamiliar concepts. Sometimes if certain cultures are associated with particular prestigious activities, it is common for the words associated with that activity to come from the language of that culture. Word borrowing is frequent in situations of language contact or dialect contact.

When a word is borrowed, it is often gradually changed so that it fits the phonological and morphological structure of the borrowing language or dialect.

All cultures that have contact are likely to borrow vocabulary from each other. English borrowed an extremely large number of lexical items from Greek, Latin, Spanish, Arabic, and especially from French during the occupation period which followed the Norman Conquest in 1066.

Greek: *electricity*, *atom*, *psychology*, *philosophy*, *mystery*, *talent* ...

Latin: *cancer*, *et cetera* (*etc.*), *e. g.* (*for example*), *i. e.* (*that is*) ...

French: *Army*, *pork*, *mutton*, *feast*, *elite*, *fiancée*, *fiancé* ...

Italian: *piano*, *tango*, *sonata*, *portico*, *spaghetti* ... (words about music, art, and food)

German: *hamburger*, *kindergarten*, *Nazi*, *Gothe*...

Chinese: *taji*, *kung-fu*, *jiaozi*, *kowtow*, *tea*, *tofu*, *tao*...

Japanese: *Judo*, *Karoshi*, *sushi*, *manga*...

Arabic: *algebra*, *soda*, *coffee*, *alcohol*, *cotton*...

......

4.2.2.4 Coinage

New words may be added to the vocabulary of a language by derivational processes. Sometimes, when a new word is needed for some purpose and there is no appropriate borrowed word available, an obvious option is coining a new word. The advertising industry has added many words to English, such as *Kodak*, *nylon*, *Xerox*, *Vaseline*...

Greek and Latin have provided prefixes and suffixes that are used productively with both native and non-native roots. The prefix ex- comes from Latin: *ex-husband ex-wife*, *ex-sister-in-law*... The suffix -able/-ible is also Latin, borrowed via French, and can be attached to almost any English verb: *writable*, *readable*, *answerable*, *movable*, etc. "While great numbers of foreign words have been taken into English from other languages, even more are formed by productive word formation processes from items that are already in the language." (Gramley & Patzold 2004: 33)

4.2.2.5 Conversion

Conversion can be defined as the derivation of a new word without any overt marking. In order to find cases of conversion we have to look for pairs of words that are derivationally related and are completely identical in their phonetic realization.

Conversion is a process which allows us to create additional lexical items out of those that already exist. That is, a word of a certain word-class is shifted into a word of another word-class without the addition of an affix. It is also referred to as *functional shift* or *derivation by zero suffix*. For example: bag — to bag...

Generally, we have such types of conversion: noun to verb (*bottle, to bottle*), verb to noun (*to call, a call*), adjective to verb and noun (*empty, to empty; poor, the poor*). Other types can also be found, but seem to be more marginal, e. g., the use of prepositions as verbs, as in *to down the can*.

4.2.2.6 Back-formation

Ignorance sometimes can be creative and a new word may enter the language because of an incorrect morphological analysis. Back-formation is this type of word-formation and means that a shorter word is derived by deleting an imagined affix from a longer form already existing in the language.

For example, *peddle* was derived from *peddler* on the mistaken assumption that the -er was the agentive suffix. Such words are called back-formation.

e. g. :

edit ← editor, hawk ← hawker, stoke ← stoker, swindle ← swindler;
resurrect ← resurrection, preempt ← preemption, televise ← television;
enthuse ← enthusiasm, liaise ← liaison.

4.2.2.7 Blends

Blends are produced by combining two words, but parts of the words that are combined are deleted. Thus we have the following words in English:

Smog: smoke + fog;
Motel: motor + hotel;
Brunch: breakfast + lunch;
Infomercial: information + commercial;
Urinalysis: urine + analysis;
Transistor: transfer + resister.

4.2.2.8 Reduced Words

Speakers tend to abbreviate words in various ways to shorten the messages they convey. Generally, they will adapt three methods to achieve this effect: **clipping**, **acronyms** and **alphabetic abbreviations.**

Clipping is the abbreviation of longer words into shorter ones. We have the examples as follows:

fax ← facsimile, telly ← television, prof ← professor, piano ← pianoforte, gym ← gymnasium, ad ← advertisement, bike ← bicycle, math ← mathematics, gas ←

gasoline, phone ← telephone, bus ← omnibus, van ← caravan, dis ← disrespect, rad ← radical…

Acronyms are words derived from the initials of several words; they are pronounced as the spelling indicates:

NASA: national aeronautics and space administration.
UNESCO: united nations educational, scientific, and cultural organization.
Radar: radio detecting and ranging.
Laser : light amplification by stimulated emission of radiation.
AIDS: acquired immune deficiency syndrome.
SARS: severe acute respiratory syndrome.
Blog: web log.
Jpeg: joint photographic expert group.
MPEG: moving picture experts group.

When the string of letters is not easily pronounced as a word, the "acronym" is produced by pronouncing each letter. This special kind of "acronym" is called **alphabetic abbreviations**:

NFL: national football league.
MRI: magnetic resonance imaging.
PDA: personal digital assistant.
MP3: MPEG layer 3.

4.3　Lexicon

In the discussion of the difficulties in defining a word, we have mentioned that it's difficult to decide whether pairs like *cat* or *cats*, *go* or *goes* belong to one or two words. In order to reduce the ambiguity of the term "word", linguists introduced a special term for it — **LEXEME**. Lexeme was a term referring to the common, abstract element which underlies the variant forms of a word. Then, in this case, *go*, *goes*, *going*, *gone*, *went* would all be forms of the same underlying lexeme: *GO*; and *BE* would be the abstract lexeme underlying the concrete forms *be*, *am*, *are*, *is*, *was*, *were*, *being*, *been*, etc. Our mental lexicon is such a repository for the idiosyncratic linguistic properties of the lexemes.

We know each word is a sound-meaning unit, and each word stored in our mental lexicon must be listed with its unique phonological representation, which determines its pronunciation and meaning. Of course each word in our mental lexicon should include other information as well, such as whether it is a noun, a pronoun, a verb, an adjective, an adverb, a preposition, or a conjunction; that is, it specifies the grammatical category or syntactic class of the word. Someone knowing the word "walk" means their lexicon contain a lexical entry *WALK* which provides several kinds of information:

(1) spelling (including its different grammatical forms: walks, walked, walking);

(2) how to pronounce all the word forms associated with the lexeme;

(3) definitions to represent the word's one or more meanings;

(4) syntactic information such as parts of speech (e.g. an intransitive verb).

Lexicon is a list of "exceptions", whatever does not follow from general principles. It provides an "optimal coding" of the idiosyncrasies of the lexeme. What we should mention here is that Chomsky's lexicon is different from the dictionary we usually understand, the theory of lexicon is the cornerstone of Chomsky's syntactic theory, and the change of the lexicon theory is the source of Chomsky's new syntactic derivation means. We won't discuss it here, readers who are interested in Chomsky's lexicon theory may refer to his *Minimalist Program* (Chomsky 1995: 235 – 241).

4.4 Summary

In this chapter, we have discussed the **morphology** of English—the study of word formation and the internal structure of words. Knowing a language means knowing the morphemes of that language, which are the elemental units that comprise words. When you know a word or a morpheme, you know both its form and its meaning; and the relationship between the form and meaning is **arbitrary**; that is, there is no inherent connection between them. Thus, the words and morphemes of any language must be learned.

In the discussion of morphology, we have classified the morphemes of English into two types: **free** and **bound** morphemes. Two kinds of morphological processes are **introduced**; they are inflectional and **derivational affixation**. Some useful concepts in the study of morphology are distinguished, including **root**, **stem**, **base**, **allomorph**, **affix** (**prefix and suffix**).

For the discussion of words, we explained the difficulty to define and identify "**word**". Linguists provided many criteria (orthographic, phonological and semantic criteria) to judge a word; but none of them is satisfactory; that's one of the reasons why we need such a kind of concept as "**morpheme**" in the study of language.

Word-formation process is the main topic in this chapter. We introduced **derivation** and **compounding** in some detail; we mentioned other methods such as **borrowing**, **coinage**, **conversion**, **back-formation**, **blending**, and **reducing words** (**clippings**, **acronyms** and **alphabetic abbreviations**); all these methods have enriched the vocabulary of English.

Lexeme is a very important concept in the study of words in a language. **Lexicon** is a repository for the idiosyncratic linguistic properties of the lexemes. Each lexical entry in our lexicon must include the phonological, syntactic, and semantic information of that lexeme.

EXERCISES

Exercises I, V, VI, VII are adapted from Fromkin, et al. 2007: 107 – 114.

Exercise I

The following steps are used to estimate the number of words in your mental lexicon. Consult any standard dictionary.
   a. Count the number of entries on a typical page. They are usually bold-faced.
   b. Multiply the number of words per page by the number of pages in the dictionary.
   c. Pick four pages in the dictionary at random, say, pages 50, 75, 125, 303. Count the number of words on these pages.
   d. How many of these words do you know?
   e. What percentage of the words on the four pages do you know?
   f. Multiply the words in the dictionary by the percentage you arrived at in (e), you know approximately that many English words.

Exercise II

Decide whether each of the following statements is true or false.
1. [s] (maps), [z] (dogs), [iz] (watches) are three allomorphs of the same morpheme expressing plurality in English.
2. Morphology studies the internal structure of words and the rules by which words are formed.
3. The structure of words is not governed by rules.
4. Free morphemes are the same as bound morphemes.
5. Sometimes bound morphemes can be used by themselves.
6. *Go*, *goes*, *going* and *went* are the same word.
7. Derivational affixes are added to an existing form to create a word.
8. Inflectional affixes may change the word class of the original stem.
9. Phonetically, the stress of a compound always falls on the first element, while the second element receives secondary stress.
10. PDA and UNESCO are both acronyms.

Exercise III

Fill in each blank below with one word which begins with the letter given.

1. The inflectional affix "-ed" conveys a g_____ meaning.
2. F_____ morphemes are independent units of meaning and can be used freely all by themselves.
3. The addition of one or sometimes more than one bound morphemes to a root to create a new word is called d_____.
4. Semantically, the meaning of a c_____ is often idiomatic, not always being the sum total of the meanings of its components.
5. There are rules that govern which a_____ can be added to what type of word to form a new word.
6. The word "modernizers" contains four m_____: *modern + ize + er + s*, among them, *-s* is an i_____ morpheme.
7. The morpheme was defined by the structuralists as the smallest unit of meaning. The variants of a morpheme are called a_____. Morphemes are either free or b_____, which are subdivided into derivational and inflectional morphemes.
8. L_____ is a repository for the idiosyncratic linguistic properties of the lexemes.
9. The advertising industry has added many words to English, *Kodak*, *nylon*, and *Xerox* are new words created by c_____.
10. A word has a fixed internal structure. If we want to insert fresh information into a sentence, then it is between the words that this information goes and not within them, words are not i_____.

Exercise IV

Divide the following words by placing a " + " between their morphemes.
Example: replaces: re + place + s.
  a. befriended b. endearment c. holiday d. airsickness e. psychophysics

Exercise V

Match each expression under **A** with the one statement under **B** that characterizes it.

A	**B**
a. noisy crow	1. compound noun
b. scarecrow	2. root morpheme plus derivational prefix
c. the crow	3. phrase consisting of adjective plus noun
d. crow-like	4. root morpheme plus inflectional affix
e. crows	5. root morpheme plus derivational suffix
	6. grammatical morpheme followed by lexical morpheme

Exercise VI

Examine the following words from Michoacan Azetic.

nokali	"my house"	mopelo	"your dog"
nokalimes	"my houses"	mopelomes	"your dogs"
mokali	"your house"	ipelo	"his dog"
ikali	"his house"	nokwahmili	"my cornfield"
kalimes	"houses"	mokwahmili	"your cornfield"
		ikwahmili	"his cornfield"

a. The morpheme meaning "house" is:
   (1) kal   (2) kali   (3) kalim   (4) ikal   (5) ka
b. The word meaning "cornfields" is:
   (1) kwahmilimes   (2) nokwahmilimes   (3) nokwahmili   (4) kwahmili
   (5) ikwahmilimes
c. The word meaning "his dogs" is:
   (1) pelos   (2) ipelomes   (3) ipelos   (4) mopelo   (5) pelomes
d. If the word meaning "friend" is mahkwa, then the word meaning "my friends" is:
   (1) momahkwa   (2) imahkwas   (3) momahkwames   (4) momahkwaes
   (5) nomahkwasmes
e. The word meaning "dog" is:
   (1) pelo   (2) perro   (3) peli   (4) pel   (5) mopel

Exercise VII

Write the one proper description from the list under **B** for the bold-faced and italicized part of each word in **A**.

A	**B**
a. terroriz*ed*	1. free root
b. **un**civilized	2. bound root
c. terror*ize*	3. inflectional suffix
d. *luke*warm	4. derivational suffix
e. **im**possible	5. inflectional prefix
	6. derivational prefix

Exercise VIII

Regular verbs in English form their past tense by "adding a -*d* (or sometimes -*ed*)": *walked*, *played*, *waited*, etc. However, this -(*e*)*d* suffix undergoes phonologically conditioned allomorphy, appearing as $[t]$, $[d]$ or $[id]$. Use the following examples to identify the phonological conditions of this allomorphy.

Hint: you will need to pay particular attention to the phonological nature of the final segment of the base form.

aged	exploded	filled	fished
kissed	laughed	played	proved
raided	rubbed	suited	screamed
walked	sipped	watched	waited

Chapter 5

Syntax

5.1 The Study Scope of Syntax

Syntax [two Greek morphemes (syn) and (tax); (syn) means "together", while (tax) means "to arrange"; thus syntax means combine or arrange something together] is probably the area where most research effort has been directed. For Norm Chomsky, grammar is the rule system which generates all the well-formed possible sentences; besides lexicon, there is a computational system for each particular language to form linguistic expressions.

Then what is a sentence? Different linguists may have different definitions for it. Generally speaking, most linguists agree that a **sentence** is built up of one or more clauses; each clause contains a subject and a predicate, and may contain one or more complements and/or adjuncts as well. Or in other words, sentences are composed of discrete units that are combined by rules; this system of rules explains how speakers can store infinite knowledge in the finite space of our brains. We say sentences are the largest grammatical unit of a language; that doesn't mean there are no units larger than the sentence; but the study of these units (such as *conversation*, *discourse*, *stories and texts*) are beyond the scope of the knowledge of language; we need to consider the other factors in the real world, such as, encyclopaedic knowledge. Thus, syntax under the generative approach to linguistics is concerned only with sentence structure.

In this sense, syntax is the study of how sentences are structured. It tries to state what words can be combined with others to form sentences and in what order. It focuses on the processes whereby words are combined to form phrases which in turn are combined to form sentences. More specifically, we can describe **the functions of syntax rules** in the following aspects:

1. They combine words into phrases and phrases into sentences; they specify the correct word order for a language.

2. It describes the relationship between the meaning of a particular group of words and the arrangement of those words. The word order of a sentence contributes significantly to its meaning.

3. It specifies the **grammatical relations** of a sentence (subject, predicate or object, etc.); they provide the information that permits the hearer to know who is doing what to whom. For example:

(1) a. Your dog chased my cat.
   b. My cat chased your dog.

4. The rules of syntax also specify other **constraints** that sentences must adhere to. For example, a transitive verb must be followed by a noun phrase as its object, while an intransitive verb must not be followed by an object; thus, the following sentences may be ungrammatical (the asterisk * or star preceding a sentence is the linguistic convention for indicating that the sentence is ungrammatical or ill-formed according to the rules of the grammar):

(2) a. *The boy found. (The boy found the ball.)
   b. *The boy found quickly.
   c. *The boy found in the house.
   d. *Disa slept the baby. (Disa slept soundly.)
   e. *Jack believes to be a gentleman.
   f. *Jack tries Tom to be a gentleman.
   g. *Jack and Tom ran the hill up. (Jack and Tom ran the bill up.)
   h. *Up the bill ran Jack and Tom. (Up the hill ran Jack and Tom.)

Our syntactic knowledge crucially includes knowledge of how words form groups in a sentence, or how they are hierarchically arranged with respect to one another. Certain words are grouped together. In the above examples (2g) and (2h), we know *ran up the hill* and *ran up the bill* are two phrases that have different syntactic structures associated with them. In *ran up the hill*, [*up the hill*] forms a unit; in *ran up the bill*, the words [*up the bill*] do not form a natural unit. (We use square brackets to indicate that a group of words forms a syntactic unit of **constituent**.)

Different linguistic schools may have different terminologies to deal with the same linguistic unit, so it is necessary for us to have a complete understanding of the terminologies used in this field.

5.2 Basic Terminology

5.2.1 Categories and Functions

Traditionally, sentences are structured out of words, phrases and clauses, each of which belongs to a specific **grammatical (or syntactic) category** (the classification of words, phrases and clauses, such as N, V, ..., NP, VP..., finite or non-finite clauses), and serves a specific **grammatical function** (the identification of function of words, phrases, and clauses, such as subject, object, case, number, ...) within the sentence containing it. Let's first illustrate the syntactic categories in a language.

5.2.1.1 Grammatical (or Syntactic) Categories

A family of expressions that can be substituted for one another without loss of grammaticality is called a **syntactic category**. Syntactic categories include both **lexical categories** (such as **N, V, P, Adj, Adv...** etc.) as well as **phrasal categories**, which correspond to its lexical category (such as **NP, VP, PP, AdjP, AdvP...** etc.). Part of a speaker's knowledge of syntax is the specification of these syntactic categories.

Besides those familiar categories mentioned above, other categories may be less familiar to us. For example: the category **determiner (Det.)**, which includes the articles *a* and *the*; and the **demonstratives** such as *this*, *that*, *these*, and *those*, and "counting words" such as *each* and *every*.

Another less familiar category is **auxiliary (Aux.)**, which includes the verbs *have*, *had*, *be*, *was*, *were*, and the **modals** *may*, *might*, *can*, *could*, *must*, *shall*, *should*, *will*, *would*.

Aux. and Det. are **functional categories**; so called because their members have a grammatical function rather than a descriptive meaning:

Determiners specify whether a noun is indefinite or definite (*a* boy vs. *the* boy), or the relation of the noun to the context (demonstratives) (*this* boy vs. *that* boy).

Auxiliaries provide the verb with a time frame, whether ongoing (John *is* dancing), completed in the past (John *has* danced), or occurring in the future (John *will* dance). Auxiliaries may also express notions such as possibility (John *may* dance) or necessity (John *must* dance) and so on.

In modern linguistics, we have a special type of words which are used to introduce complement clauses. In English, such kinds of words are *that*, *for*, and *if*; they are called **complementizers (C)**. they belong to functional categories and will be discussed later in some detail.

Lexical categories typically have particular kinds of meanings associated with them:

Verbs usually refer to actions, events, and states (*kick*, *love* ...).

Adjectives refer to qualities or properties (*lucky*, *old* ...).

Common nouns refer to general entities (*dog*, *cat*, *house* ...); **proper nouns** refer to particular individuals or places or other things (*Coca-cola* ...).

But the relationship between grammatical categories and meaning is more complex than these few examples suggest. Nouns can refer to events (*destruction*) or states (*happiness*), or properties and qualities (*beauty*).

Prepositions are usually used to express relationship between two entities involving a location (The boy is *in* the room); but this is not always the case; the prepositions *of*, *by*, *about*, and *with* are not locational.

We do not usually define categories in terms of their meanings because of the difficulties involved in specifying the precise meanings of lexical categories, but rather on the basis of their syntactic distribution (where they occur in a sentence) and morphological characteristics. For example, we define a noun as a word that can occur with a determiner (*the boy*) and that can take a plural marker (*boys*), among other properties.

5.2.1.2 Grammatical (or Syntactic) Functions

In a sentence, certain categories may achieve different functions. Let's use the following sentence as an illustration.

(3) John smokes cigars.

In sentence (3), the noun *John* serves the function of being the **subject** of the clause, in that it denotes the person performing the act of smoking; and the verb *smokes* serves the function of being the **predicate** of the clause; it describes the act being performed; while *cigars* refer to the entities on which the act of smoking is being performed; it is the **complement** of the clause (notice here we don't use the traditional term **object**, complement may have a much larger scope). The two entities involved in the act of smoking *John* and *cigars* are the two **arguments** of the predicate *smokes*. A **clause** is an expression which contains a subject and a predicate, and which may also contain other types of elements.

Generally speaking, there are a number of morphological and syntactic properties which differentiate subjects from complements. They occupy different positions in the clause, and subjects have different **case** properties to complements: subjects typically carry **nominative case**, whereas complements typically carry **objective case**. But in English, nouns like *John* and *cigars* are not overtly inflected for the case distinction. If we change the nouns into pronouns, the difference is very obvious.

(4) He / *Him smokes them / *they.

The third difference between subjects and complements is that in English verbs agree in **Person** and **Number** with their subjects. They don't agree with their complements. We all know this clearly from our traditional grammatical knowledge.

(5) The president smokes a cigar in his office after dinner.

In sentence (5), we have the subject *the president*, the predicate *smokes*, and the complement *a cigar*, but what is the function of *in his office* and *after dinner*? They do not refer to one of the entities directly involved in the act of smoking; they are not the arguments of the predicate *smokes*; they just provide additional information about the time and place when the smoking activity takes place. We say they are **adjuncts** [an expression which serves to provide (optional) additional information about the time or place (or manner, purpose, etc.) of an activity].

It is well known that sentences have a hierarchical organization; that is, the words are grouped into natural units. The natural groupings of a sentence are called **constituents**. Experimental evidence has shown that speakers do not represent sentences as strings of words but rather in terms of constituents; speakers perceive sentences in chunks corresponding to grammatical constituents. We can test the constituents of a sentence in the following way:

1. The "stand alone" test. If a group of words can stand alone, they form a constituent. For example, the set of words that can be used to answer a question is a constituent.

2. "Replacement by a pronoun or a word like *do*." Pronouns can substitute for natural groups.

(6) a. Where did you find *a puppy*? — I found *him* in the park.

b. John found *a puppy* and Bill *did* too.

3. The "move as a unit" test. If a group of words can be moved, they form a constituent.

(7) The child found *a puppy*—it was *a puppy* that the child found.

In this way, we can find that in the sentence "the puppy played in the garden", *in the garden* is a constituent:

(8) a. Where did the puppy play? —*in the garden*.

b. The puppy played *there*.

c. It was *in the garden* that the puppy played.

5.2.2 Finiteness vs. Non-finiteness

So far, we have observed many **simple sentences**, those sentences which comprise a single clause (a subject and a predicate structure, only one predicate in the sentence); however, we have **complex sentences** which contain more than one clause. Consider the following sentence:

(9) Mary knows that the president is smoking a cigar for relaxation.

We know that in this sentence, we have two predicates: *knows* and *is smoking*; thus, it includes two clauses; and we can identify its main clause *Mary knows that...* and its complement clause (because it serves as the complement of *knows*) *that the president is smoking a cigar...* Of course, we can point out its respective subject, predicate, complement, adjunct and so on. Now contrast the two different types of complex sentence illustrated below:

(10) a. We expect [John **will** win the race].

b. We expect [John **to** win the race].

Superficially, the two sentences appear to have much the same structure except that in (10 a) we have a tensed form **will** while in (10b) we have an infinitive particle **to**. In fact, in [John **to** win the race], **to** will not be changed even the main clause has been changed into the past tense, which is clearly illustrated in the following (11b).

(11) a. We expected [John **would** win the race]. (tensed).

b. We expected [John **to**　win the race]. (unspecified for tense).

To use the relevant grammatical terminology, we can say that an auxiliary or a verb is **finite** if it inflects for tense / agreement and has a nominative subject, and **non-finite** if it doesn't inflect for tense or agreement and doesn't have a nominative subject. Thus [John will win the race] is a **finite clause**; it is a clause with a nominative subject which contains a verb/auxiliary inflected for tense/ agreement; and [John to win the race] is a **non-finite clause**, that is, a clause which doesn't have a nominative subject, and which doesn't contain a verb / auxiliary inflected for tense / agreement. The following sentences may be used to illustrate the agreement and case differences in finite and non-finite clauses.

(12) a. I didn't know [John **wears** glasses].
　　　　(a finite clause, with verb inflection for agreement with its subject)
　　b. I have never known [John **wear** glasses].
　　　　(a non-finite clause, with no verb inflection for agreement with its subject)
(13) a. We expect [he / *him will win the race].
　　　　(case demands for the subjects)
　　b. We expect [him / *he to win the race].

We know that verbs in English can have up to five distinct forms, as illustrated below:

(14)　　-s　　　-d　　　　base　　　-n　　　-ing
　　　shows　　showed　　show　　　shown　　showing

The -s and -d forms are finite forms inflected for **tense** (indicating the time at which the activity took place): the -s form being the third person singular present tense form, and the -d form being the past tense form. By contrast, the -n and -ing forms are non-finite forms, inflected for **aspect** (a term used to describe the duration of the activity described by a verb): the perfect and progressive aspect respectively. The tense in the sentences with such verb forms below is marked actually by auxiliaries, not by the verb form *going* or *gone*.

(15) a. He *is / was* going home.
　　b. He *has / had* gone home.

The **base form** of the verb has a dual status, and can function either as a finite form or a non-finite form (traditionally termed as an **infinitive** form).

(16) a. You *show* little interest in syntax these days. (finite form)
　　b. He didn't *show* any emotion. (non-finite form: infinitive form)

5.3　Sentence Structure

In this section, we shall look at the ways in which words are combined together to form phrases, phrases are combined together to form clauses, and clauses are combined together to form complex sentences. We will start from the most simple **phrase structure rules and trees** to the famous **X-bar theory** of the 1980s, and continue to explain the core syntactic operation—**merger** in the 1990s.

5.3.1 Phrase Structure Rules and Trees

In the last section, we introduced the basic terminologies. Now that you know something about constituent structure and grammatical categories, you are ready to learn how the sentences of a language are constructed.

Of course, before we come to the clauses or sentences, the first step is to construct a phrase. A **phrase** is a sequence of two or more words which is not a clause, but which can nevertheless serve as a free-standing expression, and be used e. g. as a reply to an appropriate kind of question. In the discussion of syntactic categories, we have such phrases as NP, VP, AdjP, AdvP, PP, and CP; all these phrases are built around a certain word category such as Nouns, Verbs, Adjectives, Adverbs, Prepositions and Complementizers. According to our common sense, we can describe the formation of such phrases as the rules below:

(17) a. NP → Det N — a student.
    NP → NP PP — a student in the classroom.
    NP → Adj NP — good students.
    ……
  b. VP → V — run.
    VP → V NP — kick the ball.
    VP → V (P) PP — study at home.
    VP → V CP — wonder if you can come.
    ……
  c. AdjP → Adv. Adj. PP — very afraid of the snake.
    ……
  d. AdvP → Adv Adv PP — quite independently of any pressure.
    ……
  e. PP → P NP — above the desk.
    ……
  f. S → NP VP — the boy kick the ball.
  g. CP → C S — ... for you to come /... that I don't know.

Of course, we have some other rules to form different kinds of phrases. Please remember that the letter **C** represents the **Complementizer** (**C**) *for* or *that* which introduce a clause in a complicated sentence. C is a functional category, like Aux and Det. We will come back to discuss the complementizers later.

These phrase structure rules capture the knowledge that speakers have about the possible structures of a language. A speaker's knowledge of the permissible and impermissible structures must exist as a finite set of rules that "generate" any sentence in the language.

Sentence structure can also be represented by **phrase structure (PS) trees** symbolically. A tree diagram with syntactic category information can convey the same information as the nested square brackets. The hierarchical organization of the tree reflects the groupings and sub-groupings of the words of the sentence. From the PS tree below we can see that a sentence is both a linear string of words and a hierarchical structure with phrases nested in phrases.

(18) The PS tree for the sentence *"the child found a puppy"*:

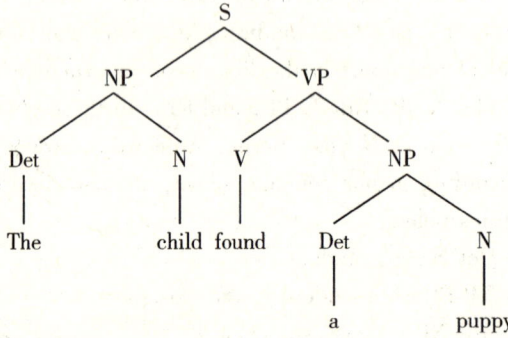

PS trees are explicit graphical representations of a speaker's knowledge of the structure of the sentences of his language; it is a formal device to represent his syntactic knowledge:

1. The linear order of the words in the sentence.
2. The identification of the syntactic categories of words and groups of words.
3. The hierarchical structure of the syntactic categories (e. g. , an S is composed of an NP followed by a VP; a VP is composed of a V that may be followed by an NP, and so on).

The syntactic category of each word is listed in our mental dictionaries. The PS tree reflects the speaker's intuitions about the natural groupings of words in a sentence; it also states implicitly what combinations of words are not syntactic categories.

The rules of syntax reveal the grammatical relations among the words of a sentence as well as their order and hierarchical organization. They also explain how the grouping of words relates to its meaning, such as when a sentence or phrase is ambiguous. In addition, the syntactic rules permit speakers to produce and understand a limitless number of sentences never produced or heard before—the creative aspect of linguistic knowledge. A major goal of linguistics is to show clearly and explicitly how syntactic rules account for this knowledge. A theory of grammar must provide a complete characterization of what speakers implicitly know about their language.

5.3.2 X-bar Theory

In the above description of the phrase structure rules, we see that a certain word can only occur with some other words. Through the analysis of those phrase structure rules, we find that for each phrasal category, we have a head word; thus different phrasal categories (NP, VP, PP, AP...) must contain a **head** (N, V, P, Adj... respectively). And the head may be followed by a **complement**, which in turn may be modified by a **specifier**; the complement and specifier may be a word or a phrase or even a sentence. During the 1980s, Chomsky developed such a phrase-structure theory which he called the **X-bar theory**, which specifies the hierarchical structure holding between heads of phrases and their specifiers and complements. Anyway, the phrasal structures may all conform to a general schema, which is illustrated in (19).

(19) XP → (Specifier) X (Complement) (e.g., the mayor of Guangzhou)

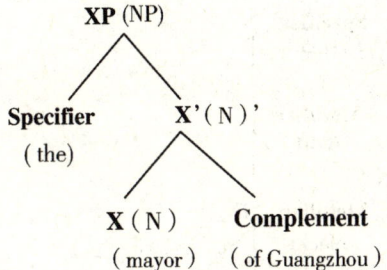

In the above tree diagram, X represents the head word of the phrase; so for the NP, the head X is a Noun, and the complement followed the head may be called the sister to the head. The head and complements together form the X-bar (X') level, which is not a complete phrase; this incomplete phrase must combine with a specifier to form an XP. Thus, we have the following phrase structures (20) which can be represented in the tree diagram similarly.

(20) a. NP → (Det.)   N (PP) ...   the students in classroom
     b. VP → (Adv.) V (NP) ...   often dream
     c. AP → (Adv.) A (PP) ...   very pessimistic of the life
     d. PP → (Adv.) P (NP) ...   mainly about the matter
     ......

Of course, the head may be modified by more than one word; for example, a noun may be modified by many different adjectives. Besides the complement, a verb may be modified by many adjuncts; in this case, a more complicated structure may be represented in (21). And the tree diagram may need more than one bar node.

(21) **XP** → (**Specifier**) (**Modifiers**) **X** (**Complement**) (**Adjuncts**)

We can use the following DP, VP, PP, AP, AdvP to illustrate the format of the tree diagrams, and **nested square brackets** may have the same function as tree diagrams; besides, it saves much more space.

(22) a. NP: The tall black **student** of English from China.
  b. VP: The detectives have all **read** the letters after lunch.
  c. PP: The arrow went right **through** the center.
  d. AP: very **afraid** of snakes.
  e. AdvP: quite **independently** of any outside pressure.

a. NP: The tall black **student** of English from China.

[$_{NP}$ [$_{Spec}$ The [$_{N'}$ [$_{Modifier}$ tall [$_{N'}$ [$_{Modifier}$ black [$_{N'}$ [$_{N}$ student [$_{Comp}$ [$_{pp}$ of English]] [$_{Adjunct}$ [$_{pp}$ from China]]]]]]] (*a detailed illustration of the sentence using nested square backets*)

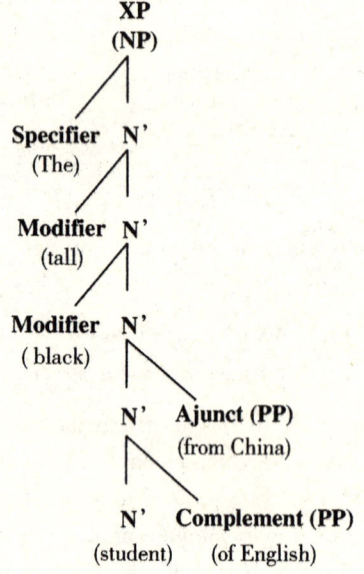

b. VP : ...all **read** the letters after lunch.

[$_{VP}$ [$_{Spec}$ all [$_{V'}$ [$_{V}$ read [$_{NP}$ the [$_{N'}$ [$_{N}$ letters [$_{PP}$ after lunch]]]]]]]]

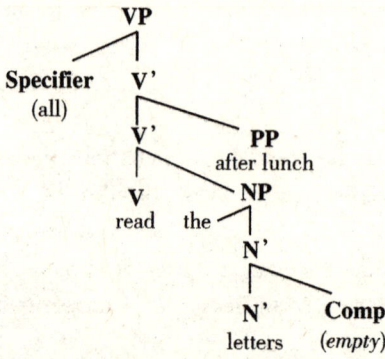

c. PP: right **through** the center.
[$_{PP}$ right [$_{P'}$ [$_P$ through [$_{NP}$ the center]]]]

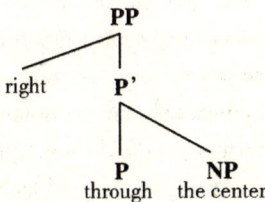

d. AP: very **afraid** of snakes.
[$_{AP}$ very [$_{A'}$ [$_A$ afraid [$_{PP}$ of snakes]]]]

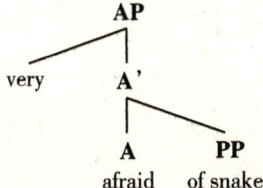

e. AdvP: quite **independently** of any outside pressure.

[$_{AdvP}$ quite [$_{Adv'}$ [$_{Adv}$ independently [$_{PP}$ [$_{P'}$ [$_P$ of [$_{NP}$ [$_{Spec}$ any [$_{N'}$ outside [$_N$ pressure]]]]]]]]]]

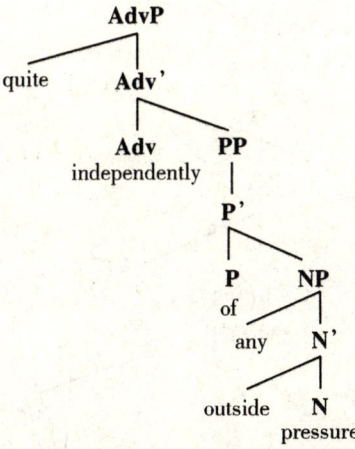

So far, we have discussed many phrase structures which can be represented by the X-bar format; all of them contained a head, and optionally a specifier, or a complement, or an adjunct. How about the clauses or sentences? Can they be represented by the same format? The answer is yes! Linguists found that *every clause or sentence may contain a head*, which is representing the tense or agreement features of the sentence. We may call it the **inflectional feature** of the sentence. In this sense, a clause may be treated as an **inflectional phrase**; hence, we have an **IP**. **I** may be represented by auxiliaries, or the marker of the tense or aspect; thus we have *-s* representing the third person singular present tense verb form, and *-ed* representing the past tense, and *is*...*-ing* representing the present continuous verb form, *has/have* ...*-n* representing the perfect verb form, etc. The infinitive marker *to*, present participle marker *-ing*, past participle marker *-n* may all be treated as the head of the non-finite clause. The tree diagrams of the sentences (23) are given below.

(23) a. John would study English.
  b. John to study English.

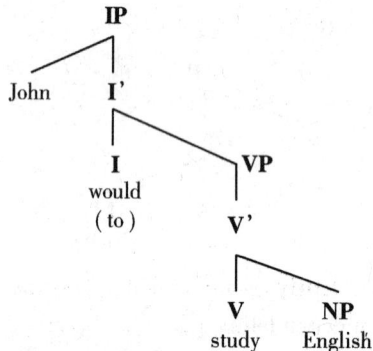

(24) a. John studies English.
  b. John is studying English.
  c. John has studied English.

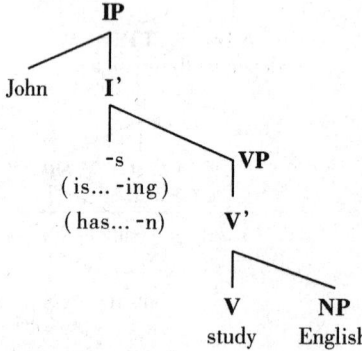

For the clauses introduced by ***that***, ***for*** (*for John to study English*), or ***if*** (*if John will study English*), we call them CPs, because these words are complementizers in English. The sentences including CPs may be diagrammed in the following tree.

(25) CP: They say **that** John will study English.

[IP They [I' I (-pres.) [VP say [CP that [IP John [I' will [VP study English]]]]]]]

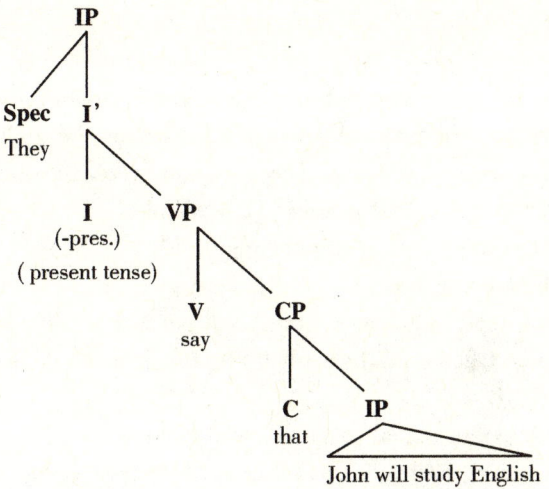

After discussing the syntactic structures of the phrases, clauses and sentences, let's come to the so-called coordinate structure. A **coordinate structure** results when two constituents of the same category (two NPs, two VPs, two IPs...) are joined with a conjunction such as *and* or *or*. We should remember that there is no limit on the number of coordinated categories before the conjunction and the coordinated categories must be of the same type. The coordinate phrase has the following structure.

(26) The cat and the dog.

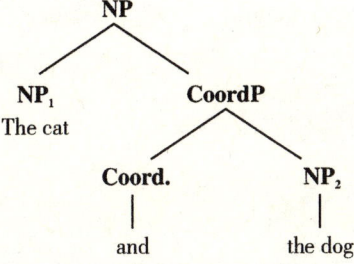

The other kinds of coordinate structures, such as VP or PP can be tree-diagrammed in the same way.

(27) a. Mary writes poetry and surfs. (VP *and* VP)
　　　b. Sam rode his bicycle to school and to the pool. (PP *and* PP)

In a coordinate structure, the second member of the coordination (NP_2) forms a constituent with the conjunction *and*. We can show this by means of the "move as a unit" constituency test.

(28) a. Tom bought a book and a CD yesterday.
　　　b. Tom bought a book yesterday and a CD.
　　　c. *Tom bought a book and yesterday a CD.

5.3.3 Merger

In the last section, we have illustrated the sentence structure in terms of the X-bar theory. In the 1990s, Chomsky abandoned this format and used another syntactic operation—**merger** to substitute for it. The operation by which two words are combined together to form a phrase is called merger. For example:

(29) a: What is the government planning to do?
　　b: Reduce taxes.

As speaker *b*'s reply illustrates, the simplest way of forming a phrase is by combining two words together. Then what are the **grammatical properties** of the phrase, a VP or an NP?

It seems that the grammatical properties of the phrase are determined by one of the words in the phrase. We can test it in two ways: the phrase can be used to replace the verb in the sentence, but it cannot replace the noun.

(30) a. The government ought to **resign**.
　　b. The government ought to **reduce taxes**.
　　c. **Taxes** are at the heart of the debate about policy.
　　d. * **Reduce taxes** are at the heart of the debate about policy.

If it is a verb phrase, then we can say the verb is the *head* of the phrase, and the phrase is the **projection** (i.e. a phrasal expansion) of the verb. We can use two methods to represent the syntactic structure of the phrase:

1. A labeled bracketing technique: [VP [V reduce] [N taxes]]
2. A labeled tree diagram:

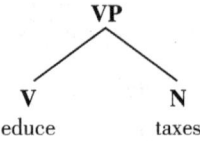

The following phrases may be tree diagrammed below in the same manner:

(31) a. DP: such a pity.
　　b. PP: right inside it.
　　c. AP: very afraid of the person.

a.
```
        DP
       /  \
    Spec   D'
   (such)  / \
          D   N
         (a) (pity)
```

b.
```
        PP
       /  \
    Spec   P'
   (right) / \
          P   N
       (inside) (it)
```

c.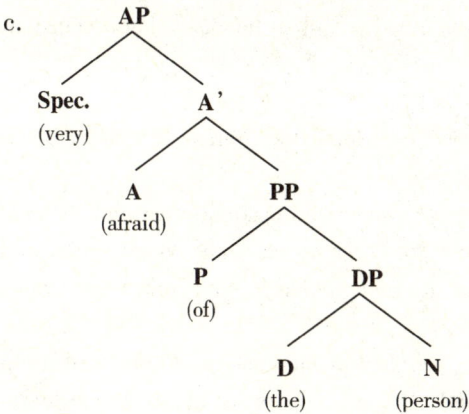

In fact, we can hypothesize that all phrases are formed in essentially the same way, namely by merging two categories together to form a larger category.

Reduce taxes → **to** [**reduce taxes**] → **try** [**to** [**reduce taxes**]]

We can build up complex structures by successively merging pairs of categories to form even larger phrases. This is a very important property of languages: **recursion**.

The simple operation of merger, as a core operation in the theory of grammar, immediately deals with the fact that English, and any other language, has a potentially infinite number of sentences, as well as the fact that the sentences can be infinitely long. The following children's rhyme about the house that Jack built will be used to illustrate such mechanism of recursion (Fromkin, et al. 2007: 133).

(32) This is the farmer sowing the corn,
    that kept the cock that crowed in the morn,
    that waked the priest all shaven and shorn,
    that married the man all tattered and torn,
    that kissed the maiden all forlorn,
    that milked the cow with the crumpled horn,
    that tossed the dog, that worried the cat, that killed the rat,
    that ate the malt, that lay in the house that Jack built.

The sentence could be infinite and become more difficult to produce and understand due to short-term memory limitations, muscular fatigue, breathlessness, boredom, or any number of performance factors. Nevertheless, these very long sentences would be well-formed according to the rules of grammar. Another typical example can also illustrate this recursion phenomenon.

(33) The cat chased the mouse.
    The cat chased the mouse that ate the cheese.
    The cat chased the mouse that ate the cheese that came from the cow.
    The cat chased the mouse that ate the cheese that came from the cow that grazed in the field...

Phrases can be formed by the operation merger; then how is it that a clause may be formed in this way?

(34) They will try to reduce taxes.

By continuous merger operation, we can form the phrase "will try to reduce taxes". But what is the status of this phrase?

Just as we do in the X-bar theory, we can treat the auxiliaries and the infinitive marker "*to*" as belonging to the same category, which was labeled inflection or **INFL** by Chomsky. Finite auxiliaries inflect for tense/agreement, and infinitival "*to*" serves much the same function in English.

Then the auxiliaries like "*will*" are assigned to the category INFL, and the phrase formed by the merger operation will be **IP**. But this sequence "*will try to reduce taxes*" is an incomplete phrase, because auxiliaries require a subject. We can assume that when we merger an auxiliary (INFL) with a verb phrase (VP), we form an incomplete inflection phrase which we shall denote as I' (I-bar). And when we merge the relevant INFL with its subject, we form an IP (A complete inflection phrase—a clause). (33) is repeated as (34) below:

(35) They will try to reduce taxes.

[$_{IP}$ They [$_{I'}$ will [$_{VP}$ [$_V$ try [$_{IP}$ [$_I$ to [$_{VP}$ [$_V$ reduce] [$_{NP}$ taxes]]]]]]]]

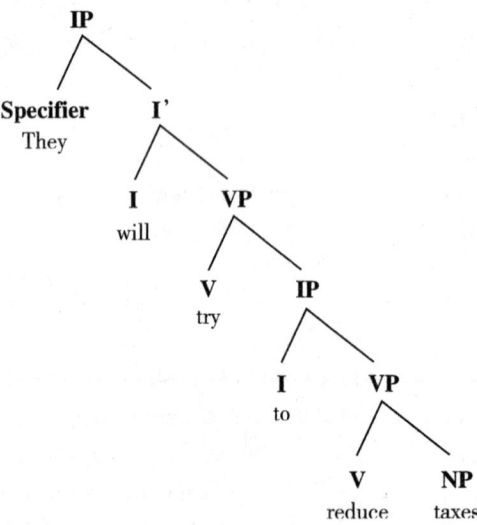

As we know, all clauses are **IPs** with the form ***subject + INFL + complement***, and each of these three constituents can be either overt or covert. But many clauses are introduced by functional elements such as ***that***, ***for***, or ***if***, they are known as **complementizers** (**Comp**, or **C** hitherto), because they are typically used to introduce a complement clause. The tree diagrams of the sentences with a CP may be shown below:

(36) a. He admitted **that** he stole it.
　　b. She's keen **for** you to go.
　　c. I doubt **if** he understands.

a. He admitted **that** he stole it.

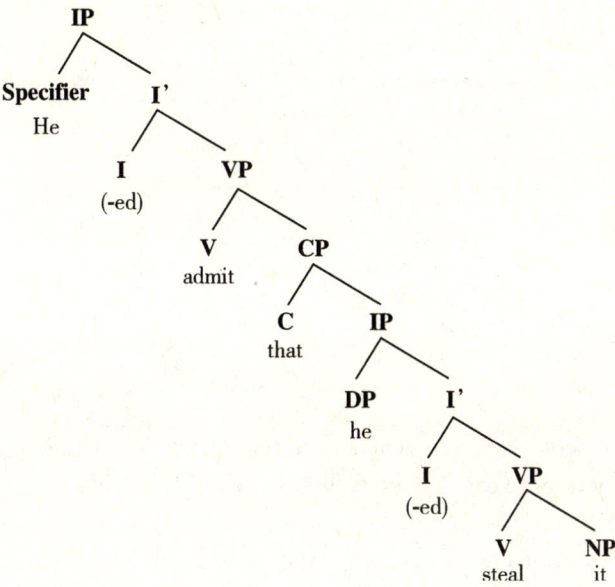

b. She's keen **for** you to go.

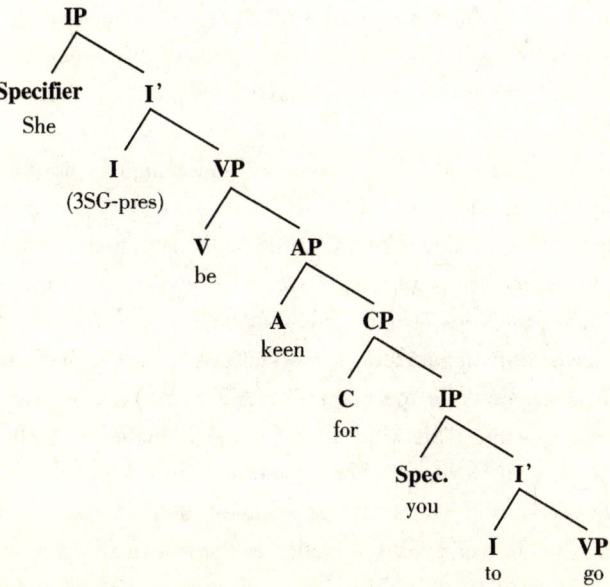

c. I doubt **if** he understands.

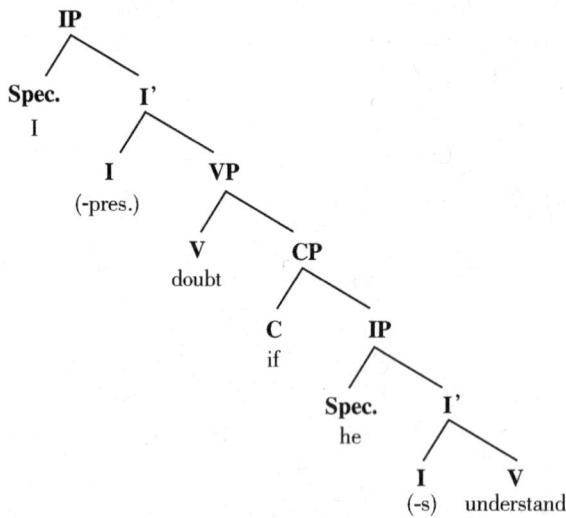

In the above sentences, the complementizer merges with the IP; thus we have a complementizer phrase (CP). Here C is the head of the clause. What we should remember is that *Spec.* refers to the specifier of the clause; that is, the subject of the clause. Sometimes we use word category [D (eterminer), or DP] directly in the tree diagram to substitute *Spec.*, and we hypothesize that all the nominal and pronominal expressions (NPs and Pronouns) as DPs with an overt or covert determiner head. As for the representation of *I*, we know it may be an auxiliary representing tense or agreement; but in the cases of lacking such an auxiliary, we use *-pres.* representing the present tense, *-s* representing the third person singular present tense form of the verb, *-ed* representing the past tense.

Although we have suggested that all phrases and sentences are formed by a simple binary merger operation, it's clear that we cannot randomly combine any pair of categories together. The combination of words is constrained by something. As we know, *syntactic structures are projections of lexical items* (i.e. words), and so must satisfy the individual properties of the words they contain.

Firstly we have **subcategorization restrictions** [or **C-selection** (C stands for categorial)]: the restrictions on the range of categories which a given item permits or requires as its complements. This kind of restriction is included in the lexical entry of the item in our mental lexicon. For example, *devour* takes an obligatory NP complement; *rely* takes an obligatory PP complement headed by *on*, and so on.

On the other hand, verbs also include in their lexical entry a specification of certain intrinsic categories; this kind of selection is called **S-selection** (S for semantic). For example, the verb *murder* require its subject and object to be human, while the verb *drink* requires its subject to be animate and its object liquid. The following sentences violate S-selection and can only be used in a metaphorical sense.

(37) a. ! The rock murdered the man.
　　 b. ! Colorless green ideas sleep furiously.
　　 c. ! You have convinced my computer.
　　 d. ! The beer drank the student.

(We will use the symbol "!" to indicate a semantic anomaly.)

The **well-formedness** of a phrase or a clause depends then on at least two factors: whether the phrase conforms to the structural constraints of the language as expressed in the PS rules; and whether it obeys the selectional requirements of the head, both syntactic (C-selection) and semantic (S-selection).

5.4　Movement

The derivation of a structure involves not only a series of merger operations combining pairs of categories together to form larger and larger phrases and clauses, but may also involve one or more movement operations, moving words or phrases from one position in a structure to another. This section will deal with such kinds of syntactic movements.

5.4.1　Head movement

So far, we have discussed the syntactic structure of phrases and clauses. We have CP, IP, DP, VP, PP, AP, AdvP and so on (remember that clauses are treated as phrases, they are CPs or IPs). As we know, in an IP, the auxiliary is the head, while in a CP, the complementizer C is the head. But for yes-no questions, we often move the auxiliaries to the left of the subject. Now compare the following two sentences:

(38) a. **If**　　the president was lying.
　　 b. **Was**　the president　　lying?

In (38) b, we say the auxiliary ***was*** undergoes inversion and moves into some position in front of the subject. It (***was***) appears to occupy the same pre-subject position that the complementizer ***if*** occupies; that's the head C position of CP.

On the assumption that *only one word can occupy a given head word position like C*, then an inverted auxiliary and a complementizer are mutually exclusive; that means a clause can be introduced by either a complementizer or an inverted auxiliary, but not by the two together. That's entirely correct:

(39)　* if was the president lying.

We say the inverted auxiliary moves from the head ***Infl*** position in IP into the head C position in CP by the operation *movement*. This kind of movement is called **head movement**. We can use a tree diagram to represent this movement process [(38) b is repeated as (40)].

(40) Was the president lying?

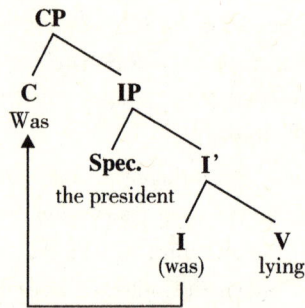

After the movement, then what happens to the head INFL position of IP once it is vacated by movement of the inverted auxiliary into C? The answer is that a moved expression leaves behind an empty **trace** of itself in its former position. The trace indicates that the INFL position "belongs to" was, and cannot be filled by another auxiliary.

(41) * Was the president is lying?

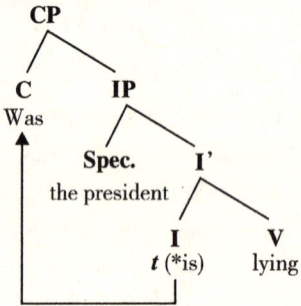

The existence of trace may be proved by the fact of **cliticization**. (42) b is wrong because the presence of the intervening trace prevents have from cliticizing onto they in inversion structure.

(42) a. Will they *t* have gone?
  b. * Will they've gone?

5.4.2 Wh-movement

We know in English the wh-word in special questions must be inverted to the sentence initial position; thus we have the sentence (43).

(43) What languages can you speak?

According to the projection principle, the original sentence should be (44), because *speak* will need a complement. This is just the form our Chinese equivalent sentence "你能说哪些语言？" adopted. And in English we have such echo questions.

(44) You can speak **what languages**?

So they are moved into some position preceding the inverted auxiliary. Obviously the preposed wh-phrases occupy the specifier position within CP. The structural description will be given below [(43) will be repeated as (45)].

A moved wh-expression leaves behind a trace at its extraction site, so this position can not be filled by any other constituent. Hence the following sentence is wrong:

(46) * What languages can you speak **any Italian**?

It seems that these expressions function as the complement of the verb at the end of the sentence. We have also the evidence to support the existence of such kinds of trace:

(47) * Which students would you say've got most out of the course?

This sentence is ungrammatical because the form *have* of the perfect auxiliary has the clitic variant *'ve* and can cliticize to an immediately preceding word which ends in a vowel or diphthong; but in the above sentence, **have** is not immediately adjacent to **say**, because there is a trace of *which students* between these two words. Similarly, in English we have the so-called **wanna contraction**; that is, *want to* can be contracted as *wanna* in certain context [(48) b, d]. But (49) b is not correct because the presence of the intervening empty NP trace between *want* and *to* blocks contraction.

(48) a. I *want to* win.
　　　b. I *wanna* win.
　　　c. Who do you *want to* beat *t*?
　　　d. Who do you *wanna* beat?

(49) a. Who might *you want   t   to* win?
　　　b. * Who might you *wanna* win?
　　　c. [$_{NP}$ Who] might you want [$_{NP}$ *t*] to win?

(45) What languages can you speak?

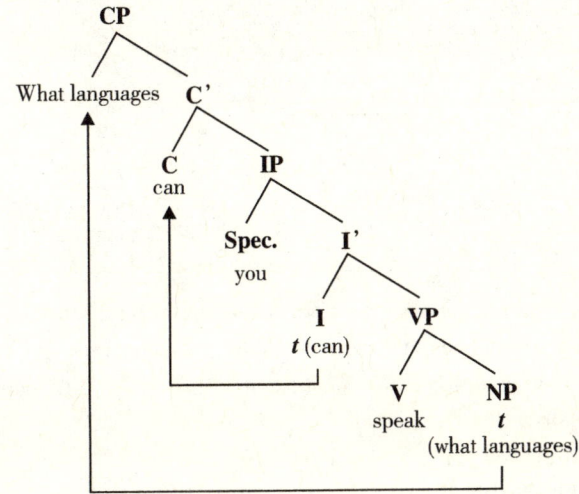

So far we have assumed that wh-expressions move into the specifier position within CP, to the left of C. But for sentence (50), the bracketed complement clause contains no overt C constituent:

(50) I'm not sure [**which senators** the president has spoken to].

In this case, we can hypothesize the head C position here is occupied/filled by a **covert complementizer**. We have evidence to support the existence of this hypothesis: we know auxiliary inversion is not permitted in complement clause questions in English; the presence of the covert complementizer also prevents an auxiliary from moving from INFL to C because one position cannot be filled by two constituents at the same time. Sentence (51) can be used to illustrate this phenomenon.

The last question is: **why wh-expressions should be moved to the front of the relevant interrogative clause in wh-questions**? Our answer is that it is the presence of the interrogative phrase in the specifier position of CP which ensures that the clause is interpreted as interrogative. We can say if it has an interrogative specifier in English sentences, then we can interpret it as a question; that is, we hypothesize that *any interrogative sentence may have an interrogative operator at the beginning of the sentence no matter it is overt (wh-question) or covert (yes-no question)*.

(51) *I'm not sure [**which senators** *has* the president spoken to].

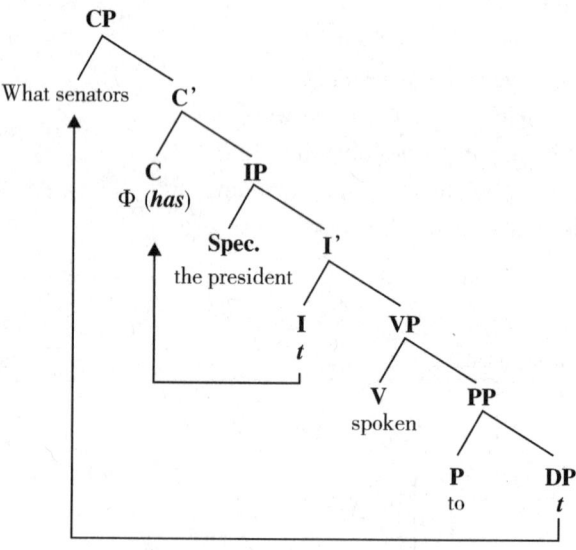

Of course, there are many other problems needing to be discussed. There are many constraints involving wh-movement, such as: Why only one wh-word can be preposed, not more than one [one position, two constituent: (52) b]? Why can't we move **what** in the sentence [short distance movement: (52) c]?

(52) a. **Who** do you think will say what?
     b. ***What who** do you think will say?

c. * **What** do you think who will say?

Due to the limitation of space, we can not discuss them in detail; you can refer to some other special syntax books to get your own answer.

We have discussed head movement and wh-movement in this section. Of course, there are many other kinds of movement:

V movement: It moves V out of VP into an empty finite *I* position, such as in the sentence (53):

(53) He had no money.

The structure before movement is (54):

(54) [$_{IP}$ He [$_{I'}$ [$_I$ 3SG-past] [$_{VP}$ [$_V$ have [NP no money]]]]].

Here *have* moved from the V position to the empty *I* position and combined with the empty inflection [3sg-past] (the third person singular past verb form), at last form the word *had*.

NP movement: It moves an NP into an empty NP position. In the passive construction, the passive subjects "originate" as the complements of their verbs; they are moved from complement position within VP into subject/specifier position within IP. For example:

(55) The car will be put in the garage.

The original structure before movement of the sentence (55) will be (56):

(56) [$_{IP}$[**NP** e][$_{I'}$[$_I$ will(***be***)] [$_{VP}$[$_V$ put[$_{NP}$ **the car**] [$_{PP}$ in the garage]]]].

The car is moved to the front empty subject position and in the **passivization** process be is added to the structure.

Topicalization: For example, in the sentence (57):

(57) You must realize that **this kind of behaviour** no teacher can tolerate.

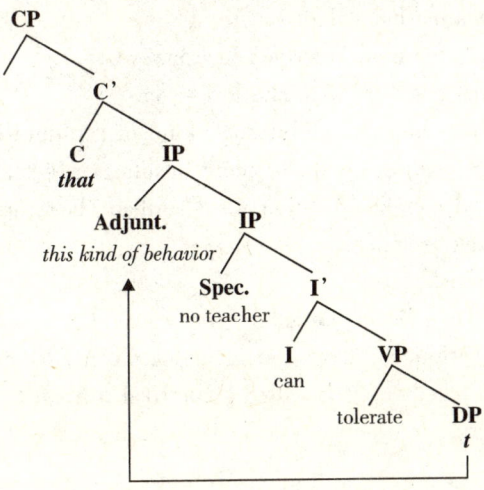

"*This kind of behavior*" originates in post-verbal position; it is then topicalized by being moved into a more prominent position at the front of the clause. It is a kind of **adjunction** (an operation whereby a given type of category is expanded into a larger category of the same type by the addition of another expression) by which it is adjoined to the left of IP, and leaves a trace behind.

Generally speaking, all these movements may be included in a general rule **Move α**, where "alpha" is a cover term for any element that can be moved from one place to another; i.e., you can move anything to any other position. Of course, there are many **constraints** for such kinds of movement and for each movement we need have some **motivation**: **wh-movement** and **head movement** are triggered by the satisfaction of the question operator (covert or overt) in the specifier of CP; **topicalization** is triggered by the topic marker; **passivization** is triggered by the passive marker and so on. One important task of linguists is trying to find those constraints and motivations for the movement operation; we cannot have a detailed discussion here on this topic.

5.5 Structural Ambiguity

In this chapter, we have discussed the structure of phrases and sentences. But how are the meanings of phrases and sentences determined? A common-sense answer would be that the meaning of a sentence is derived by combining the meanings of the words which it contains. However, there's clearly more involved than this; the interpretation of a sentence is determined by the interpretations of the words occurring in the sentence and the syntactic structure of the sentence. For example, sentence (58) a can be used to illustrate this fact, even though the sentence is composed of the same words. It is **ambiguous** (i.e. It has more than one interpretation) because of the different structure involved [(58) b, c].

(58) a. She loves me more than you.
　　 b. She loves me more than you love me.
　　 c. She loves me more than she loves you.

In English, many sentences exhibit such kind of **ambiguities**; they have two or more structures, corresponding to two or more meanings. In fact the phrase structure rules, X-bar format and merger operation we described above are convenient for us to explain these ambiguous sentences.

(59) A toy car crusher.

This noun phrase can be explained in two ways; (60) a and (60) b are the different structural descriptions. This sort of ambiguity results from the different ways the words are grouped together; it is called **structural ambiguity**.

(60) a. A car crusher which is a toy.　　　b. A crusher for toy car.

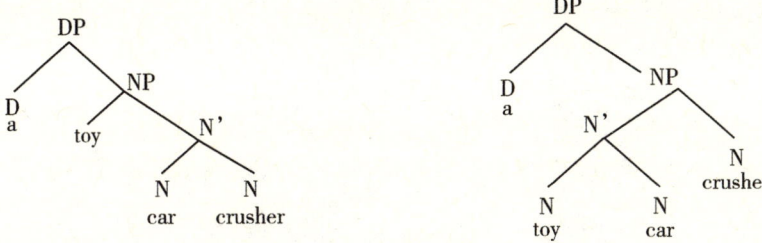

Similarly, we have (61):
(61) The girl in the car with a blue bonnet.
a. The car with a blue bonnet.

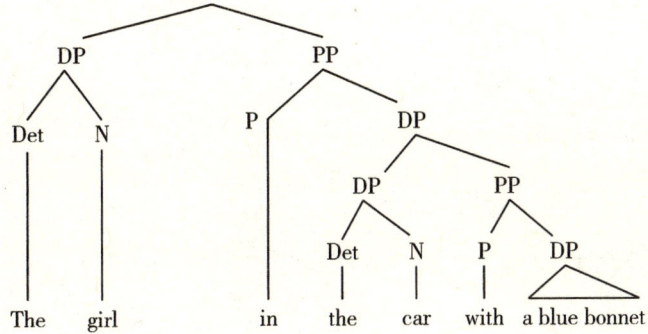

b. The girl with a blue bonnet.

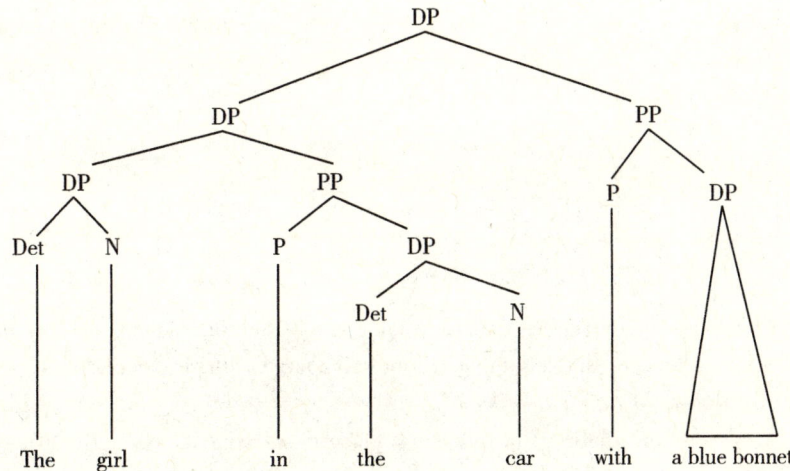

(62) The boy saw the man with a telescope.

This sentence can be interpreted in two different ways: *with a telescope* can be used to modify *the man* and *saw* respectively; thus the sentence meaning can be demonstrated clearly with the following different tree diagrams:

a. See...with a telescope.

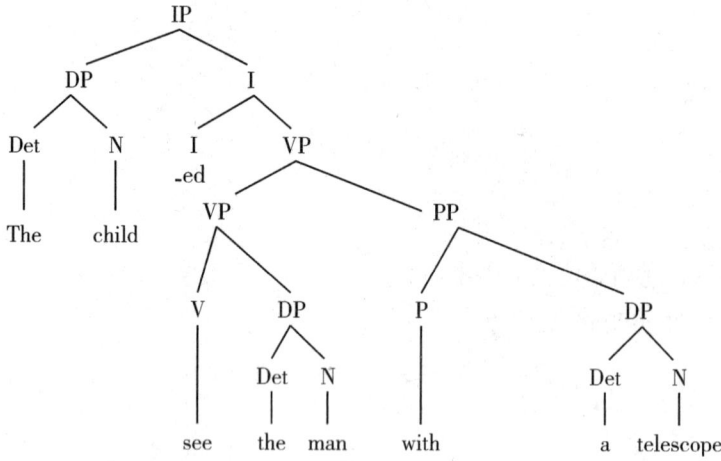

b. The man is with a telescope.

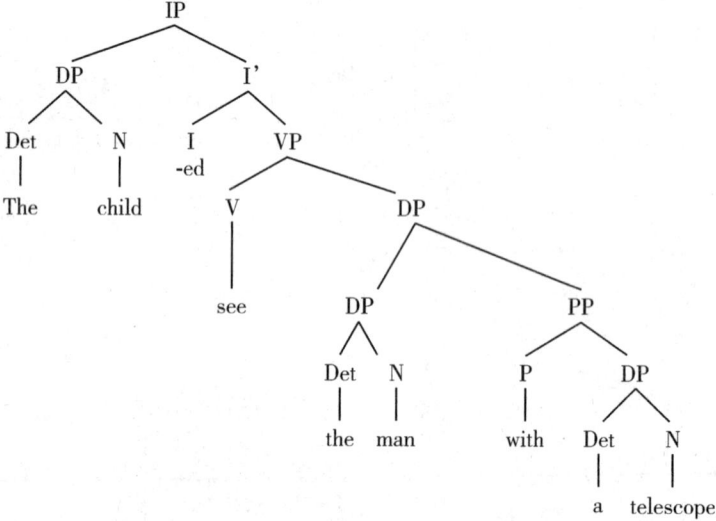

Through these sentences we can see that a single sequence of words may have two interpretations as long as the sequence can be associated with two syntactic structures—*merging constituents in different orders.*

By now, you can analyze the following ad by describing its syntactic structures:

(63) For sale: an antique desk suitable for lady with thick legs and large drawers.

The humorous reading comes from the grouping [a desk] [for lady with thick legs and large drawers] as opposed to the intended [a desk for lady] [with thick legs and large drawers], where the legs and drawers belong to the desk.

Sentences (64) may be analyzed in the same way. I'm sure the readers can deal with such syntactic ambiguities easily. You can draw the tree diagrams to demonstrate its structural ambiguity.

(64) a. Anna threw the book that Mary had been reading in the study.
b. John bought some antique books and socks in town.
c. They are hunting dogs.
d. Who would you like to visit?
e. Do Americans call cushions what the British call pillows?
f. John introduced himself to everyone that Mary did.
g. The daughter of Pharaoh's son is the son of Pharaoh's daughter.

What we should remember is that the structure of a sentence contributes to its meaning, but **grammaticality** and **meaningfulness** are not the same thing. Chomsky's famous sentence *Colorless green ideas sleep furiously* is grammatical but meaningless. Of course, there are also sentences that we understand even though they are not well formed according to the rules of the syntax: * *The boy quickly in the house the ball found*. In a word, to be a sentence, words must conform to specific patterns determined by the syntactic rules of the language.

Grammaticality also does not depend on the truth of sentences. If it did, lying would be impossible. Nor does it depend on whether real objects are being discussed or on whether something is possible. Untrue sentences or sentences discussing unicorns or sentences referring to pregnant fathers can be grammatical.

The syntactic rules that permit us to produce, understand, and make grammaticality judgments are unconscious rules. The grammar is a mental grammar, different from the prescriptive grammar rules that we are taught in school. We develop the mental rules of grammar long before we attend school.

Structural ambiguity may cause processing difficulties. In fact many of the sentences that we hear in our everyday conversations are ambiguous. Typically, however, these ambiguities do not impede communication. Indeed, we are rarely even aware of the occurrence of an ambiguity, and we generally come up with only one interpretation for each sentence, which, in the vast majority of cases, is the correct one. The grammar of English allows two different syntactic representations to be assigned to these sentences, each of which is associated with a different interpretation. Here the non-linguistic clues may indicate which interpretation is the intended one.

5.6 Summary

The rules of syntax can enable human beings to produce and understand an unlimited number of new sentences. We know when different sentences mean the same thing and we can recognize the ambiguities of the sentences in a certain situation and correctly perceive the grammatical relations in a sentence. These kind of grammatical relations may be conveniently demonstrated by tree diagrams.

In this chapter we have explained some basic terminologies in syntax, on the basis of which three kinds of syntactic operations are introduced; they are **phrase structure rules**, **X-bar theory** and **merger operation**. All of them are involved in how to combine words together to form grammatical sentences. PS rules cannot give us a complete list of the syntactic rules, merely of inductive characteristics; we don't know how many rules there are in English or other languages. On the other hand, it is not binary, which does not accord with our intuition about word combination. X-bar theory cover all phrases (including clauses and sentences) in a specific format, so it is deductive and we have such binary characteristics, but we design a bar-level for each phrase which may be beyond our mental reality. The merger operation combines the advantages of PS rules and X-bar theory and most importantly it is the essence of human language computation.

Words can be moved in a sentence, but this movement is constrained by many rules. Here we discussed in some detail about two major movement operations: **head movement** and **wh-movement**. We are clear why and how to move words and to which position the word will be moved. We have huge amounts of research in this field.

Structural ambiguities may be conveniently explained by tree diagrams. If we can analyze the structure in this way, we can greatly improve our syntactic analysis ability.

Lastly, we should say the **lexicon** represents the knowledge that speakers have about the vocabulary of their language. This knowledge includes the syntactic category of words and what elements may occur together, expressed as **c-selection** or **subcategorization**. The lexicon also contains semantic information including the kinds of NPs that can function as semantically coherent subjects and objects; this is the **s-selection** restriction of the words.

The basic design of language is universal. Syntactic rules are structure-dependent, and movement rules may not move phrases out of certain structures. These constraints exist in all languages and need not be learned; they are one part of our Universal Grammar (UG).

EXERCISES

Most of the exercises below are adapted from Radford (2000), with some minor modifications.

Exercises I

Analyze the structure of the clauses in the examples below. That is, how many clauses each sentence contains? What the grammatical function of each clause is (e.g. main clause, complement clause, relative clause)? What type each clause is (e.g.

declarative, interrogative, imperative, or exclamative)? What the constituents of each clause are? And what function each constituent serves within its containing clause (e. g. subject, predicate, complement, or adjunct)?
1. The prisoners brutally attacked the guard who spotted them.
2. Has anyone told the press the prisoners were carrying knives?
3. Which prison officer claimed the prisoners had secretly made keys?

Exercises II

Draw the sub-trees for the italicized phrases in the following sentences with the X-bar format.
1. *Angry men in dark glasses* roamed the streets.
2. *My aunt and uncle's trip* to Alaska was wonderful.
3. The reporter realized *that the senator lied*.
4. *A stranger cleverly observed that a dangerous spy from CIA lurked in the house.*

Exercises III

Using one or more of the constituency tests (i. e. stand alone, move as a unit, replacement by a pronoun) discussed in this chapter, determine which boldfaced portions in the sentences are constituents. Provide the grammatical category of the constituents.
1. Tom found **a lovely puppy** in the house.
2. The **light in this room** is terrible.
3. **Jack and Jerry** are fighting over the bone.
4. I gave a bone to Jack **and to Jerry** yesterday.
5. I gave a bone to **Jack and** to Jerry today.
6. Sam asked **if he could play soccer**.

Exercises IV

In terms of C-selection restrictions, explain why the following sentences are ungrammatical:
1. * Those women located.
2. * Robert is fond that his children love animals.
3. * The children laughed the man.
4. * Lisa gave a book.

Exercises V

Paraphrase and draw tree diagrams for each of the following sentences in two ways to show that you understand the ambiguity involved.

1. The student is a dirty street fighter.
2. They said she would go yesterday.
3. The magician touched the child with the wand.
4. Anna threw the book that Mary had been reading in the study.
5. Who would you like to visit?

Exercises VI

Analyze the following sentences, showing their structure is built up in a pairwise fashion by successive merger operations. [Assume that *don't* is a single word which belongs to the same category as words like *must*, *might*, etc., and that infinitival to sometimes (but not always) has a specifier/subject of its own.]
1. She is trying to solve the problem.
2. I would imagine she has forgotten them.
3. They don't seem keen to approve the plan to cut the budget.
4. They are expecting you to contact them.
5. He wants to try to help others.

Exercises VII

The tree diagrams below represent the structures of a variety of different sentences. For each of the five numbered positions in each structure, say what kinds of item (overt or covert) can occupy the position, and what determines the choice of item occupying each position.

a.
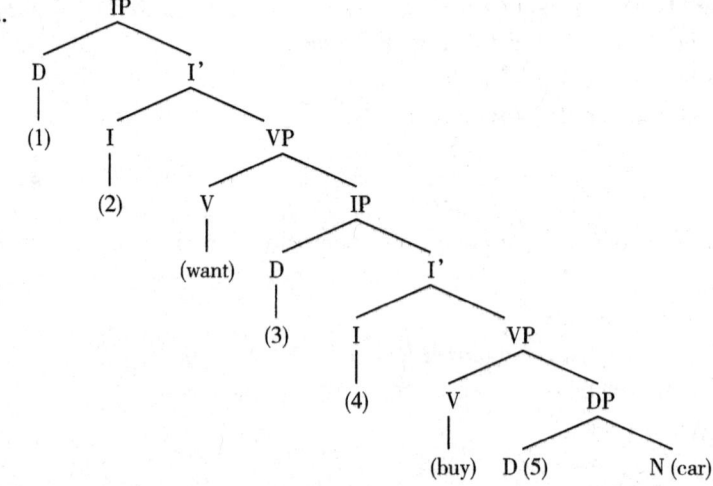

b.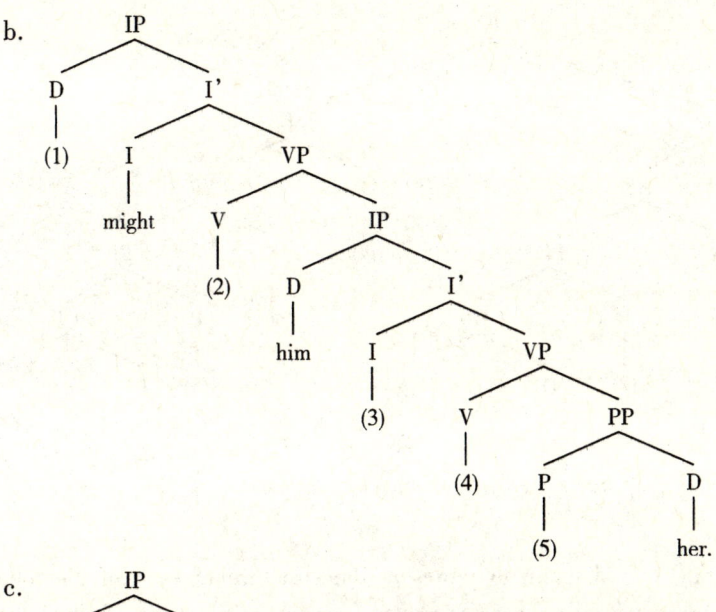

c.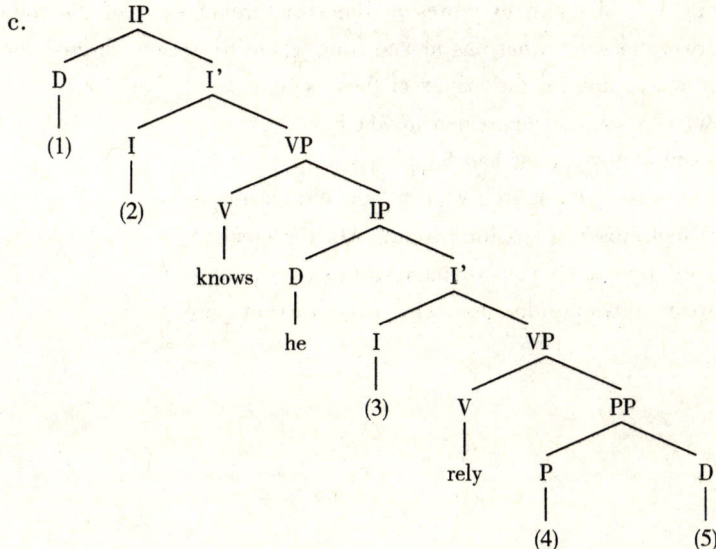

d.
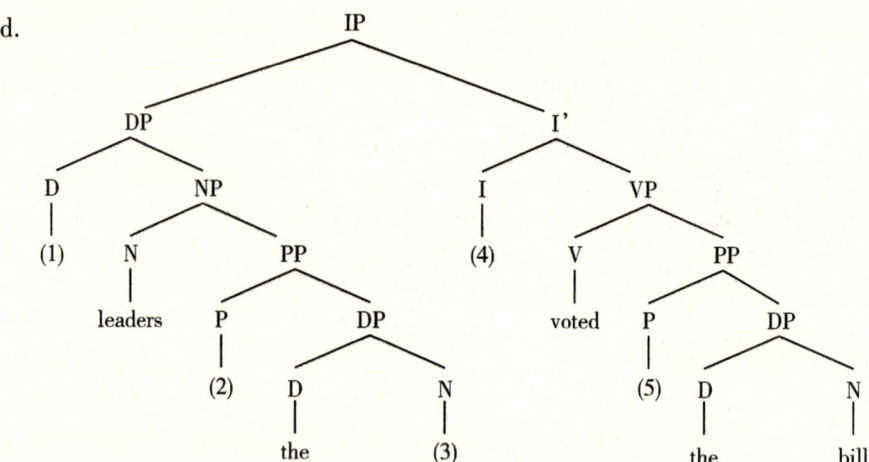

Exercises VIII

Draw a separate tree diagram to represent the structure of each of the following sentences, using arrows to show what has moved from where to where, discuss the role played by traces in accounting for the syntax of these sentences.
1. a. what did you say had happened to who?
   b. *who did you say what had happened to?
2. a. The Neofascists, I wouldn't want to win the election.
   b. *The Neofascists, I wouldn't wanna win the election.
3. a. How many people do you wanna invite to your party?
   b. *How many people do you wanna come to your party?

Chapter 6

Semantics

Meaning is not an easy subject to study. In our everyday life, we use language to convey meanings, ask questions, give commands and express wishes. When we say we know a language and we can understand its meaning, we mean a lot of things: to begin with, we know when a "word" is meaningful or meaningless (*flick* vs. ** blick*), when a sentence is meaningful or meaningless (*John swims* vs. ** swims metaphorical every*), when a word or a sentence is ambiguous ("*bear*" or "*Jack saw a man with a telescope*"), when two words or sentences are synonymous (have essentially the same meaning) (*sofa* and *couch*, or *Jack put off the meeting* and *Jack put the meeting off*), and when words or sentences have opposite meanings (*alive* vs. *dead*, or *Jack swims* vs. *Jack doesn't swim*).

You know the references of the words, and you have the capacity to discover when sentences are true or false [all *kings are male* (true), *all bachelors are married* (false)]. You know the relationships among sentences; that is, if you know the sentence *Nina bathed her dogs* is true, then you know *Nina's dogs got wet* must also be true (entailment).

Such kind of knowledge about meaning is part of the grammar of the language. The job of the linguist is to reveal and make explicit this knowledge about meaning that every speaker has. **Semantics** is the study of the *linguistic meaning* of morphemes, words, phrases, and sentences. But it took linguistics more than half a century to attempt a systematic analysis of meaning. As for the study of *how context affects meaning*, for example, how the sentence *it's cold in here* comes to be interpreted as "*close the windows*" in certain situations, it is the topic of the next chapter—**Pragmatics**.

6.1　Lexical Semantics—Word Meanings

The meaning of a phrase or a sentence is partially a function of the meanings of the words it contains; similarly, the meaning of a word is a function of the morphemes that compose it. However, there is a fundamental difference between word meaning and sentence meaning: word meaning is conventional, and you must learn them one by one; while the meaning of most sentences must be constructed by the application of semantic rules.

All the speakers of a language share a basic vocabulary—the sounds and meanings of morphemes and words; this mental storehouse of information about words and morphemes is what we have been calling the **lexicon**.

A difficulty we immediately encounter when we turn to the meanings of words is that native speakers do not provide a rich source of data; we have to resort to less direct methods for probing the semantic aspect of the words.

Dictionaries give the meanings of words by using other words rather than in terms of some more basic vocabulary; in this sense, a dictionary really provides paraphrases rather than meanings. It relies on our knowledge of the language to understand the definitions. The meanings associated with words in our mental lexicon are probably not like those we find in the dictionary, although it's very difficult to specify precisely how word meanings are represented in our minds.

6.1.1　Reference and Sense

When we are discussing the meaning of a word, we have two related but different aspects of meaning: **reference** and **sense**.

We can say the meaning of a word is its **referent**, which is the thing or things in the real world that it refers to. If meanings were reference alone, then the meanings of words and expressions would be the objects pointed out in the real world. Meaning is a connection between language on the one hand, and objects and events in the world on the other. Thus, we say *reference* deals with the relationship between the linguistic elements and the non-linguistic world of experience.

An obvious problem for such a theory about meaning is that speakers know many words that have no real-world **referents** (e.g. *unicorns*, *dragon*, *Harry Potter*), but speakers do know the meanings of these expressions. On the other hand, function words like *of* and *by*, or modal verbs such as *will* and *may* have no referents at all.

We have situations where the linguistic forms or words with the same sense may refer to different things in different contexts, and that two expressions may refer to the same individual but not have the same meaning. *Barack Hussein Obama* and *the President* currently refer to the same individual, but the meaning of *the President* is something like "the head of the state"; that is, an element of meaning is separated from its reference and is more enduring. This element of meaning is often termed sense. Thus, *unicorns*, *dragon*, and *Harry Potter* have sense but no reference in the real world.

According to the above discussion, we know *sense relates to the complex system of relationships that hold between the linguistic elements themselves*. It is an intra-linguistic relationship. It is concerned with the internal meaning of the linguistic forms. What we will focus on in this study of lexical meaning is the sense of the words, especially their sense relations.

6.1.2 Sense Relations

Sense relations are relations between word meanings. As we know, the meaning of a word is defined in part by its relations with other words in the language. Of course, every word has a semantic relation of some kind with every other word; we convey our meaning by relying on the network of sense relationships which the lexemes of the language have built up between them. Speakers have considerable knowledge about the meaning relationships among different words in their mental lexicons, and any theory must take that knowledge into account. In this section, we will deal with these kind of sense relations.

6.1.2.1 *Synonymy and Synonyms*

Synonymy refers to a kind of meaning relations; it is a kind of identity of meaning. While **synonyms** are words or expressions that have the same or a similar meaning in some or all contexts. It is doubtful whether there are lexemes in a language which can be regarded as completely identical in meaning; that is, no two words ever have *exactly* the same meaning. Some examples might be the pairs below:

sofa / couch; boy / lad; lawyer / attorney; toilet / lavatory.

These pairs show that true or exact synonyms are very rare. The synonyms often have different distributions along a number of parameters (Palmer 1981). We can classify synonyms into the following types:

a. **Dialectal synonyms**: Some words may have belonged to different dialects and then become synonyms for speakers familiar with both dialects. British English (BE) and American English (AE) are the two major geographical varieties of English; thus we have such kind of synonyms: *fall* (AE) / *autumn* (BE); *apartments* (AE) / *flats* (BE); *elevator* (AE) / *lift* (BE); *gasoline* (AE) / *petrol* (BE).

b. Words differing in "**styles** or **registers**": The words may belong to different registers; those styles of language as colloquial, formal, literary, etc. that belong to different situations. For example: *chap / man / gentleman*; *old lady / wife / spouse*; *kid / child / offspring*. The degree of formality is gradually increased in the above examples.

c. Words differing in **emotive** or **evaluative** meanings: The synonyms may portray positive or negative attitudes of the speaker. E. g. *statesman* (Positive) / *politician* (Negative); *ingenuous* (P) / *naive* (N); *thrifty* (P) / *economical* (Neutral) / *stingy* (N); *pigs* / *copper* / *cop* / *police officer*.

d. **Collocationally-restricted synonyms**: Some synonyms may be collocationally restricted; that is, they appear in a certain context. For example: *rotten* (tomatoes) / *addled* (eggs) / *rancid* (butter) / *sour* (milk); *accuse* (of) / *charge* (with) / *rebuke* (for).

e. **Near synonyms**: Those synonyms differ slightly in what they mean. E. g. *mature* / *adult* / *ripe* / *perfect* / *due*; *surprise* / *amaze* / *astound*.

6.1.2.2 Antonymy and Antonyms

In traditional terminology, **antonyms** are words which are opposite in meaning. Oppositeness of meaning is a pervasive semantic relation in the lexicons of human languages. There are a number of relations which seem to involve words which are at the same time related in meaning yet incompatible or contrasting. Antonymy comes in several varieties; we list them below.

a. **Gradable opposites**: All of the gradable antonyms are adjectives; their meanings are related to the object they modify. They may be seen in terms of the quality involved. The words do not provide an absolute scale. We know that "*a small elephant*" is much bigger than "*a large mouse*". And the members of a pair differ in terms of degree; thus, between *hot* and *cold*, we have *warm* and *cool*. The examples may include: *wide* / *narrow*, *big* / *small*, *good* / *bad*, etc.

Among these gradable pairs, one is **marked** and the other **unmarked**. The unmarked member is the one used in questions of degree, and used as a cover term. Thus we have "How *high* is the mountain"? "How *old* is Tom"? "How *tall* is Mary"? Or "ten thousand feet *high*", "ten years *old*", "five feet *tall*". We never use the marked form *low*, *young*, or *short* in these expressions.

b. **Complementary opposites**: The members of a pair in this type are complementary to each other. There is no intermediate ground between the two. The adjectives in this type do not have comparative or superlative degree. For example: *male* / *female*, *married* / *single*, *alive* / *dead*, *pass* / *fail*, *awake* / *asleep*, *present* / *absent*.

c. **Relational opposites**: These antonyms express the reversal of a relationship between items and display symmetry in their meaning. If X *gives* Y to Z, then Z *receives* Y from X. Pairs of words ending in -*er* and -*ee* are usually relational opposites (*employer* / *employee*). We have the following examples for instance: *buy* / *sell*, *husband* / *wife*, *above* / *below*, *lend* / *borrow*, *parent* / *child*, *host* / *guest*, *teacher* / *student*.

In English, you can add the prefix *un*-, *non*-, *in*- to form antonyms: *able* / *unable*, *entity* / *nonentity*, *tolerant* / *intolerant*.

6.1.2.3 Hyponymy: Superordinate or Hyponyms

Hyponymy is a relation of inclusion. A **hyponym** includes the meaning of a more general word. Thus we say that *lion* is a hyponym of *animal*, and *mother* is a hyponym of *woman*. On the contrary, *animal* is the **superordinate** of *lion*, and *woman* is the superordinate of *mother*; equivalently *lion* and *animal*, *mother* and *woman* are in the semantic relationship of hyponymy or meaning inclusion.

Superordinate: bird tool

Hyponyms: crow hawk duck etc. hammer saw chisel etc.
(or **superordinate**)
Hyponyms kestrel sparrowhawk etc. hacksaw jigsaw etc.

We can use a very straightforward test for many examples of hyponymy:
An X is a kind / type of Y.
Thus a duck is a type of bird, and a sparrowhawk is a kind of hawk.

Hyponymy is a "one-way" relation. We say that being an animal is a *necessary* condition for being a lion; it is not, however, a *sufficient* condition, an animal is of course not a type of lion.

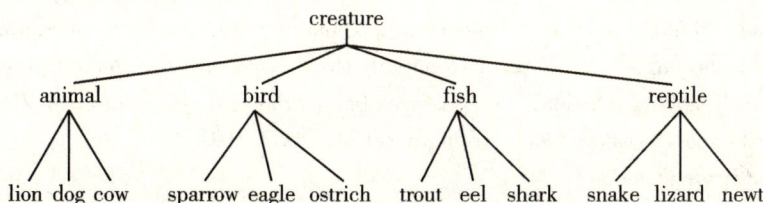

Verbs also enter into hyponymy relations. We can use the test sentence for a simple test: **X-ing is a sort of / type of Y-ing**.

Thus we can say *borrowing is a sort of getting* and *crawling is a type of moving*.

6.1.2.4 Meronymy and Meronyms

The semantic relation of hyponymy must be distinguished from another semantic relation—**meronymy**, which is a *part-whole relation* between lexical items. We can identify this relationship by using sentence frames like *X is part of Y*, or, *Y has X*. Thus *cover* and *page* are **meronyms** of *book*, and *cover* and *page* are **co-meronyms**, because a *page* or a *cover* is part of a *book*, or a *book* has a *page* or a *cover*.

We can use systems below to show this relationship:

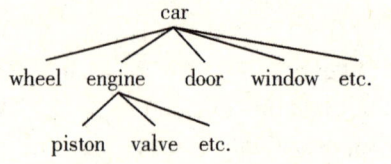
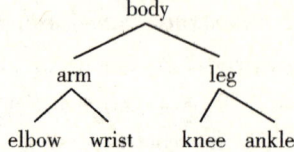

6.1.2.5 *Homonymy and Homonyms*

Homonyms are words that have different meanings but are pronounced the same, and may or may not be spelled the same. *To*, *too*, and *two* are homonyms despite their spelling differences. Homonymous words are usually given two main entries in a dictionary; polysemous variants are normally listed under a single main heading.

Some linguists distinguish between **homographs** and **homophones**; that is, different words are identical in spelling or in sound (note: the root **homo** means "*same*"; *graph* and *phone* mean "*form*" and "*sound*" respectively). When two words are identical in both sound and spelling, they are complete homonyms.

Homophones: Same sound, different meaning and spelling: *rain / reign*, *knight/ night*, *piece / peace*, *leak / leek*, *bear / bare*.

Homographs: Same spelling, different meaning and sound: *bow* (v.) / *bow* (n.), *tear* (v.) / *tear* (n.), *lead* (v.) / *lead* (n.).

Complete homonyms: Same sound and spelling, different meaning: *bank*, *ball*.

Because of these complete homonyms, sometimes we will have ambiguity; "*I'll meet you by the **bank***" is such an example. Homonyms are also good candidates for humor as well as for confusion. The passages below from *Alice Adventures in Wonderland* are good examples to show that (Fromkin, et al. 2007: 191):

"How is bread made?"

"*I know that*!" Alice cried eagerly.

"You take some **flour**—"

"Where do you pick the **flower**?" the White Queen asked. "In a garden, or in the hedges?"

"Well, it isn't picked at all," Alice explained; "it's **ground**—"

"How many acres of **ground**?" said the White Queen.

Or the following:

"Mine is a long and sad **tale**!" said the Mouse, turning to Alice and sighing.

"It is a long **tail**, certainly," said Alice, looking with wonder at the Mouse's tail, "but why do you call it sad?"

6.1.2.6 *Polysemy*

Just as we mentioned in the discussion of homonyms, polysemous words are normally listed under the same lexical entry in the dictionary. We say homonymy and polysemy both deal with multiple senses of the same phonological word, but polysemy is invoked if the senses are judged to be related; thus the criteria of "*relatedness*" is used to identify polysemy by the lexicographers in the design of their dictionaries. A polysemic word, i. e. a word with several meanings, is the result of the evolution of the primary meaning of the word, or historically, the growth and development of or change in the meaning of words. For example:

Mouth: 1. opening through which animals take in food, space behind this containing the teeth, tongue, etc.
2. place where something (e. g. a bag, a bottle, a tunnel, etc.) opens.
3. place where a river enters the sea.
4. person requiring to be fed.

These meanings of *mouth* are all closely related, maybe derived from the first primary meaning; thus *mouth* is a polysemic word.

But we should remember that such decisions are not always clear cut. Speakers may differ in their intuitions and sometimes, historical fact and speaker intuitions may contradict each other. For example:

Sole: 1. bottom of the foot.   2. flatfish.
Gay: 1. lively, light-hearted, bright.   2. homosexual.

The two meanings of these words may be unrelated intuitively; thus they should be homonyms like *bank* and *ball*. But in fact, the second meaning is derived from the first one historically, so we should treat them as polysemic words.

We have discussed a number of different types of lexical relation. A particular lexeme may be simultaneously in a number of these relations, so that it may be more accurate to think of the lexicon as a network, rather than a listing of words as in a published dictionary.

6.1.3 Semantic Features or Componential Analysis

The sense relations we have introduced above are clearly important in suggesting that there may well be links of different kinds between lexical entries, but we didn't look inside a lexical entry and see how semantic information is represented there.

Please observe the following groups of words:

man—woman—child,   dog—bitch—pup,   stallion—mare—foal,
ram — ewe—lamb,   bull—cow—calf,   hog—sow—piglet.

A range of lexical relations, including the [**male-female**] and [**adult-young**] relations, exists in above sets of words, these and other relations are characteristics of the lexicon. To explain this networking, some semanticists have hypothesized that words are not the smallest semantic units but are built up of smaller components of meaning which are combined differently to form different words, just as a phoneme is analyzed into smaller components called **distinctive features**. The meaning of a lexeme can be decomposable into a set of **semantic features**. Thus, the words like *woman*, *bachelor*, *spinster*, and *wife* have been viewed as being composed of elements such as [adult],

[human], etc. :
 woman: [female, adult, human...]
 bachelor: [male, adult, human, unmarried...]
 spinster: [female, adult, human, unmarried...]
 wife: [female, adult, human, married...]

The elements in square brackets above are called **semantic components**; thus, this kind of analysis of the word meaning is often called **componential analysis** (**CA**). It has been especially used by anthropologists in analysing the vocabulary of kinship and other important social areas within a community. Some linguists have even tried to construct an entire theoretical framework for semantic analysis by using such an approach.

For example:

	Male	Previous generation	Related by birth
aunt	−	+	−
uncle	+	+	−
mother	−	+	+
father	+	+	+
son	+	−	+
daughter	−	−	+

......

Figure 6.1 (adapted from Poole 2000: 27)

The most commonly used semantic features in the literature produced by linguists are as follows:

Nouns: [male / female, human, animate, artefact, non-living, adult / young, married / unmarried, physical object, count / mass...]

Verbs: [cause, become, have, go, change, contact, motion, in liquid, close to a surface, eventives, statives, negation ...]

There are a couple of related reasons for identifying such components: the first is that it establishes important correspondences between the semantic representations of words and the phonological representations of sounds. Distinctive phonological features have the role of distinguishing the sounds in a language and the same feature distinguishes distinct pairs of sounds. Thus, [+/ − voiced] can be used to distinguish the sounds [p] and [b]; similarly, the semantic features [male / female] can be used to distinguish the word meanings of *bachelor* and *spinster*, or *bull* and *cow*, or *stallion* and *mare*.

A second attraction is that they may allow an economic characterization of the lexical relations like synonymy, antonymy, and hyponymy, etc. And the sentence relations we will discuss later like contradiction or entailment. Decomposing the meanings of words into semantic features can clarify how certain words relate to other words. For example, two words which have the same semantic components will be synonymous with each other, while words which have a contrasting component are antonyms, and words which have all the semantic components of another are hyponyms of the later. Thus, we have:

Synonyms: bachelor: [human, adult, male, unmarried...]
unmarried man: [human, adult, male, unmarried...]
Antonyms: bachelor: [*male*, adult, human, unmarried...]
spinster: [*female*, adult, human, unmarried...]
Hyponyms: boy: [human, *male*, young...]
girl: [human, *female*, young...]
Superordinate: child: [human, *male / female*, young...]

The most ambitious claim is that in addition to these two important uses, such semantic features form part of our psychological architecture: they provide us with a unique view of conceptual structure. Semantic features are thought to be the conceptual elements by which a person understands the meanings of words and sentences.

Despite the positive views we have just sketched, there are a number of difficulties which the supporters of semantic features must face. Firstly, it is difficult to find the most primitive features to account for the word meaning; the feature set is incomplete. Secondly, it's very difficult to obtain complete feature systems like those in phonological analysis. And thirdly it is not easy to work out universal principles which can be applied consistently to whole languages or different languages.

6.2 Sentence Meaning

6.2.1 Sentence Relations— **Truth-conditional Semantics**

Semantic relations can hold between words (synonymy, antonymy, hyponymy...) and this gives a network effect to the lexicon. Similarly, semantic relations may hold between sentences of a language; sometimes, these relations are the result of particular words in the sentences; but in other cases the relations are the result of syntactic structures. Anyway, the native speaker may have this kind of knowledge about the meaning of his or her language. They may know that:

1. Sentence *a* and *b* below are **synonymous** (*a* has the same meaning as *b*; when one is true, the other must be true; when one is false, the other must also be false.):
   a. My brother is a bachelor.
   b. My brother has never married.
2. Sentence *a* below **entails** *b* (if *a*, then automatically *b*; one sentence entails

another if whenever the first sentence is true, the second one is also true, in all conceivable circumstances.):

    a. People killed the emperor.

    b. The emperor is dead.

3. Sentence *a* below **contradicts** *b* (*a* is inconsistent with *b*; two sentences are contradictory if, whenever one is true, the other is false or, equivalently, there is no situation in which they are both true or both false.):

    a. My brother John has just come from Rome.

    b. My brother John has never been to Rome.

4. Sentence *a* below **presupposes** *b*, as *c* does *d* (*b* is part of the assumed background against which *a* is said; if *a* is true, then *b* is surely true.):

    a. The Mayor of Guangzhou is a man.

    b. There is a Mayor of Guangzhou.

    c. I regret stepping on your sandwich.

    d. I stepped on your sandwich.

5. Sentence *a* and *b* are necessarily true, i.e. **tautologies** (*a* is automatically true by virtue of its own meaning, but informationally empty; their truth is guaranteed by the meaning of their parts and the way they are put together, irrespective of circumstances.):

    a. Circles are round.

    b. Sandwich is Sandwich.

6. A sentence (*a* or *b*) is necessarily false, i.e. **contradictions** (*a* or *b* is inconsistent with itself, i.e. asserts and denies the same thing, opposite in truth value.):

    a. ? He is a murderer but he's never killed anyone.

    b. ? Now is not now.

The discussion of sentence relations above involves the determination of the **truth value** of the sentences involved. Our linguistic knowledge permits us to determine the truth of sentence; then knowing the meaning of a sentence means knowing its **truth conditions**. This kind of study about sentence meaning is often called **truth-conditional semantics** because it takes the semantic knowledge of truth as basic. We have many different semantic rules which combined together to determine the truth-condition of the sentence, and reducing the question of meaning to the question of truth conditions has proved to be very fruitful in understanding the various semantic properties of language. We won't discuss this in detail here, readers may refer to Fromkin, et al. (2007: 178 – 186) and Saeed (2000: 79 – 102).

6.2.2 Sentence Analysis

6.2.2.1 *Componential Analysis for Sentences*

The meaning of words can be listed in a dictionary. But as we know, a speaker can make up novel sentences and these sentences are understood; they obey the semantic rules of the language; the meaning of the sentence must be created by rules of combination too. Semanticists often describe this by saying that sentence meaning is **compositional**. This indicates that the meaning of an expression is determined by the meaning of its component parts and the way in which they are combined. Or we may have the following **Principle of Compositionality**: *the interpretation of a sentence is determined by the interpretations of the words occurring in the sentence and the syntactic structure of the sentence* (Radford 2000: 358). Our semantic rules of grammar can account for the semantic knowledge we have, such as the truth value of the sentence, reference, entailment, and ambiguity.

How can we connect semantic information in the lexicon with the compositional meaning of sentences? One approach is to let the compositional work be done by the syntactic rules. In Chomsky's work, the phrase structure rules build sentences and thus provide the link between individual words in the lexicon and the semantic component, which then combines the meanings of individual words into overall sentence meanings. We say it is the syntactic rules which provide the bridge between word meanings in the lexicon and sentence meaning. In generative grammar, we have **selection restrictions** (C-selection and S-selection in chapter 5) between individual words and even for the semantic features of the same word; we have such kind of restrictions. The compositional analysis described in the last section may be applied to the analysis of sentence meaning.

Thus for the sentence *the man hits the colorful ball*, we know how to build the sentence structure in terms of the phrase structure rules, or X-bar theory or the merger operation; we can represent the meaning of the sentence in the following way:
The [some contextually definite] **man** [human-adult-male] **hits** [action-instancy-intensity [strikes with a blow or missile]] **the** [some contextually definite] **colorful** [abounding in contrast or variety of bright colors] **ball** [physical object- [having globular shape]]. (adapted from Saeed 2000: 237)

6.2.2.2 *Predication Analysis*

The British linguist G. Leech (1983) proposed a way to analyze the meaning of the sentence. In his framework, the **argument structure** of a verb is part of its meaning and is included in its lexical entry. **Predication** as the basic unit is the abstraction of the meaning of a sentence; by analyzing the argument structure of a verb, we know the sentence meaning because according to the **projection principle**, a VP is the projection of the verb and a sentence (or an IP) is the projection of an inflectional element (such as the marker for tense, aspect, modality, and so on).

6.2.2.2.1 Argument Structure

Propositions in logic comprise a **predicate** and a set of **arguments**. A predicate is an expression denoting (for example) an activity or event; it is something said about an argument or it states the logical relation linking the arguments in a sentence; and an argument is an expression denoting a participant in the relevant activity or event.

Verbs differ in terms of the number and types of NPs they can take as complements. **Intransitive verbs** such as *sleep* or *dance* don't take any NP as their complement as in *Mary dances well*; **transitive verbs** such as *find* or *hit* can take or **c-select** a direct object complement as in *John finds a book*; while **ditransitive verbs** such as *give* or *throw* take two object complements as in *John gave Mary a ball*. In addition, all verbs in English take a subject. The various NPs that occur with a verb are its **argument**. Thus intransitive verbs have one argument: the subject; they function as **one-place predicates**. Transitive verbs have two arguments: the subject and the object; such verbs function as **two-place predicates**. While the ditransitive verbs have three arguments: the subject, the direct object, and the indirect object; they are **three-place predicates**. But we should remember that in English we have such sentences as *it is raining*, or *it is hot*; "*it*" in these sentences can not be considered as an argument because "*it*" has no referential content; "*it*" is an expletive functioning as the subject of the sentence. Such kind of sentence may be analyzed as **no-place predication** (containing no argument). Of course, "be hot", "be raining" are still the predicates of the predication. The analysis of the verbs' argument structure is called **predication analysis**.

For example, in the sentence *the police arrested the suspects*, the DP *the suspects* is the complement and hence the **internal argument** (complements are said to be internal arguments) of the predicate *arrested*, and the DP *the police* is the subject and hence the **external argument** (subjects are said to be the external arguments) of *arrested*. We might say that the argument structure of the predicate *arrest* specifies that it is a two-place predicate which takes a DP as its internal argument and another DP as its external argument.

We can analyze the sentences below in the following way:

John sleeps: JOHN (SLEEP). The argument structure of the predicate *sleep* specifies that it is a one-place predicate which takes a DP *John* as its external argument; it has no internal argument.

The children are eating apples: THE CHILDREN, APPLES (EAT).

Mary gave Tom a book: MARY, TOM, A BOOK (GIVE).

It is raining: (BE RAINING).

As the grammatical form of the sentence does not affect the semantic predication of the sentence, then sentences with different verb forms may have the same predication.

TOM (SMOKE): Tom smokes. / Tom is smoking. / Tom has been smoking. / Tom, smoke! / Does Tom smoke? / Tom doesn't smoke.

Not all of the expressions which are associated with a verb function as arguments of the verb. For example, in the sentence *the police arrested the suspects* **on Saturday** (**in Beverly Hills / with minimum use of force**), the bold-printed prepositional phrases are not the participants in the act of *arrest*; they simply serve to provide additional information about the event (the time, place or manner in which the arrest took place); such expressions are known as **adjuncts**.

6.2.2.2.2 Thematic Roles

In the predication analysis, we say the predicate is the main element, for it includes tense, aspect, modality, etc., also, it governs the arguments because it determines the number and nature of the arguments, and it limits the semantic properties of both its subject and its complements. For example, *find* and *sleep* require (**s-select**) animate subjects; thus, Chomsky's famous sentence *colorless green ideas sleep furiously* is semantically anomalous because *ideas* (colorless or not) are not animate. Components of a verb's meaning can also be relevant to the choice of complements it can take.

However, in the predication analysis of the sentence *the police arrested the suspects*, simply saying that a verb like *arrest* takes two DP arguments fails to account for the fact that the two arguments play very different roles in relation to the act of arrest. Any adequate account of argument structure should provide a proper description of the semantic role which each argument plays with respect to its predicate.

We say that the NP subject of a sentence and the arguments in the VP are semantically related in various ways to the verb. The relations depend on the meaning of the particular verb. Such kind of relations that holds between the arguments of the verb and the type of situation that the verb describes are called **thematic roles**.

For the sentence *the boy rolled a red ball*, we have two arguments: *the boy* and *a red ball*. Obviously, *the boy* is the "doer" or "**agent**" of the rolling action; the NP *a red ball* is the "**theme**" of this action. Relations such as agent and theme and other roles we will discuss are all thematic roles mentioned above.

Linguists have attempted to devise a universal typology of the semantic roles played by arguments in relation to their predicates. Besides **agent / causer** (instigator of some action) and **theme/ patient** (entity undergoing the effect of some action), other thematic roles include **goal**, that is, the endpoint of a change in location or possession, or entity towards which something moves; or **source**, where the action originates; or **instrument**, the means used to accomplish the action; or **experiencer**, one receiving sensory input or entity experiencing some psychological state; or **recipient / possessor**, the entity receiving/possessing some entity (Radford 2002: 326); or **beneficiary**, the entity for whose benefit the action was performed; or **location**, the place in which something is situated or takes place. The components of the verb's meaning and syntactic structure may be involved in the assignment of thematic roles.

We can illustrate such kind of thematic roles in the following sentences:

1. John   sold   the book   to   Mary.
   agent   *theme*   *goal*
2. Mary   bought   the book   from   John.
   agent   *theme*   *source*
3. The boy   opened   the door   with   the key.
   agent   *theme*   *instrument*
4.   Mary   fell over.
   theme/patient
5.   John   killed   Harry.
   agent / causer   *patient*
6. They   baked   me   a cake.
   agent   *beneficiary* *patient*
7. The audience   enjoyed   the play.
   experiencer   *theme*
8. John   got   Mary   a present.
   agent   *recipient/ possessor*   *theme*
9. John   went   home.
   theme   *goal*
10. The band   played   in a hall.
    agent   *location*

Thematic roles are not assigned to the arguments randomly; there is a connection between the meaning of a verb and the syntactic structure of sentences containing the verb. Our knowledge of verbs includes their syntactic category, which arguments they select, and the thematic roles they assign to their arguments. Chomsky (1981) has a complete theory on the assignment of the thematic roles in his *Lectures on Government and Binding*; we won't discuss it in detail here.

6.3 Summary

Semantics is the study of the relationships between linguistic forms and entities in the world. It studies the linguistic meanings of words and sentences. Knowing a language means to be cognizant of how to produce and understand the meaning of an infinite number of sentences. In this chapter, we ignore the debate on meaning among philosophers, psychologists, sociologists and linguists; we just focus on the study of word meaning and sentence meaning, and deal with those concepts and content which appear commonly in books on semantics or linguistics.

Lexical semantics is concerned with the meanings of morphemes and words. In the discussion of word meanings, we distinguished **reference** and **sense**; the meaning of words may, in part, be the objects referred to by the words; that is the reference of the words. But there is more to a word than the object it denotes, and that part of meaning is called sense; it concerned with the inherent meaning of the linguistic form. Some expressions have reference but little sense, such as proper names, and some have sense but no reference, such as *the present king of France*.

There are various relations among words. We have explained six kinds of relations: **synonymy, antonymy, hyponymy, metonymy, homonymy, and polysemy**. The words in our mental lexicon exist in such a network. Similarly, sentences are related in various ways. We explained the **synonymous relation** among sentences. And sentence X may be **inconsistent / contradictory** with sentence Y; X possibly **entails / presupposes** Y; X itself may be a **contradiction** or semantically **anomalous**. Anyway, we can try to understand the **truth-conditions** of the related sentences in this way.

The meaning of a word may be further analyzed into **semantic features** such as "female", "young", "cause", or "go". And the meaning of a sentence may be decomposed in this **componential analysis**. On the other hand, we can do a **predication analysis** for the meaning of the sentence. We can analyze the **argument structure** of the predicate; thus we have no-place, one-place, two-place, three-place predication. How many **arguments** each predicate specifies is determined by the inherent feature of the verb, and each argument in a sentence has a **thematic role** to play: **agent / causer, theme / patient, recipient / possessor, goal, source, experiencer, instrument, location, beneficiary**. According to Chomsky (1981: 36), there is a principle of UG called **theta-criterion** (it is a criterion that the sentence must meet in order to be well formed): "*Each argument bears one and only one theta-role, and each theta-role is assigned to one and only one argument.*"

EXERCISES

Exercises I

Which of the following statements are true?
a. *Tennis* is a hyponym of *sport*.
b. *Pea* and *vegetable* are co-hyponyms.
c. *Plant* is a superordinate of *tree*.
d. *Lamb* is a hyponym of *creature*.
e. *Lemon* and *tomato* are co-hyponyms.
f. *Poker* is a hyponym of *game*.
g. *Game* is a hyponym of *sport*.

h. *Poker* is a hyponym of *sport*.
i. *Bread* is a co-hyponym of *butter*.
j. *Disease* is a superordinate *influenza*.
k. *Swing* and *toy* are co-hyponyms.

Exercises II

There are several kinds of antonymy. Please indicate whether the pairs in columns **A** and **B** are complementary, gradable, or relational opposites.

A	B	C
good	bad	gradable
expensive	cheap	_____
parent	offspring	_____
beautiful	ugly	_____
false	true	_____
pass	fail	_____
hot	cold	_____
legal	illegal	_____
poor	rich	_____
fast	slow	_____
asleep	awake	_____
husband	wife	_____
rude	polite	_____

Exercises III

Complete the following diagram by (a) devising a category that distinguishes the word *bus* from the word *car*, and (b) giving the appropriate symbol against each component for the word *motorcycle*.

	Powered	Carries people	Four-wheeled
bus	+	+	+
car	+	+	+
van	+	−	+
bicycle	−	+	−
motorcycle	…	…	…

Exercises IV

For each group of words given as follows, state what semantic feature or features distinguish between the classes of (a) words and (b) words. If asked, also indicate a

Chapter 6   Semantics   115

semantic feature that the (a) words and the (b) words share.
   Example: (a) widow, mother, sister, aunt, maid
            (b) widower, father, brother, uncle, valet
            The (a) and (b) words are "human".
            The (a) words are "female" and the (b) words are "male".
1. (a) bachelor, man, son, paperboy, pope, chief
   (b) bull, rooster, drake, ram
       The (a) and (b) words are _____.
       The (a) words are _____.
       The (b) words are _____.
2. (a) pine, elm, ash, weeping willow, sycamore
   (b) rose, dandelion, aster, tulip, daisy
       The (a) and (b) words are _____.
       The (a) words are _____.
       The (b) words are _____.
3. (a) walk, run, skip, jump, hop, swim
   (b) fly, skate, ski, ride, ride, cycle, canoe
       The (a) and (b) words are _____.
       The (a) words are _____.
       The (b) words are _____.
4. (a) ask, tell, say, talk, converse
   (b) shout, whisper, mutter, drawl, holler
       The (a) and (b) words are _____.
       The (a) words are _____.
       The (b) words are _____.
5. (a) absent-present, alive-dead, asleep-awake, married-single
   (b) big-small, cold-hot, sad-happy, slow-fast
       The (a) and (b) words are _____.
       The (a) words are _____.
       The (b) words are _____.

Exercises V

The following sentences consist of a verb, its noun phrase subject, and various complements and prepositional phrases. Identify the thematic role of each NP by writing *agent*, *theme*, *instrument*, *location*, *source*, *goal*, *experiencer*, *causer*, *patient*, *recipient*, *beneficiary* above the noun.

             agent   theme   source   instrument
Example: [The boy] took [the books] from [the cupboard] with [a handcart]
1. Mary found a ball.

2. The children ran from the playground to the swimming pool.
3. One of the men unlocked all the doors with a paper clip.
4. John melted the ice with a blowtorch.
5. The farmer loaded the hay onto the truck with a pitchfork.
6. Robert filled in the form for his grandmother.
7. Kevin felt ill.
8. The monster was hiding under the bed.

Exercises VI

Identify the relations between the following pairs of sentences:
1. a. Tom's wife is pregnant.
   b. Tom has a wife.
2. a. This is my first visit to your country.
   b. I have been to your country before.
3. a. Jack swims.
   b. Jack swims beautifully.
4. a. He was a bachelor all his life.
   b. He never married all his life.
5. a. My sister will soon be divorced.
   b. My sister is a married woman.
6. a. He speaks English.
   b. He speaks a foreign language.

Exercises VII

The following sentences may be lexically or structurally ambiguous, or both. Provide paraphrases showing that you comprehend all the meanings.
1. I saw him walking by the bank.
2. The police were urged to stop drinking by the fifth.
3. Wanted: Man to take care of cow that does not smoke or drink (actual notice).
4. She can't bear children.
5. Every man loves a woman.

Exercises VIII

In section 6.1.3, Figure 6.1, we have given some semantic features to distinguish the subset of English kinship vocabulary including *aunt*, *uncle*, *father*, *mother*, *son*, and *daughter*. Now try to complete the figure by including the other items representing the kinship relations such as *grandfather*, *grandmother*, *grandson*, *grand-daughter*, *sister*, *brother*, *cousin*, *nephew*, and *niece*. If necessary, please add some other semantic features to distinguish them.

	Male	Previous generation	Related by birth
aunt	−	+	−
uncle	+	+	−
mother	−	+	+
father	+	+	+
son	+	−	+
daughter	−	−	+
grandfather	...	...	...
grandmother	...	...	...
......			
niece	...	...	...

Chapter 7

Pragmatics

The study of meaning involves two main areas. In the last chapter, we discussed and concentrated on meaning that comes from purely linguistic knowledge; that is the study scope of **semantics**. On the other hand, **pragmatics** concentrates on those aspects of meaning that cannot be predicted by linguistic knowledge alone and takes into account knowledge about the physical and social world. This chapter is an introduction to general pragmatics. It covers basic concepts in considerable detail, drawing particular attention to problems in theory of meaning — the distinction between pragmatics and semantics, taking into account both social and psychological factors in the production and interpretation of utterances. During the study, the basic issues in pragmatics will be dealt with, such as **speech acts theory**, **cooperation principle**, **conversational implicature**, **linguistic politeness**, etc. All of these topics accord a central place to the roles of both speaker and hearer in the construction of meaning.

Before we discuss this detailed content, we need have a general understanding of the following questions:

What is pragmatics?
Why do we call pragmatics a wastebasket?
Why should we study pragmatics?
What's the difference among syntax, semantics and pragmatics?
What's the difference between sentence meaning and utterance meaning?
What do we mean by context?
Let's deal with them one by one in this preliminary introduction.

7.1 Some Basic Questions in Pragmatic Study

7.1.1 What Is Pragmatics?

Different linguists define pragmatics from different viewpoints. Levinson (1983: 6 - 27) listed some definitions taken from other linguists about pragmatics. I just chose six of them to do an illustration:

1. Pragmatics is the study of those relations between language and context that are grammaticalized, or encoded in the structure of a language.

2. Pragmatics is the study of all those aspects of meaning not captured in a semantic theory.

3. Pragmatics is the study of the ability of language users to pair sentences with the contexts in which they would be appropriate.

4. Pragmatics is a theory which seeks to characterize how speakers use the sentences of a language to effect successful communication.

5. Pragmatics is the study of language use and linguistic communication.

6. Pragmatics can be defined as the study of how utterances have meanings in situations.

In all these definitions, some key words or concepts are essential for us to understand: they are **meaning**, **context**, **speaker**, **relations**, **communication**, etc. In fact, George Yule (2000) defined pragmatics in some detail from four aspects: Pragmatics is the study of *speaker's meaning* (rather than what the words or phrases in those utterances might mean by themselves). Pragmatics is the study of contextual meaning (how to say? who they are talking to? where, when, and under what circumstances?). Pragmatics is the study of *how more gets communicated than is said* (i.e. the intended meaning, the invisible meaning, or what is unsaid to be understood by the listener). Pragmatics is the study of *the expression of relative distance —closeness* (which determines the choice between the said and the unsaid).

7.1.2 Why Do We Call Pragmatics a Wastebasket?

According to the definitions discussed above, we know that pragmatics cover a large area in their study scope. Generally speaking, the reasons for this phenomenon may be that the linguists and philosophers of language placed the investigation of the abstract, potentially universal, features of language (the formal system of analysis) in the center of their work table, they tended to push any notes they had on everyday language use to the edges; as the tables got crowded, many of those notes on ordinary language in use are knocked off and ended up in the wastebasket.

It is worth remembering that the contents of that wastebasket were not originally organized under a single category (i.e. pragmatics). In fact, Chomsky doesn't totally exclude performance as something useless, but rather thinks of it as something that should be done after the rules of language have been described; his third question about language use make pragmatics develop in a healthy way, and with a certain study scope. He suggested that performance should not be studied until some scientific method is found, and the grammatical system is separated from the use of language and from the context for the use of language.

As we know, for a language in use, meanings are not abstract; they are closely related to contexts. Meanings can not be determined without taking into account such contextual factors as "who says what to whom, when, where and how". When contexts are taken into consideration in the study of meanings, pragmatics hence comes into existence.

7.1.3 Why Should We Study Pragmatics?

Now let's consider the following two situations and try to answer the question: what do these children still need to learn about using language? (Peccei, J. S., 2000)

Situation 1:

A little boy comes in the front door.

Mother: Wipe your feet, please.

The child removes his muddy shoes and socks and carefully wipes his clean feet on the doormat.

Situation 2:

A father is trying to get his 3-year-old daughter to stop lifting up her dress to display her new underwear to the assembled guests.

Father: We don't DO that.

Daughter: I KNOW, Daddy. You don't WEAR dresses.

Can you figure out what's wrong with the children's behavior? You know that the problem is that the children appear to have understood what the words meant but not what their parents meant. As adults, we usually arrive at the speaker's meaning so effortlessly that we tend to be unaware of the considerable amount of skill and knowledge that we used to accomplish this.

To master a language, it is not enough to learn its pronunciation, vocabulary, and grammar exclusively. We should learn something more, such as various relations between language and language users. We should be aware of not only the literary meaning of an expression, but also its implied meaning, the presupposition of an utterance, the speaker's intention, and the hearer's inference, etc. Appropriateness is very important in linguistic communication, esp. in cross-cultural communication. If you say something grammatically incorrect, you at worst are criticized as "speaking badly"; but, if you say something inappropriate, something insincere, untruthful, or deceitful, you will be judged as "behaving badly". For these reasons, we must guard against the cultural differences which might lead us to "behaving badly". That's why pragmatics is a worthwhile area of linguistics for study.

7.1.4 What's the Difference Among Syntax, Semantics and Pragmatics?

In the research fields of philosophy, Charles Morris (1938) was the first to use the term Pragmatics. He used the term in his study of **semiotics**. He divides the research of semiotics into three branches: **syntactics** (= syntax), **semantics**, and **pragmatics**. According to him, syntactics studies the formal relationship between the signs; semantics studies the relationship between signs and the things they represent; while pragmatics studies the relationship between the signs and the interpreters of the signs.

To illustrate the differences in more details, we can say that syntax is the study of the relationships between linguistic forms: how they are arranged in sequence, and which sequences are well-formed. It doesn't consider any world of reference or any user of the forms. Semantics studies the relationships between linguistic forms and entities in the world: how words literally connect to things. Pragmatics is the study of the relationships between linguistic forms and the users of those forms. It's clear that only pragmatics allows humans into the analysis. We can use the next sentence to explain the differences in syntactical, semantical, and pragmatical analysis (yule, 2000).

(1) The duck ran up to Mary and licked her.

Syntactically, we can say that this sentence would be concerned with the rules that determine the correct structure and exclude any incorrect orderings such as:

(2) *Up duck Mary to the ran.

And there is a missing element ("and ____ licked her") before the verb, and we know how to explicate the rules that allow that empty slot. We know what kind of constituents can be combined together to form phrases and its grammatical functions. In fact, we know its syntactic tree diagram in our minds.

Semantically, we know an entity labeled "duck" has a meaning feature [animate], while a verb like "ran up to" requires something animate as its subject: the word "duck" is OK, but not a "ball" in the sentence like (3).

(3)? The ball ran up to Mary and licked her. (A question marker "?" before a sentence show that the sentence is pragmatically abnormal.)

On the other hand, semantics is also concerned with the truth-conditions of propositions expressed in sentences. You can consider the following sentence:

(4)? The duck licked Mary and ran up to her.

In formal logic, we know that if $p \& q$ is true, then logically $q \& p$ is true, but for natural language, it is not the case.

Pragmatically, we expect that sequence, in terms of occurrence, to be reflected in the order of mention. We have a principle of language use here: that is, *interpret order of mention as a reflection of order of occurrence*. That's the reason why sentence (4) is pragmatically incorrect.

Another sentence in Chinese can also be used to explain these differences:

(5) 恭 喜 你!
　　Gong xi ni!
　　Congratulations!

For this sentence, syntactically we say it is an imperative sentence without a subject, it is composed of a verb and a pronoun; semantically, we just pay attention to its literal meaning: to congratulate somebody. But pragmaticians will understand the sentence in different ways according to different contexts: who is the speaker? Is the speaker really congratulating you or just using it as an irony or show his or her anger? All these meanings may be possible in a certain situation; you can imagine such kind of contexts by yourselves.

7.1.5 Meaning: Sentence Meaning or Utterance Meaning

Semantics regards meaning as the innate property of the language proper; the property is innate, fixed, and stable, not subject to the influence of external interferences. For example: "dog" in English or "狗" in Chinese refers to a particular kind of animal in whatever situations. Now consider the sentence (6):

(6) It is cold here.

It simply expresses the semantic proposition of "the low temperature in a certain place". Semanticians do not consider the following factors as "who speaks it to whom, when, where, why, etc." In other words, they do not include context in the study of meanings. If excluding the context, this sentence is fixed in their meaning at any time in any place.

Pragmatics is different. It not only studies the meanings of the word proper, but also links those meanings with the users of the word. In other words, besides studying the word meanings of a speech, it will try to explain in what situation a speech is used, and what purposes the speakers want to achieve. In other words, pragmatics is concerned with the truth-value of a speech in a particular context. For example, we know that a "dog" refers to a dog; however, in a particular context, it can be meant as a warning or a threat. Likewise, besides stating the temperature of a place, "it is cold here" can be used by the speaker to ask the listener to do something: such as to close the window, or to turn on the heating, or to lend him a coat. These meanings are obviously not existent in the literal meanings of the utterance (6). They are inferred from the literal meanings. These inferred meanings are what the speaker aims to convey.

The task of pragmatics is to reveal the meanings that can expose the speaker's purposes or intentions in speaking an utterance. Therefore, the meanings which pragmatics is concerned with are not those existent in the words, expressions or sentences proper, but those related to the context: it involves the speaker's intention to convey a certain meaning which may, or may not, be evident from the message itself. Consequently, interpretation by the hearer of this meaning is likely to depend on context, and meaning, in this sense, is something which is performed, rather than something that exists in a static way (Leech, 1981: 320).

In linguistic literature, the distinctions between **sentence-meaning** and **utterance-meaning** are very common. To distinguish them, it is necessary to separate sentences from utterances.

A **sentence** is a grammatical concept. It is a grammatical unit of language. Its constitution should be in agreement with the grammatical rules. For example, a sentence is composed of a subject and an object. On the other hand, an **utterance** is a unit of communication. It is the smallest unit which has certain communicative functions. This smallest unit of communication can be, in length, exactly the same as a grammatically well-formed sentence; in fact during communication, most utterances are in the forms of grammatically well-formed sentences. For example:

(7) There is a dog at the gate; we'd better keep away.

These two grammatically complete sentences can have the communicative value of a "warning" or "suggestion" in certain context. However, there are also many utterances that are grammatically incomplete. For example:

(8) a. (There's) A dog (at the gate)!
    b. (I order you to) Fire!

There are still some utterances that are not in any sense sentences, but still have communicative functions, such as "Hello!", "Hi!", and "Ouch!" "Wow!", "Good morning!".

As far as meaning is concerned, sentence meaning is abstract, isolated from the context while utterance meaning is specific and related to the context under which a communication is carried out. In many situations, the utterance meaning is based on the sentence meaning; however, it contains more than the sentence meaning, because the utterance meaning is the result of the combination of the sentence meaning and the context: **Utterance M = Sentence M + Context**. For example:

(9) John is still single.

As an isolated sentence, at most, (9) tells us John's marital status. If we look at it as an utterance, then in certain contexts, besides the sentence meaning it conveys, it can also imply other meanings, for example, to encourage the listener to date John.

Grice believes that the sentence meaning is time free. The sentence meaning is not always the same as the intention of the speaker in the use of this sentence in particular context.

(10) He is a fine friend.

The sentence meaning is perpetual. However, if you say this when your friend deserted you at a time when you are in trouble, you will mean something quite different.

We can list the differences between sentence meaning and utterance meaning in the following way:

Sentence meaning	**Utterance meaning**
1) Sentence meaning — Literal meaning of a sentence;	1) Speaker meaning — Intended meaning of a speaker;
2) Non-context-dependent meaning;	2) Context-dependent meaning;
3) Having a dyadic relation as in What does X mean?	3) Having a triadic relation as in What did you mean by X?

Example:

(11) Today is Sunday.
Today is the first day of the week.

Today is Sunday.
By this the speaker wants
to express an order,
to convey information,
to make a suggestion,
to give an invitation,
to make a request,
to ask for permission,
......

7.1.6 Meaning and Context

Meaning and Context are the two basic concepts in the study of Pragmatics. Pragmatics, as a topic in linguistics, is the study of the use of context to make inferences about meaning.

As early as in 1930s, the famous British linguist J. R. Firth put forward the contextual theory of meanings. Firth believes that we *should know a word according to the company it keeps*. Meaning is to be studied through a hierarchy of contexts. Words are analyzed in the context of sentences which are then analyzed in situational contexts or settings which are in turn seen in cultural contexts.

Pragmatics is concerned with the interpretation of linguistic meaning in context. Context plays an important role in the study of meanings in pragmatics. Then what is context? Different linguists have different interpretations as to what is included in the scope of context. Generally, context refers to the environment or conditions in which something exists or occurs. Two kinds of contexts are relevant: the linguistic context and the situational context. For the linguistic context, it refers to the context the sentence appears; that is, the discourse that precedes the phrase or sentence to be interpreted, or the discourse surrounding a word or passage that helps make its meaning clear. As for the situational context—virtually, everything nonlinguistic in the environment of the speaker, it involves A: the relevant features of participants: (1) the verbal action of the participants, (2) the non-verbal action; B: the relevance of objects; and C: the effect of the verbal action.

Pragmatics can be compared to semantics which in one sense is the study of the literal meaning of a sentence. The speaker, however, often speaks something that means more than, or is even apparently different from, what he/she actually says, and yet the hearer understands this additional or altered meaning.

In certain situations or contexts, the following sentences may mean more than the literal meaning; readers can imagine the context with some special meaning for each sentence.

(12) a. You are a fool!
b. Lights, please!
c. What's on TV? —Nothing!
d. Say cheese!
e. Do you like rice? — I'm a Cantonese, you know.

By doing pragmatic study, you can talk about people's intended meanings, their assumptions, their purposes or goals, and the kinds of actions that they are performing when they speak. But we should be aware that all these very human concepts are extremely difficult to analyze in a consistent and objective way. The following conversation may be used as an example to illustrate such difficulties:

(13) *Her*: So—did you?
Him: Hey—who wouldn't?

Without any background knowledge or a certain context, we are not sure what was communicated here. We say pragmatics is appealing because it's about how people make sense of each other linguistically, but it can be a frustrating area of study because it requires us to make sense of people and what they have in mind.

7.2 The Conversational Principles and Implicature

7.2.1 The Cooperative Principle

In the last section, we have shown that the meaning of an utterance may be decided by the nonlinguistic context. In fact, speakers and listeners involved in conversation are generally cooperating with each other; people having a conversation are not normally assumed to be trying to confuse, trick, or withhold relevant information from each other. And collaboration is a necessary factor to be successful in conversation.

The advanced theory of **cooperative principle** from American philosopher Grice (1975), contributes a lot to the explanation of communicative activities by means of language. Listeners normally have to assume what a speaker mentioned is not trying to mislead them, and speakers may sometimes mean more than what they actually say. In that case, how do listeners know this and fill the gap between semantic content and pragmatic inference? Grice's hypothesis states: there must be a principle to govern it — the Cooperative Principle (Grice 1975):

"*Make your conversational contribution such as is required, at the stage at which it occurs, by the accepted purpose or direction of the talk exchange in which you are engaged.*"

In order to make this principle to be more concrete and understandable, Grice used four **maxims** to illustrate it. They are:

The maxim of quantity:

1. Make your contribution as informative as is required (for the current purposes of the exchange).
2. Do not make your contribution more informative than is required.

The maxim of quality: Try to make your contribution one that is true.

1. Do not say what you believe to be false.
2. Do not say that for which you lack adequate evidence.

The maxim of relation: Be relevant.

The maxim of manner: Be perspicuous.

1. Avoid obscurity of expression.
2. Avoid ambiguity.
3. Be brief (avoid unnecessary prolixity).
4. Be orderly.

In short, these maxims specify what participants have to do in order to converse in a maximally efficient, rational, co-operative way: they should speak sincerely, relevantly and clearly, while providing sufficient information.

According to Grice, both the speaker and the hearer should cooperate in conversation to express each other's intention. If the response violates the cooperation, this violation is actually another way to observe the cooperation. That is to say, the speaker might run counter to the maxims of the CP, but the listener must try to make out the underlying cooperation, with the belief that the speaker does follow the CP. The meaning of the underlying cooperation is the **conversational implicature.**

7.2.2 Conversational Implicature

The theory of conversational implicature proposed by Grice intends to analyze the true meaning or implied meaning of the speaker during the conversation. The basic assumption in conversation is that, unless otherwise indicated, the participants are adhering to the cooperative principle and the maxims. But conversation participants do not always observe the maxims strictly. For various reasons, these maxims are often violated. In other words, when we violate any of these maxims, our language becomes indirect, so there will be conversational implicatures.

(14) *Man*: Does your dog bite?
Woman: No.
(*The man reaches down to pet the dog. The dog bites the man's hand.*)
Man: Ouch! Hey! You said your dog doesn't bite.
Woman: He doesn't. But that's not my dog.

Why is the situation so funny? We understand the problem is the man's assumption about the dog (the woman's dog—more was communicated than was said). In fact, the woman has given less information than is expected.

Implicature are naturally interpreted as communicating more than is said. Something must be more than just what the words mean. It is an additional conveyed meaning; the speaker knows the answer.

Now let's observe some conversations violating the maxims of cooperative principle to achieve such conversational implicatures.

1. Violating the requirement of *the quantity maxim*.

(15) A: Would you like to come to our party tonight?
B: I'm afraid I'm not feeling so well today.

(B's answer does not provide enough information and may be not telling the truth; the conversational implicature (CI) is *I don't want to go to your party tonight.*)

2. Violating the requirement of *the quality maxim*.

(16) This woman is made of iron.

(The CI here is: *She has a strong character.*)

3. Violating *the maxim of relation*.

(17) A: The hostess is an awful bore, don't you think so?
B: The roses in the garden are beautiful, aren't they?

(B's answer is not relevant to A's question; B is changing the topic. The CI may be that *I wouldn't like to discuss the hostess here, it's inappropriate.*)

(18) An interview:

Boss: What are your qualifications?
Smith: I have a wife and six children at home. My wife is a helpless cripple. My children have nothing to eat, no clothes to wear, no shoes on their feet, no coal in the cellar and winter is coming.

(Smith's answer is of course irrelevant; the CI here is very clear: *I don't have any qualifications for the job, but I beg you give me the job because I need it.*)

4. Violating *the maxim of manner*.

(19) *Ann*: Where are you going with the dog?

　　　　Sam: To the V—E—T. (vet)

　　(Sam's answer violates the maxim of manner; the spelling of one letter after another for the word *vet* is not brief of course. Why should Sam spell the word? Maybe the dog is familiar with the word, and Sam wouldn't like the dog to understand the meaning of the word. The CI here is that *we don't tell the dog where we are going.*)

　　A similar conversation may be understood in the same way.

　　(20) *A*: Shall we get something for the kids?
　　　　B: Yes. But I veto I-C-E-C-R-E-A-M.

　　It is important to note that it is speakers who communicate meaning via implicatures and it is listeners who recognize those communicated meanings via inference. The inferences selected are those which will preserve the assumption of cooperation.

　　The implicature is calculable. Even if the utterance flouts the CP, the meaning can be inferred—from the literal meaning or the sense of the utterance on the one hand; and the co-operative principle and the maxims on the other. The listener would make the inference in question to preserve the assumption of co-operation. Levinson (1983: 113 – 114) introduced the general pattern for working out an implicature:

　　(i) S (peaker) has said that p;

　　(ii) There's no reason to think S is not observing the maxims, or at least the cooperative principle;

　　(iii) In order for S to say that p and be indeed observing the maxims or the cooperative principle, S must think that q;

　　(iv) S must know that it is mutual knowledge that q must be supposed if S is to be taken to be co-operating;

　　(v) S has done nothing to stop me, the addressee, thinking that q;

　　(vi) Therefore S intends me to think that q, and in saying that p, *has* implicated q.

　　The description here is a little bit complicated, but the reader can infer the implicature according to these steps one by one.

7.2.3　Politeness Principle

　　After we have discussed the cooperative principle and its four maxims, we know that speakers may sometimes violate these maxims so as to achieve some conversational implicatures. But the important question is why we violate these maxims, and the answer may be that we would like to say something indirectly; that is, we violate CP maxims to follow **Politeness Principle** (**PP**). Leech (1983) presented his politeness principle which is similar to Grice's Cooperative Principle. Politeness concerns a relationship between two participants whom we may call *self* and *other*. *Self* will normally be identified with S (peaker), and *other* will typically be identified with H(earer), but speakers also show politeness to third parties. Generally speaking, politeness is focused more strongly on *other* than on *self*.

According to Leech, we have six maxims for PP:
1. **The Maxim of Generosity**
   A: Minimize benefit to *self*.
   B: Maximize cost to *self*.
2. **The Maxim of Tact**
   A: Minimize cost to *other*.
   B: Maximize benefit to *other*.
   (maximize the expression of beliefs which express or imply cost to *other*.)
3. **The Maxim of Approbation**
   A: Minimize dispraise of *other*.
   B: Maximize praise of *other*.
4. **The Maxim of Modesty**
   A: Minimize praise of *self*.
   B: Maximize dispraise of *self*.
5. **The Maxim of Agreement**
   A: Minimize disagreement between *self* and *other*.
   B: Maximize agreement between *self* and *other*.
6. **The Maxim of Sympathy**
   A: Minimize antipathy between *self* and *other*.
   B: Maximize sympathy between *self* and *other*.

We clearly attach great importance to "speaking politely". The need to be polite can often account for why we choose to imply rather than assert an idea or why we choose to use an indirect speech. Suppose you were considering X for a job that needed good writing skills, you have written to his English teacher asking her to assess his performance in this area. You receive the following reply:

"*X has regularly and punctually attended all my classes. All his assignments were handed in on time and very neatly presented. I greatly enjoyed having X in my class.*"

The questions are:
1. What maxim does the teacher seem to flout?
2. What implicature would you draw about X's writing skills?
3. Why do you think the teacher phrased her response this way?

We say that the teacher's response appears to flout the maxim of **quantity**; there is insufficient information about X's writing skills, yet we would assume that as his English teacher, she would have this information. On the other hand, most people may infer that X's writing skills are not very good even though at no point is this explicitly stated. This is a classic example of "damning with faint praise". At last, the teacher knows that she should give an informative answer to the question (**quantity**), she also knows that she should only say what is truthful (**quality**). The teacher does not want to state baldly that the student's performance was not very good (**polite**), at the same time she does not want to lie, so she makes her response in such a way that the reader can infer this without her having to state it.

Grice has proposed a way of analyzing implicatures based on the co-operative principle and its maxims of relevance, quantity, quality, and clarity. In Grice's analysis, the speaker's flouting of a maxim combined with the hearer's assumption that the speaker has not really abandoned the co-operative principle leads to an implicature. Implicatures are inferences that cannot be made from isolated utterances. They are dependent on the context of the utterance and shared knowledge between the speaker and the hearer. We violate CP maxims to follow PP.

7.3 Speech Act Theory

John Austin was a prominent figure in what became known as Ordinary Language Philosophy and he was the initiator of **speech act theory**. His series of lectures, known as the William James Lectures, were given at Oxford and also delivered at Harvard in 1955. After his sudden death in 1960, Austin's lectures were brought together in book form by his student Urmson. This book was entitled *How to Do Things with Words*. The speech act theory is of significance in the study of pragmatics. It has become the core theory in this field and greatly influenced such linguistic fields as psycholinguistics, sociolinguistics and applied linguistics.

As we know, in attempting to express themselves, people do not only produce utterances containing grammatical structures and words; they perform actions via those utterances. E. g. :

(21) a. You are fired.
　　 b. They are so delicious.
　　 c. You are welcome.
　　 d. You are crazy.

By saying these kinds of sentences, we are making a declaration of ending your employment (21a), giving a compliment (21b), showing an acknowledgment of thanks (21c), or expressing your surprise (21d). Actions performed via utterances are generally called speech acts. In English, more specific labels such as apology, complaint, compliment, invitation, promise, or request are given to them.

7.3.1 One Utterance, Three Related Acts

According to Austin, on any occasion, the action performed by producing an utterance will consist of three related acts. They are **locutionary act**, **illocutionary act**, and **perlocutionary act.**

Locutionary acts are acts of saying something. It is the basic act of utterance, or the act of producing a meaningful linguistic expression. If someone has difficulty with actually forming the sounds and words to create a meaningful utterance in a language, then he might fail to produce a locutionary act. If I said the sentence *I will come tomorrow*, then the locutionary act I am performing is *I moved my tongue and uttered a sequence of sounds, and said such a grammatical sentence with the literal meaning of I will come tomorrow*.

Illocutionary acts are acts performed in saying something. We form an utterance with some kind of function in mind; we have our intentions, or so-called illocutionary force in uttering a sentence. Following the formula **In saying X, I was doing Y**, we have the example as in saying *I will come tomorrow*, I was making a promise.

Perlocutionary acts are acts performed as a result of saying something. We do not simply create an utterance without intending it to have an effect; this is the perlocutionary act. This is the actual result of the utterance; it may or may not be what the speaker wants to happen, but it is nevertheless caused by the utterance. Following the formula **By saying X and doing Y, I did Z**, we have a clear result.

By saying *I will come tomorrow* and (thus) making a promise, I reassured you that we have said something and intended it to have an effect; that is, tomorrow, I will come.

Of these three related acts, the most discussed is **illocutionary force**. "Speech act" is generally interpreted quite narrowly to mean only the illocutionary force of an utterance. We should be clear that different locutions can have the same illocutionary force; similarly, the same utterance can potentially have quite different illocutionary forces depending on the contexts. For example, for the same utterance *I'll see you later* (represented as A), in different contexts, the illocutionary act may be:

(22) a. I predict that... (A) ...
   b. I promise you that... (A) ...
   c. I warn you that... (A) ...

Sometimes, the speaker may draw attention to the illocutionary force of their utterances explicitly. Imagine a telephone conversation between a man trying to contact Mary, and Mary's friend.

(23) *Him*: Can I talk to Mary?
   Her: No, she's not here.
   Him: I'm asking you—can I talk to her?
   Her: And I'm telling you—SHE'S NOT HERE!

In this scenario, each speaker has described their illocutionary force clearly by using such kind of performative verbs as *ask* and *tell*.

There are certain expected or appropriate circumstances for the performance of a speech act to be recognized as intended. They are Austin's **felicity conditions**. For example:

(24) I sentence you to six months in prison.

This sentence is said by a judge in a courtroom. However, it will be infelicitous if the speaker is not a specific person in a special context. We won't discuss this aspect in detail here.

7.3.2 Speech Act Classification

Illocutionary acts can be classified according to their purposes. Below are Searle's five types of illocutionary acts based on Austin's classification: **declarations**, **representatives**, **expressives**, **directives**, and **commissives**.

Declarations are those kinds of speech acts that change the world via their utterance. These kinds of speech acts are quite special in that they can only "count" if the speaker has the appropriate authority to perform these acts. The performative verbs used in this speech act include *declare*, *resign*, *appoint*, *name*, *pronounce*, *fire*, *sentence*, etc. Sentence (24) is such a declaration. The other examples are:

(25) a. *Guilty*! (The jury declares in the court of law.)
　　b. *Priest*: I now pronounce you husband and wife.
　　c. *Referee*: You're out!
　　d. I now declare the meeting open.

Representatives are those kinds of speech acts that state what the speaker believes to be the case or not. Speakers represent external reality by making their words fit the world as they believe it to be. The performative verbs used in this speech act include *assert*, *claim*, *affirm*, *state*, *deny*, *inform*, etc. Statement of facts, assertions, conclusions, and descriptions are examples of the speaker representing the world as he believes.

(26) a. The earth is flat.
　　b. It was a warming day.
　　c. Chomsky didn't write about peanuts.
　　d. I have never seen the man before.

Expressives are those kinds of speech acts that state what the speaker feels. They express psychological states and can be statements of pleasure, pain, likes, dislikes, joy, or sorrow. The speaker makes words fit the world (of feeling). The performative verbs used in this speech act include *apologize*, *thank*, *congratulate*, *boast*, *welcome*, etc. For example:

(27) a. What a nice picture!
　　b. I am sorry.
　　c. Congratulations.
　　d. You're very kind.

Directives are those kinds of speech acts that speakers use to get someone else to do something. They express what the speaker wants. Speakers' direct hearers to perform some future act which will make the world fit the speakers' words. They are commands, orders, requests, suggestions, and they can be positive or negative. The performative verbs used here are *request*, *ask*, *urge*, *tell*, *demand*, *command*, *advise*, etc.

(28) a. Turn off the radio.
  b. Don't touch that.
  c. Could you lend me a pen, please?
  d. Clean it up!

Commissives are those kinds of speech acts that speakers use to commit themselves to some future action. They express what the speaker intends. They are promises, threats, refusals, pledges, and can be performed by the speaker alone, or by the speaker as a member of a group. The speaker makes the world fit the words (via the speaker). The performative verbs used in this speech act include *promise*, *threaten*, *consent*, *refuse*, *offer*, *guarantee*, *commit*, etc.

(29) a. If you don't get up by 8:10, I'll lock you up in the room.
  b. I'll return you the money tomorrow.
  c. We will not do that.
  d. I'll call you tonight.

7.3.3 Direct and Indirect Speech Acts

Different types of speech acts can be made on the basis of structure. There is an easily recognized relationship between the structures and their functions.

  Examples   **Structural forms — communicative functions**
(30) a. You wear a seat belt.   Declarative — statement
  b. Do you wear a seat belt? Interrogative — question
  c. Wear a seat belt!   Imperative — command/request

Whenever there is a direct relationship between a structure and a function, we have a **direct speech act** (for example, we use a declarative sentence to express a statement, or an interrogative to express a question). But as we know, declarative or indicative sentences are not specifically for statements or assertions; imperatives are not necessarily for requests or commands; and interrogatives are not only for questions. Whenever there is an indirect relationship between a structure and a function, we have an **indirect speech act**. For example:

A. A declarative or indicative sentence has even more functions.
(31) It's going to rain.
(as a statement, a warning, a hypothesis, a description, a report, etc.)
B. An interrogative form can be used to perform other functions.
(32) Would you pass the salt?
(as a question, a request, a demand, a plea, a command, etc.)
C. An imperative form does not necessarily issue a command; it may have the

function of a suggestion, or an expectation:

(33) Go to see the doctor, and you'll be all right.

Sentence (34) is a good example to show this point. *a* is a declarative for a statement, so it is functioning as a direct speech act. *b* is used to make a command or request, so it is functioning as an indirect speech act.

(34) It's cold outside.

a. I hereby **tell** you about the weather.

b. I hereby **request** of you that you close the door.

Direct speech act is a very common and easy speech act, because you can get the meaning literally and you needn't guess what someone really wants to say. Indirect speech acts may be a little bit more difficult for us to interpret, because we need be clear about the context and understand it according to the situation. Of course, indirect speech acts make our speech more polite.

One of the most common types of indirect speech acts in English has the form of an interrogative, but is not typically used to ask a question (i.e. we don't expect only an answer, we expect action).

(35) Can you close the door?

This sentence is uttered with the intention to convey a request to close the door even though it is in a question form.

(36) *Mary*: What I would like to eat tonight is a big dinner.

    Peter: I had a long day. I'm tired.

Judging from Peter's words, we know that: 1) Peter is tired. 2) If Peter is tired, he wishes Mary would make the dinner. 3) Peter wishes Mary would make the dinner. The conclusion is that Peter wants Mary make dinner by herself.

(37) a. Move out of the way!

    b. Do you have to stand in front of the TV?

    c. You're standing in front of the TV.

    d. You're making a better door than a window.

Here (37) *a* is a direct speech act; we use an imperative sentence to express a command. But *b*, *c*, *d* are all indirect speech acts expressing the same meaning.

We can also use different ways to make a request of "pass me the milk". You can classify each of the following utterances as declarative, interrogative, or imperative, and then decide what the speaker is using the utterance to do.

(38) a. You can pass me the milk.

    b. Why don't you pass the milk?

    c. Have you got the milk?

    d. I could use the milk.

    e. Get me the milk.

    f. Send the milk down here.

We have different ways for performing indirect speech acts. If you want to make a request, you can do it by way of asking the hearer's *ability*, or by way of expressing the speaker's *wish*, or by way of asking the hearer's *intention*, or by way of stating a *fact*:

(39) a. Are you able to reach the book on the top shelf?
     b. I'd rather you didn't do that anymore.
     c. Would it be too much (trouble) for you to pay me the money today?
     d. Officers will wear ties at dinner.

What I should mention is that indirect speech acts are generally associated with greater politeness in English than direct speech acts. In the interpretation of such kind of indirect speech act, we need consider the linguistic or non-linguistic context.

7.4 Summary

In this chapter, we have discussed some questions on pragmatics, including the definition of pragmatics, the significance in pragmatic study, the distinction among **syntax**, **semantics** and **pragmatics**. We have illustrated the differences between sentence meaning and utterance meaning and explained the relationship of meaning and **context.**

For the main content in pragmatic study, we introduced two conversational principles and their respective maxims: **cooperative principle** and **politeness principle**. We know that the maxims of cooperative principle can be flouted to meet the demands of politeness principle, but such kind of violation will lead to **conversational implicatures**.

Another main theory in pragmatic study is the **speech acts theory**, a framework originally proposed by J. L. Austin. According to this theory, utterances can be analyzed as speech acts on three levels: **the locutionary act** (the words the speaker uses), **the illocutionary act** (what the speaker is doing by using those words), and **the perlocutionary act** (the effect of those words on the hearer). On the other hand, according to Searle, the illocutionary acts can be grouped into general categories which are based on the relationship between "the words" and "the world" and who is responsible for bringing about the relationship; thus, we have **declarations**, **representatives**, **expressives**, **directives**, and **commissives**. Speech acts can also be classified as a direct or indirect speech act. In a **direct speech act** there is a direct relationship between its linguistic structure and the work it is doing. In **indirect speech acts** the speech act is performed indirectly through the performance of another speech act. The true illocutionary force of an indirect speech act can be inferred from the context; it will make our speech more polite.

EXERCISES

Exercises I

There are incomplete passages and utterances in this section. Complete them by filling in each blank with word(s) according to the context.

1. Pragmatics not only studies the meanings of the _____ proper, but also links those _____ with the users of the word. In other words, besides studying the word meanings of a speech, it will try to explain in what _____ a speech is used and what _____ the speakers want to achieve. Pragmatics is the study of meaning as _____ by a speaker (or writer) and _____ by a listener (or reader).

2. _____ studies the formal relationship between the signs. _____ studies the relationship between signs and the things they represent. _____ studies the relationship between the signs and the interpreters of the signs.

3. American philosopher H. P. Grice, advanced the theory of _____.

4. Whenever there is a direct relationship between a structure and a function, we have _____ (that is, for example, we use a declarative sentence to express a statement, or an interrogative to express a question). Whenever there is an indirect relationship between a structure and a function, we have _____.

5. _____ are those kinds of speech acts that speakers use to get someone else to do something. They express what the speaker wants. Speakers direct hearers to perform some future act which will make the world fit the speaker's words.

6. _____ are acts performed as a result of saying something. We do not simply create an utterance with function without intending it to have an effect. This is the actual result of the utterance; it may or may not be what the speaker wants to happen; but it is nevertheless caused by the utterance. By saying X and doing Y, I did Z.

7. Language speakers may sometimes violate cooperative maxims so as to achieve some _____, but the important question is why we violate these maxims. The answer may be that we would like to say something indirectly; that is, we violate CP maxims to follow _____.

8. The meanings which pragmatics is concerned about are not those existent in the word, expressions or sentences proper, but those related to _____.

Exercises II

What might the second speaker "mean" in each of the following dialogues? Write a pragmatic paraphrase in each case, and decide which maxim was flouted by the second speaker in each dialogue.

1. *Virginia*: Do you like my new hat?
   Mary: It's pink!
2. **Maggie**: Coffee?
   James: It would keep me awake all night.
3. *Linda*: Have you finished the student evaluation forms and the reading lists?
   Jean: I've done the reading lists.
4. *Phil*: Are you going to Steve's barbecue?
   Terry: Well, Steve's got those dogs now.
5. *Annie*: Was the dessert any good?
   Mike: Annie, cherry pie is cherry pie.

Exercises III

Provide a semantic meaning and a pragmatic meaning for "it's cold here" in the context below.

The Queen and her butler, James, are in the drawing room. The window is open. The Queen says: it's cold here.

Exercises IV

Draw the implicature from the second speaker's response in the following dialogues.
1. *John*: Did you get the milk and the eggs?
   Dave: I got the milk.
2. *John*: Did you manage to fix that leak?
   Dave: I tried to.
3. *John*: I hear you've invited Mat and Chris.
   Dave: I didn't invite Mat.
4. *John*: What happened to your flowers?
   Dave: A dog got into the garden.
5. *John*: Who used all the printer paper?
   Dave: I used some of it.
6. *John*: Are you going to Mark's party tonight?
   Dave: My parents are in town.
7. *John*: What's with your mother?
   Dave: Let's go into the garden.
8. *John*: Where's the salad dressing?
   Dave: We've run out of olive oil.
9. *John*: Want some fudge brownies?
   Dave: There must be 20,000 calories there.

10. *John*: Did you buy the car?
   Dave: It cost twice as much as I thought it would.

Exercises V

An utterance can simultaneously perform three actions. Analyze the following utterance made by Mike to Annie in terms of locutionary, illocutionary and perlocutionary act.

Annie: You've interrupted me again!
Mike: I was rude.

Exercises VI

The following two scenes may be humorous and interesting. Can you do a pragmatic analysis and explain why it is interesting?

Situation 1:
Visitor: Excuse me, do you know where the Ambassador Hotel is?
Passer-by: I know where it is (and walks away).

Situation 2:
Mr. Logic is in the post office.
Mr. Logic (L): Do you sell postage stamps?
Saleswoman (S): Of course, how many do you want?
L: I do not necessarily require any. I merely asked whether or not you sold postage stamps. However I do at present require one first class stamp.
S: That's 16 pence please.
L: You assume that I wish to make a purchase? I merely stated that I required a stamp. A purchase does not necessarily follow. However I do at this point intend to purchase the stamp. Accordingly I remit the sum 16 new pence.

Exercises VII

In each of the following utterances, decide whether the second speaker's utterance is a representative, a commisive, a directive, an expressive or a declaration.

1. I sentence you to 10 years in prison.
2. Clean it up!
3. I'll take her to the vet.
4. It's raining.
5. I'm sorry.

Chapter 8

Language Acquisition

Language is extremely complex. Yet very young children — before the age of five — already know most of the intricate system that comprises the grammar of a language. They can make sentences, ask questions, use appropriate pronouns, negate sentences, form relative clauses, and inflect verbs and nouns, and in general have acquired the phonological, morphological, syntactic, and semantic rules of the grammar.

No one teaches grammar to the children; their parents are no more aware of the rules of grammar than the children. Children seem to act like efficient linguists equipped with a perfect theory of language, and they use this theory to construct the grammar of the language they are exposed to.

It is very clear that the children do not learn a language simply by memorizing the sentences of the language and storing them in the mind; no one can remember all the sentences in a language; rather, children acquire a system of rules that enables them to construct and understand sentences, no matter whether or not they have heard or produced them before. Children are creative in their use of language.

From the phenomena described above, we know that the tasks for linguists are to describe the child's development in terms of a sequence of grammars, and secondly, try to explain the uniformity and rapidity in the pattern of children's linguistic development. A theory of language acquisition must seek to explain such characteristics.

On the other hand, we need some theories or hypotheses in the explanation of the second language learning process. In this chapter, we'll briefly introduce the major theories and hypotheses in the **first language acquisition (FLA)** and **second language acquisition (SLA)**. FLA and SLA cover a large scope; readers may refer to other materials to have a detailed understanding for some of the specific topics.

8.1 First Language Acquisition (FLA)

There have been various proposals concerning the psychological mechanisms involved in acquiring a language. The **behaviorists** believe that language learning is a matter of imitation and habit formation; children learn language through imitation, reinforcement, analogy, and similar processes. But this kind of theory cannot explain the acquisition of more complex grammatical structures of the language. Norm Chomsky showed that language is a complex cognitive system that could not be acquired by behaviorist principles; we have much evidence to show that language is not learned in this way (Fromkin, et al. 2007: 314–316):

Example 1: **Language is not learned through imitation.**
Child: My teacher **holded** the baby rabbits and we patted them.
Adult: Did you say your teacher **held** the baby rabbits?
Child: Yes.
Adult: What did you say she did?
Child: She **holded** the baby rabbits and we patted them.
Adult: Did you say she **held** them tightly?
Child: No, she **holded** them loosely.

Example 2: **Language is not learned through reinforcement.**
Child: Nobody **don't like** me.
Mother: No, say "nobody **likes** me".
Child: Nobody **don't like** me.
(*Dialogue repeated eight times.*)
Mother: Now, listen carefully; say "nobody **likes** me".
Child: Oh, nobody **don't likes** me.

Example 3: **Attempts to correct a child's language are doomed to failure.**
Child: Want **other one** spoon, Daddy.
Father: You mean, you want **the other** spoon.
Child: Yes, I want **other one** spoon, please, Daddy.
Father: Can you say "**the other** spoon"?
Child: **Other...one...** spoon.
Father: Say...**other**.
Child: **Other**.
Father: Spoon.
Child: Spoon.
Father: **Other**...spoon.
Child: **Other**...spoon. Now give me **other one** spoon?

Imitation, reinforcement, error correction and analogy cannot account for language development because they are based on the assumption that what the child acquires is a set of sentences or forms rather than a set of grammatical rules.

Theories that assume that acquisition depends on a specially structured input (such kind of input is called **motherese**, or **caretaker talk**, or **baby talk**; this is an **interactionist view of language acquisition**) also place too much emphasis on the environment rather than on the grammar-making abilities of the child. These proposals do not explain the creativity that children show in acquiring language.

Chomsky maintains that the most plausible explanation for the uniformity and rapidity of first language acquisition is to posit that the course of acquisition is determined by a biologically endowed innate language faculty within the human brain. This provides children with a genetically transmitted set of procedures for developing a grammar which enables them to produce and understand sentences in the language they are acquiring, on the basis of their linguistic experience:

"We may usefully think of the language faculty, the number faculty, and others as 'mental organs', analogous to the heart or the visual system or the system of motor coordination and planning." (Chomsky, 1980: 39)

8.1.1 The Innateness Hypothesis

According to Chomsky, in human brains, there is an innate Universal Grammar which lies in one part of human brain called the **language acquisition device (LAD)**. Chomsky's hypothesis that the course of language acquisition is determined by an innate language faculty is known popularly as **the innateness hypothesis.**

In this sense, "learning" is not the right word to describe how language develops. We say *language grows*. The growth is the realization of the genetic potential (UG) in conjunction with "triggers" (language input) from the environment. Language acquisition is the growth of the mental organ of language triggered by certain language experience; it is not learned in the same way as learning to ride a bicycle. The way in which Chomsky visualizes the acquisition process can be represented schematically below:

Experience of L ⟶ Language Faculty or LAD ⟶ Grammar of L

Acquisition is the process through which language data goes into the LAD (the "black box"), and a grammar comes out; the LAD evaluates alternative grammars to see which best fits the incoming data.

We can summarize the **mentalist view of language** and language acquisition as follows:

1. Language is species-specific; that is, only humans speak language. Language grows in a way similar to other parts of a child's body, such as hands and feet. For this

reason, Chomsky even calls language as a mental organ.

2. Language exists as an independent faculty in the human mind; that is, although it is part of the learner's total cognitive equipment, it is separate from the general cognitive mechanisms responsible for the intellectual development.

3. A child is born with a language acquisition device (LAD) in his or her brain. The genetically endowed LAD consists of only a few very abstract principles, which can make the child to master the L1 within a remarkably short period of time.

4. The process of acquisition consists of **hypothesis testing**. By using the limited number of abstract principles in UG, the child can make more examples and develop the capacity to create an infinite number of sentences.

5. The efficiency of the language acquisition device (LAD) can decline as the child grows older. This explains why adults can no longer learn a language as easily and as gracefully as children.

According to Chomsky, the LAD was described as an imaginary black box existing somewhere in human brain. The black box is said to contain principles that are universal to all human languages. He assumes that the LAD probably consists of three elements — linguistic universals, a hypothesis making device, and an evaluation procedure.

To sum up, the so-called LAD has a number of linguistic universals, or **Universal Grammar (UG)** in store. Children's grammar is rendered from the innate Universal Grammar instead of from the real language around them by induction or generalization. The real language around them is also necessary, but what role it plays in children's language acquisition is no more than that of a trigger to the transformation from the innate Universal Grammar to the Individual Grammar.

In Chomsky's (1988: 68) analogy, the **principles of UG** specify what is invariant (the network itself) and that each **parameter** corresponds to a switch. All that the child has to learn are those grammatical properties which are subject to parametric variation across languages.

8.1.2 The Logical Problem of Language Acquisition

In history, **Plato's problem** is well known to the researchers in the domain: *How do we come to have such rich and specific knowledge, or such intricate systems of belief and understanding, when the evidence available to us is so meager?* We need account for the richness, complexity, and specificity of shared knowledge, given the limitations of the data available. Plato's solution is from memories of prior existence. Similarly in language acquisition research we have a sharp and clear form which has sometimes been called "Plato's problem", the problem of "**poverty of stimulus**", or a learnability problem. In the same manner, **Descartes** proposed his problem regarding language acquisition: *How do children come to learn something so complex as language so quickly* *and effectively, with limited exposure to language, or with "poverty of stimulus"?* Chomsky's solution to Descartes' problem is in terms of the innate properties of the mind. The acquisition of a grammar must be mediated by UG; there is an interaction between the innate UG and the linguistic input from the language being acquired.

8.1.3 Poverty of the Stimulus

The theoretical need for an innate language faculty is based on a negative argument. The claim is that on the basis of input alone, children cannot attain the complexities of adult grammars. Innate linguistic properties fill in where the input fails. Even with explicit correction, children's grammars are often unchangeable. Certain aspects of child (or adult) competence are known without experience, and hence must be part of the genetic blueprint for language with which we are biologically endowed at birth.

All children come to acquire with ease and complete success a rich and complex body of linguistic knowledge despite both their lack of cognitive sophistication and the poverty of the stimulus. There is a mismatch between the primary linguistic input and the system actually attained. One ends up knowing far more than is provided by linguistic input. The input that children are exposed to is *degenerate*, *finite*, and *under-determinate*; that is, the input to the language learner under-determines the end result; the input is insufficiently precise to account for linguistic competence. Language acquisition is more similar to growing than to learning. It is the maturing of the mind according to a preset biological clock.

The "**poverty of the stimulus**" argument has a clear and simple form: On the one hand there is the complexity of language knowledge, and on the other is the insufficient data available to the learner. If the child's mind could not create language knowledge from data in the surrounding environment, the source must be within the mind itself. In Cook's deduction (1988: 86), we can see the structure of the above argument more clearly:

(**Step1**) A native speaker of a particular language knows a particular aspect of syntax (principle), (**step2**) which could not have been learned from the language input typically available to children, (**step3**) and not learned from outside the child's mind through any form of learning, (**step 4**) then it must be built-in to the mind.

That children are born with certain aspects of language is justified by evidence about language knowledge. We can say each piece of final knowledge that is not derived from experience is innate (such as **structure-dependency**, **binding theory**, and so forth). The input, standing alone, is simply insufficient to allow the child to attain full adult competence: children and adults can understand and produce sentences that they have never heard before; they know that certain structures are not possible and that others are ambiguous without being explicitly taught such things. Adults achieve the same result in the end (a complex competence grammar), despite varying exposure to data in the course of acquisition — they may have heard different input, or the same input in a different order, or they may not have been exposed to certain kinds of input at all (White, 1996). On the other hand, under widely varying environmental circumstances, learning different languages, under different conditions of culture and child-growing, and with different motivations and talents, all normal children acquire their native language at a high level of proficiency within limited time.

Without some innately endowed UG, language learning would be impossible because the input data are insufficiently "rich" to allow acquisition ever to occur, much less to occur (so uniformly and so quickly) in about five years for child language, and especially not if children were only equipped with general inductive learning procedures with which to attempt to make sense of that input. The bottom line is, the reason children learn language speedily, easily, and uniformly, whereas apes and computers do not, is that UG narrows down the choices open to them. Despite the fact that certain properties of language are not explicit in the input, native speakers end with a complex grammar that goes far beyond the input, resulting in knowledge of grammaticality, ungrammaticality, ambiguity, paraphrase relations, and various subtle and complex phenomena, suggesting that universal principles must mediate acquisition and shape knowledge of language.

As mentioned above, we know there is a gap between available experience and attained competence formed in first language acquisition and the gap is bridged by an innate UG. Abstractly, the logical problem of adult foreign language learning is the same as childhood language learning. Adult L2 learners are able to attain grammatical knowledge which can neither be learned through positive evidence nor is generally explicitly taught in the foreign language classroom; and given enough time, input, and effort, with the right attitude, motivation, and learning environment, many adult learners achieve very high levels of proficiency; then the logical problem of foreign language acquisition becomes that of explaining the quite high level of competence (Bley, 1989). If some fact of grammar is unlearnable, without invoking some even more mysterious source for this knowledge, then it must be related to UG, independent of whether or not we are able to provide an exact and complete UG-account of that fact.

The next section will introduce the general study scope of second language acquisition and the main hypotheses made in the field. We seldom discuss whether the hypotheses are proved to be true or wrong; readers may use their own judgment.

8.2　Second Language Acquisition (SLA)

Second language acquisition (SLA) refers to two important aspects in the field: the first is the conscious or unconscious processes by which people learn (or acquire) a second language; furthermore, it refers to the study of these processes, which is a very important part of applied linguistics.

8.2.1 Some Basic Distinctions

In the study field of SLA, researchers often make a distinction between "**second language**" and "**foreign language**", with **second language** referring to the language which plays an institutional and social role in the community (i.e. it functions as a recognized means of communication among members who speak some other language as their mother tongue), while **foreign language** referring to the language which plays no major role in the community. According to this distinction, English studied in Hong Kong may be treated as a second language for the people there, while English studied in mainland China may be treated as a foreign language. Of course, L2 may also be called "**target language**", the language people are trying to learn or acquire.

SLA takes place in two kinds of settings: (1) **Natural settings** (or **naturalistic settings**). In the same way that children acquire their mother tongue: no one teaches children any grammar rules; but by the age 5 or 6, they are said to be in good command of almost all the basics of their mother tongue. (2) **Classroom settings**. This is called instructed or tutored SLA: you go to a class to learn the L2; you often have to pay conscious attention to grammar rules and vocabulary items and have to make an effort to commit them to memory.

A radical difference in both what is learned and how it is learned for second or foreign languages may be that the learner is focused on communication in naturalistic SLA and thus learns incidentally, while in instructed SLA the learner typically focuses on some aspect of the language system. The distinction reflects the settings and activities in which learners typically participate. Thus in SLA literature, we also distinguish "**acquisition**" and "**learning**": "acquisition" refers to the subconscious process of "picking up" a language through exposure. "Learning" refers to the conscious process of studying it. But as we know, it's difficult to demonstrate whether the knowledge learners possess is of the "acquired" or "learned" kind; it's problematic for this distinction.

In this book, we don't distinguish "second language" from "foreign language", or "acquisition" from "learning"; henceforth, we may just use second language acquisition and foreign language learning to mean the same thing; both refer to the study of a foreign language, disregarding whether it is studied in natural settings or classroom settings, and no matter whether this foreign language plays a social role or not in the community.

8.2.2 The Study Scope in the Field of SLA

Since the establishment of this discipline around the end of the 1960s, SLA researchers have been interested in describing the characteristics of L2 learning and how these change as acquisition takes place, what people actually do in the process of developing this additional language, regardless of whether or not they themselves are consciously aware of the details of this process. There has also been a growing interest in theory construction; different frameworks, models, hypotheses, and theories appeared to explain the process of SLA. According to Ellis (1994), there are four general questions in second language acquisition research:

1. What do second language learners acquire?

This is about the description of the characteristics of the language that learners actually acquired when they tried to learn an L2. Researchers collected samples of learner language and tried to describe their main features. We document what kind of language learners produced, and tried to work out whether it manifested regularities of some kind or another; thus we have the theories for **error analysis** and **interlanguage** (a special term for the transitional system reflecting the learner's current L2 knowledge).

2. How do learners acquire a second language?

After the description of the interlanguage or the errors produced by the language learners, researchers wanted to explain why learners made errors, why their language displayed marked regularities, and why it changed systematically over time. We need to consider what contribution external factors (the social situation, input, output) make to L2 acquisition, and what contribution internal factors (such as different learning processes, communicative strategies, and different existing knowledge of the individuals learning a second language) make to L2 acquisition. We need to take into account both external and internal factors and how the two interrelate.

3. What differences are there in the way in which individual learners acquire a second language?

This question is about the individual learner differences. As we know, different learners may vary greatly in their rate of learning, their approach to learning, and in their actual achievement. They have different ages, cognitive styles, attitudes and motivation, personalities, aptitude; all these differences may lead to great differences in their final learning result.

4. What effects does instruction have on second language acquisition?

Classroom learning of a second language is the main method used in China; so it's of great significance for us to study the effects that instruction of various kinds has on L2 acquisition. As we know, the classroom affords an opportunity to control very precisely the nature of the input that learners are exposed to; the researchers can formulate and test very specific hypotheses regarding how particular features of an L2 are acquired.

SLA research is not capable of providing teachers with recipes for successful practice; there is no comprehensive theory of SLA, nor even any single theory that is widely accepted. In the field of SLA, there is much disagreement and controversy; this reflects the highly complex nature of L2 acquisition and the relative immaturity of the field. Nevertheless, knowing something about SLA will be of great help for L2 learners and especially for L2 teachers. With this nature of knowledge, we are more clear about the object we are learning and more aware of the individual differences; thus we can find our own learning method or teaching theory to achieve a good learning or teaching result.

Based on the four questions discussed above, we can conclude that the study of SLA consists of two major tasks: firstly we must describe the processes of language learning as they are (description). Secondly, we need explain the reasons for the way they are (explanation). The related research areas for exploring SLA given by Ellis (1994) are as follows:

Table 8.1 A Framework for Investigating L2 Acquisition

Focus on learning			Focus on the learner
Description	Explanation		
Area 1	Area 2	Area 3	Area 4
Characteristics of learner language	Learner-external Factors	Learner-internal mechanisms	The language Learner
Errors	Social context	L1 transfer	General factors e.g. motivation
Acquisition orders and developmental sequences	Input and interaction	Learning processes	Learner strategies
Variability		Communication strategies	
Pragmatic features		Knowledge of linguistic universals	

We have access to huge amounts of research in all these areas; as for how to finish the description task, we have two steps. We firstly collect samples of L2 learner language; then, we record, classify and analyze it. For an explanation of the data, we can try to discover any learner-external factors, or learner-internal factors, and of course we can consider the individual learner differences. Maybe one phenomenon is caused by the interaction of more than one factor. In any case, SLA research can provide some insights for the L2 learning process.

8.2.3 Contrastive Analysis and Error Analysis

An obvious starting point in the study of SLA is the study of the language that learners produce at different stages of their development. Learner language can provide the researcher with insights into the process of acquisition. In this section, let's discuss two methods that deal with learners' errors.

8.2.3.1 *Identification and Classification of Errors*

Language learning is fundamentally a process involving committing errors. In second language learning, errors are inevitable, and no matter what painstaking efforts might we make, errors will always occur. Errors could be significant in three ways (Ellis 1994: 48):

(1) They provide the teacher with information about how much the learner has learned.

(2) They provide the researcher with evidence of how language was learned.

(3) They serve as devices by which the learner discovers the rules of the target language.

Errors are important, surely, the identification and classification of errors may be the first task for the researchers. In fact, identification of errors is closely connected with the recognition of aims and methods of the research and causes of errors. Different classifying criteria result in different results. Generally speaking, the psycholinguistic sources of errors could be described as follows (Ellis, 1994: 58):

Errors: performance mistakes and competence errors

Performance mistakes: 1. processing problems
         2. communication strategies

Competence errors: 1. transfer errors
        2. intralingual errors
        3. unique (e.g. induced) errors

In fact, any deviation from target-language norms may reflect either a problem in performance or in competence. According to Corder (1967), an **error** takes place when the deviation arises as a result of lack of knowledge; it represents a lack of competence. A **mistake** occurs when learners fail to perform their competence as a result of memory limitations and lack of automaticity. But it is competence errors that have been considered central to the study of L2 acquisition.

1. Transfer or interference errors

Transfer or interference errors occur as a result of using elements from one language while speaking another. This mother tongue transfer can play a large part in causing errors. Because of the grammar differences between the mother tongue and the second language, when translating Chinese into English, learners often make errors with word orders, articles and making sentences without a subject. The lack or misuse of articles may be such a transfer error, because in Chinese, the article part of speech is nonexistent, and consequently, learners are very likely to neglect them. Some transfer errors are given below:

(1) a. * We like to *kick* the football.
　　b. We like to play the football.
(2) a. * I was too *thick-hearted* that I failed my exam.
　　b. I was too careless that I failed my exam.
(3) a. * I was very easy to find her.
　　b. It was very easy for me to find her.
(4) a. * He still has *not* come *until* now.
　　b. He has still not come so far (to this moment).
(5) a. * Some students go online is not in order to study.
　　b. Some students do not go online for study.

2. Intralingual errors

Intralingual errors are not relevant to the mother tongue. They originate from the structure of the target language, so any second language learner will come across them. Intralingual errors reflect the general features of rule learning such as faulty generalization, incomplete application of rules and failure to learn conditions under which rules apply. Learners usually over-generalize, ignore or misunderstand the rules and forms. Below are some examples of intralingual errors:

(6) * They fell in love at the first sight.
　　(The over-generated rule: a superlative has to be preceded by "the".)
(7) * He made me to rest.
　　(Just as the pattern: "He asked/wanted/invited me to go.")
(8) * You like to sing?
　　(A declarative word order in question instead of "Do you like to sing?")
(9) * It aims to arise students' interest to make them happy while learning by doing something.
　　(The misuse of *arise* as another similar word *raise*.)
(10) a. * Sorry, I forget my dictionary at home.
　　　b. Sorry, I left my dictionary at home.

3. Unique or Induced errors

These errors occur when learners are led to make errors by the nature of the instruction they have received or by over training of certain language forms and grammar rules. While teaching a second language, teachers sometimes give lots of exercises for students to practice difficult language points; however, the over practice of certain language forms leads students to set up a stereotype when meeting with similar forms. The use of "any" to mean "none" when the students were told that "any" has a negative meaning is such an example. Drills performed without consideration for meaning can also result in error. For example:

(11) a. The coffee is very hot.
　　　b. I can't drink it.

c. → The coffee is too hot to drink.
(12) a. The apricot is sour.
  b. I can't eat it.
  c. → * The apricot is too sour to eat it.

8.2.3.2 *Contrastive Analysis*

Contrastive analysis (**CA**) is an inductive approach based on the distinctive elements of a language. Under the influence of behaviorism, researchers of language teaching began the study of learners' errors. By comparing systematically the language and the culture to be learned with the native language and culture of the students, we can predict and describe the patterns that will cause difficulty in learning and those that will not cause difficulty.

According to the theory of Lado (1957), the **Contrastive Analysis Hypothesis** includes the following three aspects: the main source of errors in L2 is from the transfer of L1 habits, which is also the main difficulty in second language learning. Secondly, the task of contrastive analysis is to compare the forms and meanings across the two languages and find the mismatches or differences so that people can predict learners' difficulties; and the ideal textbooks should be based on contrastive analysis so as to reduce the interference of L1. The method is a simple procedure made up of four steps (Ding, 2004):

  a. Describing L1 and L2;
  b. Selecting a linguistic feature;
  c. Making L1 – L2 comparison on this feature;
  d. Using the result to predict or explain errors in learners' L2 performance.

Contrastive Analysis sought to predict the errors that learners make by identifying the linguistic differences between their L1 and the target language. The underlying assumption of CA was that errors occurred primarily as a result of interference when the learner transferred native language "habit" into the L2.

Contrastive analysis had a strong form and a weak form: the strong form held that we could use contrastive analysis to **predict** errors by identifying the differences between L1 and L2; learners make errors where L2 differs from L1. The weak form held that we could use contrastive analysis to **diagnose**, i.e. to **explain** the reasons for errors by identifying them as a result of interference.

CA was eventually abandoned mainly because of its faulty theoretical assumption and its exclusive attribution of learner errors to L1 transfer. We won't discuss it here due to the limitation of space.

8.2.3.3 *Error Analysis*

The popularity of interlanguage research led to important changes in methodology. In the 1970s, contrastive analysis gradually gave way to error analysis (EA), an approach that analyzes both interlingual (transfer errors) and intralingual errors. While CA regarded all errors as interlingual and traced their origin to L1, EA was ready to consider all possibilities.

Error analysis is the process of determining the incidence, nature, causes and consequences of unsuccessful language learning, in other words, the study and analysis of the errors made by foreign language learners.

It was S. P. Corder who first advocated the importance of error analysis in the language learning process. Initially, he systematically illustrated the nature, significance and classification of learners' errors in accordance with his cognitive psychology, and brought forward a full set of exhaustive methodologies for carrying out error analysis research.

Corder (1974) also suggests the five steps in EA research:
1) Collection of a sample of learner language.
2) Identification of errors.
3) Description of errors.
4) Explanation of errors.
5) Evaluation of errors.

After much research completed by different experts, there are some findings which are very valuable for any future research. For example, transfer errors are more common in the phonological and lexical levels of language than in the grammatical level. They occur more often with adult learners than with child learners. All these studies are providing useful information for the students, teachers and researchers on how much the learner has learned and how language is learned.

The behaviorist, habit-formation account of L2 acquisition treated errors as the result of the negative transfer of L1 habits, while according to the mentalists' creative-construction account, errors were predicted to be similar to those found in L1 acquisition because learners actively construct the grammar of an L2 as they progress. It's difficult to summarize the results of attempts to explain errors in learner language; but the following appear to be some of the main findings (Ellis 1994: 61 – 62):

1. A large number of the errors that the learners produce are intralingual in origin rather than transfer.

2. Learners at an elementary level produced more transfer errors than learners at an intermediate or advanced level, while learners at an intermediate or advanced level produced more intralingual errors.

3. Transfer errors are more common in the phonological and lexical levels of language than in the grammatical level.

4. Errors can have more than one source.

Because of the weaknesses in methodological procedures and the limitations in scope, EA was criticized during 1970s and 1980s. For example, EA fails to provide a complete picture of learner language; it neglects the learner's non-errors; EA has not proved very effective in helping us understand how learners develop knowledge of an L2 over time. Anyway, EA was one of the first methods used to investigate learner language.

8.2.4 The Major Hypotheses in SLA

SLA covers a large study area and involves many theories and hypotheses. In fact, we have already illustrated some hypotheses in FLA and SLA, such as the **innateness hypothesis**, the **poverty of the stimulus hypothesis**, and the **contrastive analysis hypothesis**. Here in this section, some major hypotheses in SLA will be introduced briefly; of course, all of them may be testified or falsified to some extent; you may agree or disagree with some specific hypotheses. If you are interested in one of them, you can find your own evidence to prove it or tear it down; you can also modify them or come up with your own hypothesis. In any event, that's the way we study SLA.

8.2.4.1 *Interlanguage Hypothesis*

Interlanguage is a term coined by Selinker (1972). It refers to the systematic knowledge of language that is independent of both the learner's L1 and the L2 system he or she is trying to acquire. It is a unique linguistic system because it is neither L1 nor L2 but at the same time bears resemblance to both. Interlanguage is transitional; it is undergoing changes as long as learning continues. The claim that *interlanguage is systematic yet unique and transitional is hypothetical*; this is why it is usually referred to as the interlanguage hypothesis.

The key questions in the interlanguage theory study are (Ellis 1994: 351):

1. What processes are responsible for interlanguage construction?

2. What is the nature of the interlanguage continuum?

3. What explanation is there for the fact that most learners do not achieve full target language competence?

Selinker (1972) identifies five principal cognitive processes responsible for L2 acquisition. These are:

1. Language transfer: Some knowledge of the learners' interlanguage system may be transferred from the first language; "transfer" refers to L1 influence, which remains one of the sources for learner errors.

2. Transfer of training: Some interlanguage elements may derive from the training or the ways in which the learners were taught. Teaching sometimes creates language rules that are not part of the L2.

3. Strategies of second language learning: Learners often develop some peculiar ways of learning.

4. Strategies of second language communication: An identifiable approach by the learner to communicate with native speakers. In the following example, the learner

discerned a problem and was able to explain the error in some sense, though immediate correction was not made until the policeman provided it.

For example:
Learner: **I lost my road.**
Policeman: What?
Learner: I lost my road.
Policeman: You lost your road?
Learner: Ahh...I lost myself...I got lost....
Policeman: Oh, you **lost your way.**
Learner: Oh, yes, I lost my way.

5. Overgeneralization of the target language material: This refers to the situation in which an erroneous rule enters the learner's system as a result of instruction. For example: want—wanted, then, we have: go—goed, do—doed.

Selinker also noted that L2 learners failed to reach target language competence; that is, they do not reach the end of the interlanguage continuum. They stop learning when their interlanguage contains at least some rules different from those of the target language system. He referred to this as **fossilization** — the phenomenon of permanent halt in L2-learning progress.

8.2.4.2 The Hypothesis-Testing Hypothesis

Interlanguage processes have been discussed in terms of hypothesis-testing. Corder (1976) suggested that *learners form hypotheses about the structural properties of the target language on the basis of the input data they are exposed to*. In this way, they build a "hypothetical grammar", which is then tested productively. Hypotheses are confirmed if learners' interpretations are plausible and their productions accepted without comment or misunderstanding. They are disconfirmed if their understanding is defective and if their output fails to communicate and is corrected. In such cases, learners may reconstruct their hypotheses.

Originally, this hypothesis is used to explain the process of the first language acquisition; it emphasizes the child's effort to derive rules of the mother tongue. It holds that language development is a stage-by-stage process of cyclical movement between hypothesis application and reformulation. The process can be described in the following way: firstly, the child may form hypothesis about the language according to UG and his or her language input; then, the hypotheses that the child subconsciously sets up are tested in its use of language, and continuously matched with the new linguistic input that the child obtains by listening to what is said in his immediate environment, in his interpretation and production of the language; the child may abandon or revise, or reinforce the hypothesis. This process causes the child's hypotheses about the structure of language to be changed and adapted regularly, through the evaluation procedure, and through a process of systematic changes towards the adult rule system. A child learns not through imitation but by creative hypothesis testing.

But according to Ellis (1994: 352), the main problem of such accounts is that it is not clear how learners obtain the linguistic information they need to modify hypotheses during communicative exchanges. And linguistic theories of interlanguage maintain that hypothesis-testing cannot provide an adequate account of interlanguage development.

8.2.4.3 Natural Order Hypothesis

In the field of FLA, we have a hypothesis stating that *all children acquiring their first language acquire linguistic forms, rules, and items in a similar order*. For example, in English children acquire progressive (-ing), plural (-s), and active sentences before they acquire third person (-s) on verbs, or passive sentences.

In second language and foreign language learning, grammatical forms may also appear in a natural order, though this is not identical with the order of first language acquisition. SLA follows a "universal" route that is not influenced by factors such as the learner's L1, age, and the context in which acquisition takes place (i.e. whether it takes place in natural or classroom settings); and no matter which rules are taught first, and which are taught later.

The natural order hypothesis states that we acquire the rules of a language in a predictable order, some rules tending to come early and others later. The order does not appear to be determined solely by formal simplicity and there is evidence that it is independent of the order in which rules are taught in language classes. Thus it is not always a good idea to start with a rule by considering only whether it is simple in terms of structure. Some rules are simple in structure, but difficult in use, or less often used in real communication. To make learners' communication in the target language easier, it might be better to teach those more often used rules first, before the rules used less often.

Krashen (1977) provided the proposed "natural order" for L2 morpheme acquisition (in Ellis 1994: 94): (-ing), plural (s), copula (is) → auxiliary, article (a, the) → irregular past → regular past (ed), 3rd person singular (s), possessive ('s).

And some researchers claimed that the acquisition order of pronouns may be like that: I, me → you, he → we, they → she/he → your, our, their.

And the acquisition order of the present tense marker will be like (Chang 2006): is → (read) s → does.

Of course, there are some other specific findings in the morpheme study. People agreed that the end point of this natural sequence was a full competence in L2, the point at which the learners showed no difference from a native speaker. But for the starting point of the acquisition order, there are different opinions; some researchers claimed that it's the learner's L1; i.e. they are restructuring the L1 system to make it into an interlanguage system. But most researchers hold the starting point to be the learners' rudimentary knowledge of L2 which help them recreate a new system. The L2 learner may borrow L1 rules and features into this rudimentary body of L2 knowledge. We don't discuss this issue here.

8.2.4.4 *Comprehensible Input Hypothesis*

In the field of SLA, Krashen's theory may be the most famous; in fact his comprehensible input hypothesis is made up of a set of five interrelated hypotheses, as summarized below:

1. **Acquisition-learning hypothesis.**
2. **Natural order hypothesis.**
3. **Input hypothesis.**
4. **Monitor hypothesis.**
5. **Affective filter hypothesis.**

In the last section, we have discussed his natural order hypothesis; here we just discuss the other hypotheses briefly.

In his **Acquisition-learning hypothesis**, he claimed that *Acquisition is a subconscious and intuitive process of constructing the L2 system, just like the process used by children in FLA; and this process is unaffected by teaching or error correction.* While **Learning** *a language, on the other hand, is a conscious process, much like that which one experiences in school. Learners tend to form, analyze the structure, and commit rules to memory.* According to Krashen, this process often involves teaching and error correction; it is less effective than acquisition.

Comprehensible input hypothesis is also called the "$i + 1$" theory, and originally called the **Input Hypothesis**. According to Krashen, *we acquire language only when we receive comprehensible input (CI).* L2 development is a matter of quantitative accumulation. In this hypothesis, input whose content is comprehensible to learners but whose linguistic forms are slightly in advance of their current level of ability ("slightly" meaning one step above their proficiency) may be helpful to the acquisition. That is, if a learner is at stage i, the input conducive to acquisition should contain $i + 1$; if the input is at the level of $i + 1$, Krashen claims that learners can understand most of the language but are still challenged to make progress. If the input is at a higher or lower level (e.g. $i + 2$ or $i + 0$), in contrast, no acquisition will take place. The Comprehensible Input Hypothesis can be restated in terms of the natural order hypothesis. For example, if we acquire the rules of a language in a linear order (1, 2, 3...), then i represents the last rule or language form learned, and $i + 1$ is the next structure that should be learned.

In his **Monitor Theory,** Krashen claims that *before the learner produces an utterance, he or she internally scans it for errors, and uses the learned system to make corrections.* Self-correction occurs when the learner uses the Monitor to correct a sentence after it is uttered. According to the hypothesis, such self-monitoring and self-correction are the only functions of conscious language learning. But for the Monitor to be successfully used, three conditions must be met: that is, the acquirer/learner must know the rule. Secondly, the acquirer must be focused on correctness. And lastly, the acquirer/learner must have time to use the monitor.

According to the **Affective filter hypothesis**, *the affective filter is an impediment to learning or acquisition caused by negative emotional ("affective") responses to one's environment*; these negative emotions prevent efficient processing of the language input. The blockage can be reduced by sparking interest, providing low anxiety environments and bolstering the learner's self-esteem. Optimal acquisition will take place in contexts where the "affective filter" is low (low anxiety).

Since the appearance of Krashen's theory, there are different opinions in the field. The criticism may be stated as follows: the definitions of learning and acquisition are only clear in theory. Furthermore, there is no interaction between the "learned" and "acquired" systems. On the other hand, L2 performance varies in patterns that are much more complicated than just having two alternatives, using or not using the monitor. And comprehensive input alone does not necessarily lead to L2 acquisition. Language teachers oppose Krashen's hypothesis because according to this hypothesis L2 teaching would be a useless profession due to his claim that teaching has no effect on acquisition or on spontaneous L2 performance.

8.2.4.5 *The Frequency Hypothesis*

The frequency hypothesis was proposed by Hatch & Wagner-Gough in 1976. It stated that input and interaction may facilitate L2 development by modeling specific grammatical patterns with a high frequency. *The higher the frequency is at which learners experience the use of L2 grammatical patterns, the sooner they acquire those patterns*. This hypothesis calls for more interaction, more input and more repeated practice in second language teaching. But as we know, it is incomplete; there are many other linguistic features that are difficult to learn even though they occur frequently in language (e.g. English articles and prepositions). On the other hand, certain items are easier to learn than others even though they appear less frequently (e.g. dirty words).

8.2.4.6 *The Interaction Hypothesis*

Based on Krashen's comprehensible input hypothesis, Michael Long (1985) proposed an interaction hypothesis; that is, *the input and interaction may facilitate L2 development by providing comprehension input*, i.e. input that is $i + 1$, one step ahead of the learner's existing L2 knowledge. Long agreed with Krashen that SLA depends on the availability of comprehensible input before the learner's internal processing mechanism can work. While Krashen believes comprehensible input will happen by itself, Long holds that this kind of input is made comprehensible as a result of interactional modification when communication problems arise. According to Long, in a non-native speaker (NNS) - native speaker (NS) encounter, both parties will experience difficulty in comprehension and expression and will therefore modify the interaction; in most cases, the native speaker will adjust the speech to a level that is appropriate to the non-native speakers. The more L2 interaction the learner holds with others, the more negotiation of meaning will happen and subsequently the more comprehensible input the learner will receive.

Merrill Swain (1995) criticizes Krashen and Long's failure to recognize the importance of "comprehensible output" and argues for an output hypothesis.

8.2.4.7 Swain's Comprehensible Output Hypothesis

The output hypothesis holds that *learners need the opportunity for meaningful use of their linguistic resources*. Swain calls such meaningful use of the target language "pushed language". Swain says that comprehensible output refers to the need for a learner to be "pushed toward the delivery of a message that is not only conveyed, but that is conveyed precisely, coherently, and appropriately" (1985: 249). According to her, output may stimulate learners to move from semantic, open-ended, nondeterministic, strategic processing commonly existing in comprehension to the complete grammatical processing needed for accurate production. Output, thus, would seem to have a potentially significant role in the development of syntax and morphology.

The output practice has at least three functions:
1. Output encourages hypothesis testing.
2. Output facilitates the metalinguistic development.
3. Output contributes to consciousness-raising.

Swain's argument is based on her observation of the problems with the French immersion programs in Toronto in the 1980s. It occupies an undeniable place in SLA literature.

8.2.4.8 The Critical Period Hypothesis

As is well known in the field of SLA, younger L2 learners are generally better at learning second languages than older learners. This is supported by Lenneberg's **Critical Period Hypothesis (CPH)**, which claimed *language may be learned only within a particular period of time between 2 months and 13 years of age* (Lenneberg 1967). There is a fixed span of years during which language learning can take place naturally and effortlessly, and after which it is not possible to be completely successful. Children cannot fully acquire language unless they are exposed to it within the critical period — a biologically determined window of opportunity during which time the brain is prepared to develop language. Though Lenneberg himself did not extend the CPH directly to L2 learning, we have reasons to believe that it will be true for SLA. As we know, few adult L2 learners reach the competence child learners do.

Moreover, the critical period is linked to brain lateralization. Adolescents lose the ability to achieve native-speaker competence because they experience brain specialization during this critical period (puberty, the first ten years of life); the brain retains its plasticity then. This period was equated with the period taken for lateralization of the language function to the left side of the brain to be completed. Chomsky also claims that the LAD atrophies once the adolescent passes this critical period.

The CPH is controversial; there is evidence for and against it. If you say that few adult L2 learners reach the competence child learners do, we can also claim that there are the few adult learners who do reach near-native competence. So we will leave the topic here no matter whether you believe it or not.

What I should mention is that the notion of a critical period is true of many species and seems to be species-specific biologically triggered. Certain species of birds develop their bird song during a biologically determined window of time. Instances of children who grew up in environments of extreme social isolation constitute "experiments in nature" for testing the critical-age hypothesis. We have so called "wild" children, or children reared by wolves; none of them, regardless of the cause of isolation, was able to speak or knew any language at the time they were reintroduced into society. Under these circumstances, we can say, language acquisition, though an innate, neurologically based ability, must be triggered by input from the environment

All together we have discussed more than ten major hypotheses in the field of SLA. Of course, there are some other hypotheses which are beyond our illustration, and there are a vast array of factors influencing our second language acquisition. The cognitive, affective and personality variables like age, cognitive style, personality, attitudes, motivation, and aptitude will certainly affect the route, rate and ultimate attainment of SLA.

8.3 Four Conditions for Language Learning

Language learning involves many different factors such as previous learning experience, cognitive style, motivation, as well as **aptitude**, age, personality and so on. Most of these factors cannot be changed by the teacher, but it is important to recognize them, and we can often regulate classroom activities to suit as many people as possible. There are certain basic principles that can help us select and devise useful classroom activities that are most likely to stimulate learning. So under what conditions does effective language learning take place? In this last section we will try to illustrate the four conditions for language learning in some detail.

What we have discussed above in FLA and SLA has demonstrated that in order for anyone to learn a language with reasonable efficiency, besides the genetic endowment (UG) and the principles not specific to the faculty of language, we need have language experience [they are Chomsky's (2005) three factors that enter into the growth of language in the individual]. In order to obtain the language experiences, three essential conditions must be met: they are language input, language output, and motivation; there is also one additional condition that is desirable, though not essential; that is instruction (Willis 1996).

1. **Language input** (or Exposure)

All good language learners take full advantage of their exposure to the target language in use. They let themselves to be involved in an appropriate language environment; that is, to be exposed to a rich but comprehensible input of real spoken and written language in use. Krashen's comprehensible input hypothesis may be used to explain this point. In a word, the language input the learners are exposed should be real, or authentic, with good language quality; on the other hand, it should be rich enough. It is best to select a range of materials that will give them a varied language experience, and to choose things they enjoy in order to sustain their motivation.

2. **Language output** (or use of language)

As well as input, output is now generally considered essential for language development, especially if learners wish to speak and write in the target language. If learners know that in class they will be expected to make real use of the target language themselves, this leads them to pay more attention to what they hear and read, and to process the input more analytically, to notice useful features of language. Thus output can encourage intake.

3. **Motivation**

The third essential condition students need is **motivation** to learn: motivation to process the exposure they receive, and motivation to use the target language in order to benefit from exposure and use. Success and satisfaction are key factors in sustaining motivation. If students feel they have achieved something worthwhile, through their own individual effort, they are more likely to participate the next time. Hence the teachers need to set achievable goals and to highlight students' successes in the classroom.

As we have illustrated just now, language input, output and motivation are three essential conditions for language learning. One without the others, or even two without the third, will not be sufficient. All three can be met outside the classroom, learners can learn a language quite successfully by living, working or socializing in an environment where the target language is used, simply because these three conditions naturally coincide.

4. **Instruction**

It is generally accepted that instruction which focuses on language form can both speed up the rate of language development and raise the ultimate level of the learners' attainment. But what we should remember is that students will not necessarily learn what we teach them when we teach them. Instruction can certainly help students notice specific features of the target language; it can give students the opportunity to process grammatical and lexical patterns and to form hypotheses about their use and meaning. Learners are then more likely to recognise these features occurring in the input they are exposed to.

According to the above discussion, we can say our whole teaching aim is to reproduce the essential conditions for learning, and thus to enlarge and open up those opportunities. A task-based language teaching method may be such a good way for us to achieve this goal.

8.4 Summary

In this chapter, we have managed to answer Chomsky's second question on how the knowledge of language is acquired (including that of the first language and the second language), and the **logical problem of language acquisition**. We have mainly introduced the **mentalist view** of language acquisition. The ease, rapidity, and uniformity of children's language acquisition, despite the **poverty of the stimulus** they receive, suggest that the language faculty is innate; with the help of this faculty (UG), children create grammars, extract rules (and much of the lexicon) from the language around them. Children are not taught language; language grows in their mind.

For second language acquisition, we have introduced the study scope in this field and the study methods as **contrastive analysis** and **error analysis**; some major **hypotheses** have been illustrated briefly without any comments on whether they are right or wrong; you can testify or falsify them in your own way. We didn't discuss the individual differences in SLA, that doesn't mean they are not important; in fact, the final achievement of SLA may be due to such kind of internal factors as age, motivation, personality, aptitude, or learning strategies. Readers may refer to other materials in this area.

Language learning or acquisition involves four conditions: **language input**, **output**, **motivation**, and **instruction**. The first three conditions are necessary and can be met in everyday life in the case of FLA; thus in the case of SLA, the teachers must try their best to create this kind of environment to meet the demands of these conditions. Instruction focusing on language form is beneficial for language learning; it will help students notice the specific features of the language and promote awareness of language structures. In fact, language teachers have their roles to play in the language classroom.

EXERCISES

Exercises I

Children overgeneralize rules such as the plural rule or the past tense formation

rule, producing forms such as *mans* or *mouses*, and *goed* or *doed*. What might a child learning English use instead of the adult words given?
    a. children   b. went   c. better   d. best   e. brought   f. sang
    g. geese   h. worst   i. knives   j. worse   k. saw   l. had

Exercises II

According to SLA researchers, there are differences between errors and mistakes. What are they? Try to give examples to illustrate them.

Exercises III

Identify all the errors in the following note written by a student to her teacher. For each of the errors, discuss the possible reasons (taken from Ding 2004: 57 – 60).
Teacher Din:
    I got a fever and feel painful this morning. Due to this reason, I can't come to class. My classmate Wang Yin agreed to brought my home work. I hope this won't create too much problem for you.

                                                                               Sincerely, Lin Min

Exercises IV

According to the research into the order of acquiring interrogation, people found roughly four stages. Please describe the features of each stage for the sentences given below.
    1. You are reading? Or I writing on this paper?
    2. What you doing? Or what "ring" mean? Or what the color? Or where your sister work?
    3. Are you a student? Or where is the girl? Or do you work in the station?
    4. He ask me what happened. Or I don't know where he is.

Exercises V

Choose one of the hypotheses introduced in this chapter to do a detailed study. You can find materials from other books, journals or the internet, then present it in class. The content of your presentation should include:
    1. Who presented this hypothesis?
    2. What is the major content of the hypothesis?
    3. The evidence to support or falsify the hypothesis.
    4. Your opinion about it.

Exercises VI

We all have strongly held beliefs about the ways that foreign or second languages are learned; all these beliefs are based on our own experiences as language learners and as language teachers. According to what we have learned in this chapter, please judge whether these beliefs are true or wrong, and make a brief comment on them.
1. You can learn to speak a foreign language quite well without lessons.
2. You must use the language freely, or learn to speak it, even if you make a lot of errors.
3. Teachers should always correct students' errors.
4. People of all intellectual abilities can successfully learn another language.
5. The younger you are the better you will learn another language.

Chapter 9

Neurolinguistics

The biological basis of how people speak, listen and comprehend, and how all of this mental equipment evolved, is largely mysterious. But the study of language has been crucial to understanding the brain/mind relationship. Conversely, research on the human brain is helping to answer questions concerning the neurological basis for language. Human beings are the only organisms in which one particular part of the left half of the brain is larger than the corresponding part of the right half; this has led to the belief that human language is biologically, or more exactly, neurologically, based.

So far, we have attempted to answer Chomsky's first three questions; let's come to his fourth question: *How is linguistic knowledge represented in the brain?* This is the study scope of neurolinguistics, which studies the relationship between brain and language: how the structure of the brain affects language learning; how and in which parts of the brain language is stored; and how damage to the brain influences the ability to use language. The study of the biological and neural foundations of language is called **neurolinguistics.**

The neuroscientist Vernon Mountcastle once claimed that "*Things mental, indeed minds, are emergent properties of brain*". This thesis is widely accepted, often considered a distinctive and exciting contribution of the current era. It is an "astonishing hypothesis", the bold assertion that mental phenomena are entirely natural and caused by the neuro-physiological activities of the brain and that capacities of the human mind are in fact capacities of the human brain (Chomsky 2002). Properties termed mental are the result of the organic structure of the brain and the human nervous system generally. On the other hand, we have no direct method to do intrusive experimentation on the human brain because of the consideration of ethics; we can only rely on less controlled methods of investigation; for example, by studying brain damaged patients who suffer from language disorders. To understand the structure of the brain, obviously, the extent and precise nature of the damage is not known without the neuroanatomical study of the brain; thus the conclusion will be tentative. Anyway, we have obtained much knowledge about the brain by the study of language. In this chapter we will introduce the achievements in neurolinguistic study and make a brief survey on Chomsky's biolinguistic perspective.

9.1 The Brain Structure and Its Lateralization

The brain is an extremely complex organ, consisting of several "layers". The most important part of the brain is the outside surface of the brain; the folded surface of the cerebral hemispheres is called the **cerebral cortex**, which contains the **grey matter**. This is where the higher intellectual functions, such as sophisticated reasoning, linguistic skills, and musical ability are located. The cerebral cortex is the decision-making organ of the body and storehouse of "memory". It receives messages from all the sensory organs and initiates all voluntary actions. The cerebral cortex can be damaged in various ways; it may suffer injury from a blow to the head or other types of wounds, or internal damage due to disease or a blockage in a blood vessel.

The study of patients with different types of damage demonstrated that different parts of the brain are related to different functions; that is, we can locate different functions in the brain as indicated below [a combination of three pictures in Radford (2000: 13, 14) and Pinker (2004: 327)]:

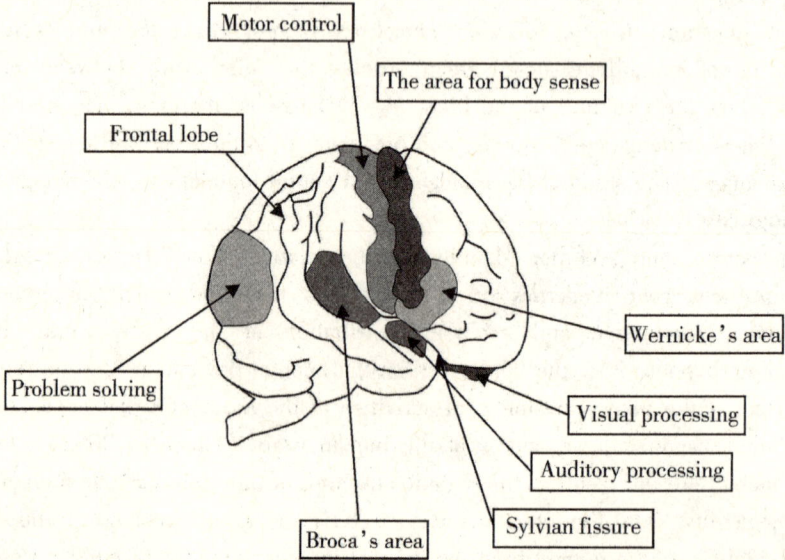

Figure 9.1 The Human Cerebral Cortex, with the Functions of Some Areas Indicated

Lateralization is the term used to refer to any cognitive function that is localized primarily on one side of the brain or the other. In the early nineteenth century, Franz Joseph Gall proposed this theory, which is the idea that different human cognitive abilities and behaviors are localized in specific parts of the brain. His view that the brain is not a uniform mass, and that different human abilities and behaviors are traceable to specific parts of the brain, has been upheld by scientific investigation of aphasia and other disorders and more recently by functional brain imaging.

The cortex is separated into two parts: the left brain and the right brain. Each hemisphere controls the opposite half of the body in terms of muscle movement and sensation. Various experiments have provided information on the different capabilities of the two hemispheres. The **left hemisphere** has primary responsibility for analytic tasks such as arithmetic and language, and it is not superior for processing all sounds. It is only better for those sounds that are linguistic. Whereas the **right hemisphere** controls visual and spatial skills, it processes stimuli more holistically. We can briefly summarize the brain lateralization in the following way (adapted from He & Mei 1998: 213):

(1) **Left hemisphere**　　　　　　　**Right hemisphere**
analytic reasoning　　　　　　　holistic reasoning
language and speech　　　　　　perception of nonlinguistic sounds
temporal ordering judgment　　 visual and spatial skills
reading and writing　　　　　　pattern-matching tasks
mathematical thinking　　　　　recognition of musical melodies
associative thought　　　　　　 recognition of familiar faces
rhythmic perception.　　　　　　nonverbal information.

Language is generally said to be lateralized to the left hemisphere; but as more research has been done, it has become clear that language functions cannot be easily and directly located in specific cortical regions; rather, several different areas of the brain are involved in performing linguistic tasks.

The Japanese language has two writing systems. One system, *kana*, is based on the sound system of the language; each symbol corresponds to a syllable. The other system, *kanji*, is ideographic; each symbol corresponds to a word. *Kanji* is not based on the sounds of the language. Japanese people with left-hemisphere damage are impaired in their ability to read *kana*; whereas people with right hemisphere damage are impaired in their ability to read *kanji*. Also, experiments with normal Japanese speakers show that the right hemisphere is better and faster than the left hemisphere at reading *kanji*, and vice versa (Fromkin, et al. 2007: 49). If this is true, then what about the situation for our Chinese people with such ideographic Mandarin Chinese words?

In recent years, new techniques have been developed for studying the activity of the brain as it performs a specific linguistic task. These so-called imaging techniques such as **Magnetic Resonance Imaging (MRI)**, **functional Magnetic Resonance Imaging (fMRI)**, **Positron Emission Tomography (PET)**, and **Magnetic Encephalography (MEG)**, and **Event-related Brain Potential (ERP)** measurements reveal activity in specific parts of the brain in response to specific stimuli, providing images of the brain "at work", and reveal the lateralization or asymmetry of function of the two hemispheres. We may hope that they will eventually lead to a growth in our knowledge about the physiological mechanisms underlying the knowledge of language.

9.2 Brain Plasticity in Early Life

Lateralization of language to the left hemisphere is a process that begins early in life. Experiments prove that infants as young as one week old show a greater electrical response in the left hemisphere to language and in the right hemisphere to music.

Whereas the left hemisphere is innately predisposed to specialize for language, there is also evidence of considerable **plasticity** (i.e. flexibility) in the system during the early stages of language development. This means that under certain circumstances, the right hemisphere can take over many of the language functions that would normally locate in the left hemisphere. There is much evidence to prove this: in children who have had the diseased left hemisphere surgically removed after language acquisition has begun. These children firstly experience an initial period of **aphasia**, and then reacquire a linguistic system that is virtually indistinguishable from that of normal children; they also show many of the development patterns of normal language acquisition (Fromkin, et al. 2007).

In adults, however, surgical removal of the left hemisphere inevitably results in severe loss of the language function; whereas adults (and children) who have had their right hemispheres removed keep their language abilities. That means the plasticity of the brain decreases with age and with the increasing specialization of the different hemispheres and regions of the brain.

Some evidence suggests that the right hemisphere plays a role at the earliest stages of language acquisition. Many children who have had removed a diseased right hemisphere do not develop language, even though they still have a left hemisphere.

Various findings show that the human brain is essentially designed to specialize for language in the left hemisphere but that the right hemisphere is involved in early language development. Under the right circumstances, the brain is remarkably resilient; if brain damage or surgery occurs early in life, normal left hemisphere functions can be taken over by the right hemisphere.

Michael Merzenich is one of the foremost researchers of neuro-plasticity; his work has shown that the brain retains its ability to alter itself well into adulthood. This suggests that brains with injuries or disease might be able to recover function, even later in life. In a word, the brain has a powerful ability to change itself and adapt.

9.3 Language Disorder — Aphasia

The study of aphasia is the most important tool in the investigation of language in the brain. **Aphasia** is the neurological term for any language disorder that results from brain damage or lesion caused by an accident, a stroke, a disease or trauma, after language has been acquired in the normal way. This sort of brain damage almost always occurs in the left side of the brain (the two sides of the **Sylvian fissure**). Aphasics who lose their language completely are said to suffer from **global aphasia**. In many cases, the brain damage is extensive enough to affect other intellectual functions; sometimes patients maintain a good many of the cognitive capacities they had before the injury. Although they cannot produce or understand language, they can often solve intellectual puzzles which don't rely on language.

It is reasonable to suppose that we might learn how a machine works by investigating how it goes wrong; thus aphasia provides us with a potentially valuable source of information as to how linguistic representations are implemented in the brain. In aphasic patients, there is typically some language ability left after brain damage, indicating that the knowledge of language can be selectively impaired by brain lesions. We can learn something about the inter-connections of the brain mechanisms underlying language.

In the study of aphasia, researchers found at least three important language disorders: **Broca's Aphasia (BA)**, **Wernicke's Aphasia (WA)** and **Specific Language Impairment (SLI)**; they have different locations of damage and show different characteristics in morphological and syntactic disorders. We will try to illustrate them in some detail in this section.

9.3.1 Broca's Aphasia

In 1861, a French neurologist, Paul Broca, described a patient who had suffered a stroke and who could say only one word, but appeared to understand everything that was said to him. After the patient's death, Broca studied his brain and discovered a large area of damage in the frontal lobe of the left hemisphere indicated in Figure 9.1, **Broca's area**. Broca said this was the area of the brain responsible for controlling the production of speech.

Agrammatism (literally meaning "lack of grammar") is considered to be the characteristic symptom of Broca's aphasia. It is defined as the omission of function words in speech production; whereas in comprehension, agrammatic patients perform in the normal range. It affects function words such as articles, auxiliaries, prepositions, pronouns, complementizers, and bound morphemes such as those marking tense (-ed) and agreement (-s) in English and also gender, case, etc., in those languages such as Italian and Russian which are inflectionally richer than English. It does not affect content words such as nouns, verbs, and adjectives.

Broca's aphasia is characterized by labored speech and certain kinds of word-finding difficulties but it's primarily a disorder that affects the person's ability to form sentences with the rule of syntax. This combination of properties produces the characteristic **telegraphic speech**:

(2) "Ah ...little boy... cookies, pass...a...little boy...Tip, up...fall".

[The description of a picture of a child stealing a biscuit by a Broca's aphasic (Radford 2000: 244).]

(3) Doctor: Could you tell me what you have been doing in the hospital?
   Patient: Yes, sure. Me go, er, uh, P. T. [physical therapy] none o'cot, speech...two times...read...r...rip...rike...uh. Write practice... get ... ting...better.
   Doctor: And have you been going home on weekends?
   Patient: Why, yes...Thursday uh...uh...uh...no... Friday ...Bar...ba...ra... wife ... and oh car...drive...purpike...you know...rest... and TV.

[An excerpt of a conversation between a patient with Broca's aphasia and a doctor (Fromkin, et al. 2007: 39).]

The sentences Broca's aphasics produce in spontaneous speech are characterized by their simplicity or reduced syntactic complexity. These sentences are often incomplete, with functional elements being omitted. For example (adapted from Radford 2000: 407):

(4) a. He going bus. (He's going *on the* bus.)
   b. This happened? (*When did* this happen?)
   c. Woman is packing the case. (*The* woman *is* packing the case.)
   d. Only passed my test afternoon. (*I* only passed my test *in the* afternoon.)
   e. Pulling it. (*They are* pulling it.)

From the above examples, we can see the realizations are syntactically less complex than the target reconstructions, and omissions and simplifications typically affect functional projections (DP, IP and CP). The head I (*is*) and P (*on*) and D (*the*) in sentence *a* are omitted; in sentence *b*, the wh-operator *when* is omitted from Spec-CP, and the preposed auxiliary *did* is omitted from C. In sentence *d* and *e*, the pronominal D (I, *they*) in spec-IP are omitted.

It is true that English-speaking agrammatics omit many function words, but this observation cannot be generalized; studies on other languages lead to the following conclusions about agrammatics (Radford 2000: 246):

1. They never produce words, stems or roots that would violate word-structure

properties of their language.

2. They still have inflectional paradigms.

3. They seem to know the categorial identity of affixes, in the sense that they retain knowledge of the categories to which specific affixes can be attached.

In a word, agrammatics have a grammar that is selectively impaired, but the architecture of the system is identical to that of linguistically normal people.

Phonologically, the speech of Broca's aphasics is very halting. They speak very very slowly and have a lot of hesitation, and a lack of normal sentence intonation. It's difficult for them to produce accurately the needed phones.

Broca's aphasics have problems in comprehending functional categories as well as in producing them; they may also have difficulties in understanding complex sentences in which comprehension depends exclusively on syntactic structure and where they cannot rely on their real-world knowledge. For example, they might be confused as to who is chasing who in a passive sentence (5), because here it is plausible for either animal to chase the other.

(5) The cat was chased by the dog.

But they have less difficulty with (6):

(6) The car was chased by the dog.

Here the meaning of the sentence can be provided by nonlinguistic knowledge. They know that it is implausible for cars to chase dogs and can use that knowledge to interpret the sentence.

The phenomenon of agrammatism is perhaps the clearest case of impairment to the central cognitive system that underlies the production and comprehension of sentences. The deficit can be characterized in syntactic terms, namely as an impairment to *the internal feature specification of functional categories*. We won't discuss it here anymore; readers may refer to Radford's explanation (2000: 406 – 419).

Generative linguists have shown interest in syntactic disorders. Many generative linguists (particularly Norm Chomsky and his followers) claim that humans possess a language-specific cognitive system that underlies the production and comprehension of sentences. Syntactic principles are said to be unique to language, and autonomous of non-linguistic cognitive systems such as vision, hearing, reasoning, or memory. This view of syntax makes two interesting predictions about language disorders: first, we would expect to find cases of language disorders in which knowledge of syntax is impaired while other cognitive systems remain unaffected. If the syntactic system is indeed autonomous, then it should be possible for it to be selectively impaired. The second prediction is that syntactic disorders should involve impairments of both language production and language comprehension. It seems that the syndrome of Broca's aphasia does provide some evidence to support this.

9.3.2 Wernicke's Aphasia

There is a second group of aphasic patients who have considerable difficulty in understanding language. Such patients appear to produce language reasonably fluently, but they often speak in a confused or misleading fashion. This pattern of deficit is often referred to as **Wernicke's aphasia**. It is associated with damage to another area of the left hemisphere known as **Wernicke's area** (see Figure 9.1), which is named after the German neurologist Carl Wernicke who first described this phenomenon in detail in the 1870s.

Those errors in the use of content words that typically occur in Wernicke's aphasics are the common phenomena of **paraphasias**; function words seem to be unaffected in these cases. The speech of such patients is fluent and effortless, and the rate of production of words can exceed the normal rate. However, the content of the speech can be remarkably empty and convey little information. Wernicke's aphasics do not demonstrate difficulties in grammar and function words, but rather these patients make many errors in content word usage:

(7) "*They have the cases, the cookies, and they were helping each other with the good*".

[The description of the picture of a child stealing a biscuit by a Wernicke's aphasics (Radford 2000: 244).]

(8) "*I felt worse because I can no longer keep in mind from the mind of the minds to keep me from mind and up to the ear which can be to find among ourselves*".

[One patient replied to a question about his health (Fromkin, et al. 2007: 40).]

(9) "*The spy filed to grain*".

(The sentence "*The spy fled to Greece*" is read aloud by a Wernicke's aphasics.)

Unlike Broca's patients, people with Wernicke's aphasia produce fluent speech with good intonation, and they may largely adhere to the rules of syntax. However, their language is often semantically incoherent. They have difficulties in naming objects presented to them and also in choosing words in spontaneous speech; they may make numerous lexical errors (word substitutions).

Performance of Wernicke's aphasics on content words is affected by the frequency of the word in the vocabulary, and the structures which characterize the mental lexicon; that is, the meanings of words and their associative links (e.g. semantic relatedness) in the mental lexicon. The following effects have been found in content-word paraphasias from aphasics (Radford 2000: 249):

1. Frequency effects: low-frequency content words yield more paraphasias than high-frequency words. Or infrequent words take longer to retrieve and are more often inaccurately retrieved than frequent words.

2. Categorization-level effects: hyponym exchanges (from *sparrow* to *owl*) or use of superordinates (from *sparrow* to *bird*).

3. Similarity effects: semantic exchanges (from *hair* to *comb*) or pragmatic exchanges (from *flowers* to *visit*) (flowers and visits are often associated in everyday life).

In general, the content-word usage of Wernicke's aphasics is markedly poorer than in normal speakers. But there do not seem to be any qualitative differences in content word usage between aphasics and normal speakers, and the organizational principles of the mental lexicon, in terms of levels of categorization and associative processes are not affected by the deficit.

The basic structure of the mental lexicon does not globally change as a result of the impairment. The relevant variables controlling content-word usage in aphasics are the same as for normal subjects: namely word frequency, semantic similarity and categorization level.

At first sight, the spontaneous speech of Wernicke's aphasics appears to be fluent, with normal prosody and syntactic structure. However, they are not always syntactically well formed and contain various kinds of errors, e. g. word exchanges and exchanges of whole constituents as well as blends of different constituents. This cluster of properties is called **paragrammatism** in the clinical literature.

Paragrammatic errors do not result from an independent syntactic disorder; they are just indicative of patients' lexical problems, specifically their word-finding difficulties. It has been found that blends, constituent substitutions, and syntactic errors typically occur at the time when the patient is trying to retrieve content words, particularly nouns. They start to produce a sentence and if they experience word-finding problems, they will change the sentence plan or start again. The paragrammatism is not a genuine syntactic disorder, but rather a secondary effect of patients' lexical disorder.

For example: a Wernicke's aphasic was asked to name a lady's shoe that was shown to him (taken from Radford 2000: 412).

(10) *Experimenter*: What is this? (= a lady's shoe)
      Patient: Yes sir. Now there there I remember. I have you there what I thought was the ... a lady. one. another. with a very short. very very clever done. do that the one two, go, but there's the liver. And there is the new. and so on. It is a document. late ...

9.3.3 Specific Language Impairment (SLI)

The language disorders suffered by Broca's aphasia and Wernicke's aphasia are caused by damage to the brain, but there are cases of children without brain lesions who nevertheless have difficulties in acquiring language or are much slower than the average child. They show no other cognitive deficits; they are not autistic or retarded, and they have no perceptual problems. Such children are suffering from **Specific Language Impairment** (**SLI**). SLI is a term covering disorders in the normal acquisition of language without there being any clear primary deficit.

SLI children and adults have normal non-verbal IQs, no hearing deficits and no obvious emotional or behavioral difficulties. Only their linguistic ability is affected; and often only specific aspects of grammar are impaired. It occurs in families; it is more frequent in boys than in girls and it affects both members of a pair of identical twins more frequently than it affects both members of a pair of fraternal twins. All these things suggest its likely to be from a genetic source. The nature of the impairment affects aspects of grammatical inflection, and certain complex syntactic processes; unlike aphasics, SLI subjects have never acquired language in the normal way.

SLI children have problems in the area of *inflectional morphology*, and specifically, they often omit grammatical function words and bound morphemes, or they use them incorrectly. Within the area of inflection, subject-verb agreement, case marking, gender and auxiliaries appear to be more strongly affected than noun plurals. It also seems that in SLI children, the development of inflectional morphology comes to a standstill at an early stage and that beyond this point the acquisition process cannot advance without difficulties.

The following sentences are produced by a ten-year-old SLI child (adapted from Radford 2000: 250):

(11) a. You got *a* tape recorders.

　　　　　　　　　　　　　　　　　　(A problem in number marking)

　b. When the cup break *he* get repair.

　　　　　　　　　　　　　　　　　　(An inappropriate pronominal choice)

　c. *The* Marie-Louise look at the bird.

　　　　　　　　　　　　　　　　　　(An inappropriate determiner choice)

　d. The superman *is say* good-bye and *hiding*.

　　　　　　　　　　　　　(Difficulties with participle forms and auxiliary verbs)

　e. The ambulance *arrive*.

　　　　　　　　　　　　　　　　　　(Difficulties in subject-verb agreement)

SLI subjects can retrieve irregular verbs such as *got* and *is* from memory — equivalently from the relevant lexical representations — but that they cannot generate the third person singular forms of verbs. That is, SLI individuals' ability to learn inflectional rules is impaired relative to their ability to memorize and store individual words. They have problems learning regular inflectional rules, while their ability to retrieve irregular forms, which are stored as part of a verb's lexical entry remains intact. That is, SLI subjects' knowledge of inflection is selectively impaired; they have problems with regular rules of inflection than with accessing irregulars from memory.

Children with SLI have particular problems with the use of function words such as articles, prepositions, and auxiliary verbs. They may also have difficulties with inflectional suffixes on nouns and verbs such as markers of tense and agreement. For example [The sentences are taken from a four-year-old boy with SLI (Fromkin, et al. 2007: 50).]:

(12) a. Meowmeow chase mice.
     b. Show me knife.
     c. It not long one.

An experimental study of several SLI children showed that they produced the past tense marker on the verb (as in *danced*) about 27 percent of the time and the plural marker -s (as in *boys*) only 9 percent of the time as compared to normal children, who produced them 95 percent of the time respectively.

In SLI subjects, the normal development of grammar is selectively impaired, and that the impairment mainly affects inflection; word order appears to develop normally.

9.3.4 The Implications of the Study for the Aphasic Patients

The study of the language disorders of aphasic patients has provided many important implications for brain scientists, neurolinguists and biolinguists. They have provided the evidence for Chomsky's claim that the Language Faculty is a mental organ and linguistics is a natural science, and confirmed *the modular characteristics of the brain and the ideas of language organ, linguistic modularity and the genetic properties of human languages*. We will discuss them in some detail.

Human beings are biologically equipped from birth with an autonomous language faculty that is highly specific and that does not derive from general human intellectual ability. SLI children show that language may be impaired while general intelligence stays intact, supporting the view of *a grammatical faculty that is separate from other cognitive systems*.

The historical descriptions of language loss and disorders after brain damage, together with the later controlled scientific studies of aphasia, have provided substantial evidence that *language is predominantly and most frequently a left-hemisphere function*. Deaf signers with damage to the left hemisphere show aphasia for sign language similar to the language breakdown in hearing aphasics, even though sign language is a visual-spatial language. They may have difficulties in sign production and comprehension with the damage to the Broca's area or Wernicke's area. This shows that the *left hemisphere is lateralized for language—an abstract system of symbols and rules—and not simply for hearing or speech. Language can be realized in different modalities, spoken or signed*. In most cases, lesions to the left hemisphere result in aphasia but injuries to the right do not (although such lesions result in deficits in facial recognition, pattern recognition, and other cognitive abilities).

The idea of *a grammar as a cognitive (ultimately, neurological) structure* is common to the field of generative linguistics. The kind of selective impairment that we find in people with aphasia has provided important information about the organization of different cognitive abilities, especially grammar and the lexicon. It tells us that *language is a separate cognitive module*—so aphasics can be otherwise cognitively normal—and also that *separate components in language can be differentially affected by damage to different regions of the brain*. Mental grammar, like the brain itself, is not an undifferentiated system, but rather consists of distinct components or modules with different functions. In view of the fact that damage to different parts of the brain results in different kinds of linguistic impairment (e. g. syntactic versus semantic).

Language disorders such as aphasia and SLI do not involve global disorders of the mental lexicon, but rather selective deficits to otherwise normal lexical and morphological systems. The kind of **word substitutions** that aphasic patients produce also tell us about *how words are organized in the mental lexicon*. Sometimes the substituted words are similar to the intended words in their sounds (*pool* for *tool*, or *sable* for *table*), or in meaning (*table* for *chair*, or *boy* for *girl*). The substitution of semantically or phonetically related words tells us that *neural connections exist among semantically related words and among words that sound alike*. Words are not mentally represented in a simple list but rather in an organized network of connections.

The omission of **function words** by agrammatic aphasics shows that this class of words is mentally distinct from **content words** like nouns. Those errors suggest that *the content words and function words of the mental dictionary in our brains are located in different places, and they are processed in different brain areas or by different neural mechanisms*. This point further supports the view that both the brain and language are structured in a complex, modular fashion.

Chomsky has proposed that the language faculty is a "mental organ", analogous to a physical organ like the heart or the visual system. That is to say, the brain consists of subcomponents, or modules, each specialized for different purposes such as vision, the language faculty, the number faculty. Moreover, when one examines the different subsystems of the language faculty such as syntax, morphology, and lexicon, further distinguishing properties are found; they are controlled by different places in the brain.

If we can find individuals who develop their language normally when general intelligence is impaired, it will strongly argue for the view that *language does not derive from some general cognitive ability*. We do have such individuals to show this, which will be described in the next section.

9.4 Language Savants

There are numerous cases of intellectually handicapped individuals who show remarkable talents in other fields, despite their disabilities in certain aspects. We have excellent scientists, musicians and artists who lack the simple abilities required to take care of themselves; we have calendrical calculators who can tell you without pause on which day of the week falls any date in the last or next century. Most such savants have been reported to be linguistically handicapped, and the literature reports cases of language savants who have acquired the highly complex grammar of their language (as well as other languages in some cases) but who lack nonlinguistic abilities of equal complexity. Laura and Christopher are two such cases (taken from Fromkin, et al. 2007: 50 – 52). Their situations argue against the view that linguistic ability derives from general intelligence, because they developed language despite other intellectual deficits.

Laura

Laura was a retarded young woman with a nonverbal IQ of 41 to 44. She lacked almost all number concepts, including basic counting principles, and could draw only at a preschool level. Her drawings of humans resembled potatoes with stick arms and legs. She had an auditory memory span limited to three units. She could neither read nor write nor tell time; that is, she had not the concept of time. She could not add 2 + 2, she did not know who the president of the United States was or what country she lived in or even her own age.

Yet, when at the age of sixteen Laura could produce syntactically complex sentences like:

(13) a. *He was saying that I lost my battery-powered watch that I loved.*
   b. *Last year at school when I first went there, three tickets were given out by a police last year.*

Laura produced complex sentences with multiple phrases. She used and understood passive sentences, and she was able to inflect verbs for number and person to agree with the subject of the sentence. In a sentence imitation task, she both detected and corrected grammatical errors.

Laura is but one of many examples of children who display well-developed grammatical abilities, less-developed abilities to associate linguistic expressions with the objects they refer to, and severe deficits in nonlinguistic cognition. In *the genetic properties of human languages* (Yang & Ning 2002), we have many such cases to prove these genetic properties.

Christopher

Christopher has a nonverbal IQ between 60 and 70; he is unable to take care of himself. The tasks of buttoning a shirt or cutting his fingernails are difficult for him. However, linguists found that his linguistic competence is as rich, and as complex as that of any native speaker. Furthermore, when given written texts in some fifteen to twenty languages, he translates them quickly, with few errors, into English. The languages include Danish, Dutch, German, French, Italian, Portuguese, Spanish, as well as Polish, Finnish, Greek, Hindi, Turkish, Welsh, etc. ... He learned these languages from speakers who used them in front of him, or from grammar books. Christopher loves to study and learn languages; his linguistic ability is independent of his general intellectual ability.

From those language savants with good language abilities but who are intellectually handicapped, we can conclude that any notion that linguistic competence results simply from communicative abilities, or develops to serve communication functions, is proved to be wrong by studies of people with good linguistic skills, but nearly no or severely limited communicative skills. The acquisition and use of language seem to depend on cognitive skills different from the ability to communicate in a social setting.

Evidence from aphasia, SLI and other genetic disorders, along with the asymmetry of abilities in linguistic savants, strongly supports the view that *the grammatical aspect of the language faculty is an autonomous, genetically determined module of the brain.*

9.5 Language Gene

In the last several sections we have described the syndromes of aphasics, SLI patients and language savants. It seems that, *biologically speaking, we have an innate language organ which controls the different aspects of language including syntax, mental lexicon, or the sound system.* The inheritable capability to learn any language must be encoded in the DNA of our chromosomes. We can say that the critical difficulty which all linguists and geneticists should face up to is try to find the language gene(s); this localization of the genes controlling the language faculty will be an epoch-making revolution in human history.

If our knowledge of language and, specifically of grammar, is indeed controlled by our genes, then we should expect to find genetically caused disorders of grammatical development. We do have such SLI patients to prove this view.

SLI runs in families. One entire family missing a gene called FOXP2 has problems with many language skills such as grammatical competence.

Hurst (1990), Gopnik and Crago (1991) studied three generations of the KE family in Britain in detail. All of the people in the study are adult native speakers of English. Some linguistic disabilities appear in this family through several generations. The patients can not control the movement of the tongue and the lip automatically and they show difficulties in the organization of words and grammar and in naming objects (*glass* or *tea* may be used to replace *cup*).

Phonologically, they have difficulties in pronunciation: problems reading consonant clusters or omitting the onset of words and some syllables in multi-syllable words (*spoon* is read as *boon*, *table* as *able*).

Syntactically, they cannot understand sentences like:

(14) a. The knife is longer than the pencil. (Comparative sentences)
b. The girl is chased by the horse. (Passive sentence)
c. The boy chasing the horse is fat. (Reduced relatives)

They cannot use the *grammatical inflections* freely. For the number, tense or aspects of verbs and plural or single nouns, they often make mistakes (*walk* for *walked*, *sing* for *singing*, *a books* for *a book*, *three book* for *three books*). All these patients understand the concept of numbers and time (they know the meaning of *yesterday*), one of them is even good at mathematics and computing, but when it comes to using numbers and time in grammar they are unable to deal with it. The members of the family have normal IQs but problems with language.

The impaired members of this family do not reliably indicate the tense of the verb. They often make such sentences as (15):

(15) a. She *remembered* when she *hurts* herself the other day.
b. He *did* it then he *fall*.
c. The boy *climb* up the tree and *frightened* the bird away.

The research group found that at the same spot of the chromosome, there is a mutation of the same FOXP2 gene among the patients with severe disorders in speech and language. They thought that this mutation of FOXP2 might be involved in the language disorder because of its inability to control or adjust the other genes. On the basis of all the evidence of familial transmission of speech disorders, we can reasonably conclude that *there are specific properties of language that appear to have a genetic basis.*

Studies of genetic disorders also reveal that *one cognitive domain can develop normally along with abnormal development in other domains*, and they also reinforce the strong biological basis of language. Some scientists even claim that there are more than 10 and less than 1000 genes similar to FOXP2 which are related to human linguistic abilities. "*It is clear to everyone that FOXP2 is not 'the' language gene, but it is also clear that FOXP2 and the genes it interacts with provide a concrete example of the long-anticipated genetic basis of language.*" (Boeckx 2011: 451) More research needs to be done to prove this.

9.6 Chomsky's Biolinguistic Perspective

In the last section of this textbook, the author feels a responsibility to introduce that famous linguist, Norm Chomsky, to the readers; we cannot, of course, do a detailed and comprehensive introduction of his achievements in linguistics; we won't discuss his technical generative processes of language expressions, which are narrowly involved in this textbook here and there; but we can focus on his recent thinking on **biolinguistics**. The content of this section is completely based on Chomsky's articles, most of them are Chomsky's original sentences, the author simply rearranged them in a fashion to be more easily understood by the students; we will omit the quotation marks and occasionally indicate the place where it is taken from. His biolinguistic perspective on language will be a guiding program for 21st century linguistic study.

Norm Chomsky is one of the leading intellectual figures of modern times. He has had a major influence on linguistics, psychology, and philosophy, and a significant effect on a range of other disciplines from anthropology to mathematics, education to literary criticism. His influence can be compared to **Einstein**, **Picasso**, and **Freud**. He has shown that there is really only one human language; he has revolutionized linguistics and made it a natural science. He has demonstrated that a substantial part of our knowledge is genetically determined and provided evidence that "unconscious knowledge" is what underlies our ability to speak and understand. In a word, Chomsky has changed the way we think of ourselves and our conception of the mind, gaining a position in the history of ideas on a par with that of **Darwin** or **Descartes** (Smith 2008).

9.6.1 What Is a Biolinguistic Perspective?

The term "**biolinguistics**" was first coined in 1974 by Massimo Piatelli. Just like modern linguistics, biolinguistics rejects everyday notions of language, and insists on applying a biological, pluralist, bottom-up, decompositional perspective on the human language faculty. Biolinguistics is neither your typical (popular) linguistics, nor your typical (popular) biology (Boeckx 2011). According to Chomsky (2005: 12), if we treat human language as a particular object of the biological world, then the study of language has come to be called the biolinguistic perspective.

Within the biolinguistic perspective, we admit that there exists a language faculty which provides the blueprint for the growth of human language in human brains. We claim that (Chomsky 2005, 2007a, 2009):

1. Along with other cognitive systems, the language faculty is an "organ of the body"; it is one of many subcomponents of an organism that interact in its normal life.

2. A person's language is a state of some component of the mind, while this component is more or less the same as the visual or digestive or immune systems, more or less on a par with the systems of insect navigation, and others.

3. We can think of language as a mental organ, where the term "mental" simply refers to certain aspects of the world, to be studied in the same way as chemical, optical, electrical and other aspects.

4. The study of language is changed into the effort to determine the genetic endowment of the faculty of language (FL), which is understood to be a cognitive organ, shared among humans and in crucial aspects unique to them, hence a kind of species property. So interpreted, language is a kind of **I-language** (where I is understood to suggest "internal", "individual", and "intensional"), a state of FL,

and universal grammar (UG) is reinterpreted as the theory of the initial state of FL.

The biolinguistic approach focuses attention on a component of human biology that enters into the use and acquisition of language, however one interprets the term "language". It is commonly assumed that whatever the human intellectual capacity is, the faculty of language is essential to it.

Within the biolinguistic framework, several tasks immediately arise (Chomsky 2007a):

The first is to construct generative grammars for particular languages that yield the facts about sound and meaning.

The second task is to account for the acquisition of language, the problem of explanatory adequacy.

Another question is how the faculty of language evolved; that is, developed gradually from a simple form to a complex form.

And the forth question is how the properties "termed mental" relate to "the organic structure of the brain".

In a word, the goal of the study of language is to unearth "the great principles underlying the grammars of all language", to "gain a deeper insight into the innermost nature of human language and of human thought" (Chomsky 2008). One of the most fundamental questions of the biology of language is "*to what extent does language approximate an optimal solution to conditions that it must satisfy to be usable at all, given extralinguistic structural architecture*" (Chomsky 2005: 9 – 10).

Perhaps the major advance in biolinguistics has been the discovery of the FOXP2 gene; moreover, FOXP2 appears to be so well-conserved a gene which allows for experiments with other species (mice, birds, bats, etc.) that could not be possible with humans for ethical reasons. In addition, the FOXP2 discovery promises to shed light on the nature of various linguistic disorders and deficits (Boecks 2011). On the other hand, the renaissance of biolinguistics may result from the formulation of Chomsky's Minimalist Program (1995) in theoretical linguistics, which has provided a platform for the biolinguistic study.

9.6.2 The Nature of Language

Chomsky's view on language is totally different from our everyday notion about language. According to him, language is a species property of human, a common endowment with a significant variation apart from serious pathology, unlike anything else known in the organic world in its essentials, and surely central to human life since its emergence. It is *man's intellectual and moral nature*.

The term "language" means internal language, a state of the computational system of the mind/brain that generates structured expressions, each of which can be taken to be a set of instructions for the interface systems within which the faculty of language is embedded (Chomsky 2007b: 14).

A part of the human biological endowment is a specialized "language organ", the faculty of language. Its initial state is an expression of the genes, comparable to the initial state of the human visual system, and it appears to be a common human possession. Accordingly, a typical child will acquire any language under appropriate conditions, even under severe deficit and in hostile environments. **The initial state** changes under the triggering and shaping effect of experience, and internally-determined processes of maturation, yielding later states that seem to stabilize at several stages, finally at about puberty (Chomsky 2002).

The most elementary property of our shared language capacity is that it enables us to construct and interpret a **discrete infinity** of hierarchically structured expressions: discrete because there are 5 word sentences and 6 word sentences, but no five and half word sentences; infinite because there is no longest sentence. Language is therefore based on a **recursive generative procedure** that takes elementary word-like elements from some store, call it the lexicon, and applies this procedure repeatedly to yield structured expressions, without bound. To account for the emergence of the language faculty, we have to face two basic tasks: to account for the "atoms of computation", the lexical items; the second is to discover the computational properties of the language faculty, including the generative procedure that constructs infinitely many expressions in the mind, and the methods by which these internal mental objects are related to two interfaces with language — external (but organism-internal) systems: **the system of thought**, on the one hand, and also to **the sensorimotor system**, thus, externalizing internal computations and thought (Chomsky 2009).

9.6.3 The Evolution of Language

In the discussion of language development, Chomsky used an evolution story to illustrate this process of the appearance of language. He said that the current best guess about the unity and diversity of language and thought may be something like the following description:

In some completely unknown way, our ancestors developed human concepts. At some time in the very recent past, maybe about 75,000 years ago, or between 100,000 years ago and 50,000 years ago, an individual in a small group of hominids in East Africa underwent a minor **mutation**; this mutation took place in an individual, not in a group, that provided the operation **Merge** — an operation that takes human concepts as computational atoms, and yields structured expressions that provide a rich language of thought. After the mutation, that individual could think; it could form complex thoughts; it could plan; it could interpret and so on (Chomsky 2009).

The innovation or the mutation of this individual had obvious selectional advantages, and controlled the small group. The property propagated through the descendants, so some descendants had the same property. After a while or at some later stage, maybe some series of generations, some of them might have had the bright idea to try to externalize what was going on in their heads. This internal language of thought was connected to the sensorimotor system, a complex task that can be solved in many different ways and at different times, and quite possibly a task that involves no evolution at all.

In the course of these events, the human capacity took shape, yielding a good part of our "moral and intellectual nature". The outcomes appear to be highly diverse, but they have an essential unity, reflecting the fact that humans are in fundamental respects identical. There is only one language with minor dialectal variation, primarily — maybe entirely — in mode of **externalization**. And the core systems of syntax and semantics, constructing expressions and interpreting them, seem close to optimal. The above story looks almost exactly like what we discover (Chomsky 2009, 2010).

In the evolution history of the human beings, it seems that brain size reached its current level about 100, 000 years ago, which suggests to some specialists that human language probably evolved, at least in part, as an automatic but adaptive consequence of increased absolute brain size, leading to dramatic changes of behavior. This "**great leap forward**" must have taken place before about 50, 000 years ago, perhaps by some slight mutation. Some small rewiring of the brain gave rise to unbounded operation Merge, yielding a language of thought, later externalized and used in many ways (Chomsky 2007a). The Great Leap was effectively instantaneous, in a single individual, who was instantly endowed with intellectual capacities far superior to those of others, transmitted to offspring and coming to predominate, perhaps linked as a secondary process to the sensorimotor system for externalization and interaction, including communication as a special case (Chomsky 2005: 12).

From the descriptions above, we can see clearly that for Chomsky and many other linguists, communicative needs would not have provided "any great selective pressure to produce a system such as language, with its crucial relation to development of abstract or productive thinking; language is virtually synonymous with symbolic thought. The role of language as a communication system between individuals would have come about only secondarily" (Chomsky 2005).

9.6.4 Internal Thought, Externalization and Communication

Chomsky's story about language evolution tells us that language is originally used to express our internal thought; there is only one human language. Then the question is why there are so many languages in the world; we say the reason might be that the problem of externalization can be solved in many different and independent ways. We have no reason to suppose that solving the externalization problem involved an evolutionary change — that is, genomic change. Emergence of the language faculty involved evolution, while historical change (which continues constantly) does not. When you study a second language, all you study is externalization; you study the sounds, the particular lexical choices, which are arbitrary, and the inflectional system. You know how to change verb forms in different tenses and aspects; you know some facts about word order, and so on. That's just about all you have to learn. You don't have to learn the syntax and the semantics because that's there already (Chomsky 2009).

The linear property (of the language) has to do with externalization and that's where languages differ. German puts the verb here, but English puts it there, and so on. It is the kind of thing you have to learn, but there is no evidence that any of that enters into the thought system. Sentences are understood exactly the same way in your internal thought system no matter whether you put the verb at the end or at the beginning or in the middle and so on (Chomsky 2010).

Language is very well designed for thought and very badly designed for communication. Language is virtually not an instrument of communication. The displacement property or inflectional changes of the language are surely not a good system for communication. Language can of course be used for communication, as can any other thing that we do: our style of dress, gestures, traffic lights and so on. And language can be, and commonly is used for much else. But the overwhelming use of language is internal — for thought, expressing meaning, and sound is sort of tacked on there and it doesn't work very well (Chomsky 2010). The core properties of human language appear to differ sharply from animal communication systems, and to be largely unique in the organic world.

Any approach to "evolution of language" that focuses on communication, or the sensorimotor system, or statistical properties of spoken language, and the like, may well be seriously misguided (Chomsky 2009). This means that almost the entire study of language for 2,500 years is kind of off track. It's studying a secondary problem, namely how the sensory motor system links to an internal system that is language. That's not, strictly speaking, a linguistic problem (Chomsky 2010). It is no wonder that Chomsky claimed that he thinks it is no exaggeration to say that more has been learned about languages in the past twenty-five years than in the earlier millennia of serious inquiry into language (Chomsky 2007a).

After reading the above discussions of biolinguistic perspective, you may doubt whether these kinds of views about language are really true or not, because superficially they are not the same as our common sense view about language. We can just say that is the mainstream view about the nature of language shared by most linguists in the world nowadays. Readers interested in biolinguistics may surf the internet and find the website www. biolinguistics. eu for materials to read.

9.7 Summary

Neurolinguistics studies the brain mechanisms and anatomical structures that underlie linguistic competence and performance and how they developed over time.

The brain is the most complicated organ of the body, controlling motor and sensory activities and thought processes. Research conducted for over a century reveals that different parts of the brain control different body functions. The verve cells that form the surface of the brain are called the **cortex**, which serves as the intellectual decision maker, receiving messages from the sensory organs and initiating all voluntary actions.

The brain is divided into two parts: the **left cerebral hemisphere** and the **right cerebral hemisphere**. Each hemisphere exhibits contralateral control of functions. The left hemisphere controls the right side of the body, and the right hemisphere controls the left side. Much evidence suggests that the brain is asymmetric, with the left and right hemispheres lateralized for different functions.

Neurolinguists have many tools for studying the brain. We didn't mention those experiments and scans of various types in this chapter, but we know these techniques permit the study of the living brain as it processes language and reveals the **lateralization** or asymmetry of function of the two hemispheres, with the left hemisphere specialized for language. Through the study of people with **aphasia**, we know that different areas of the brain can be associated with particular language functions. For example, damage in the part of the brain called **Broca's area** may cause **Broca's aphasia**, which results in impaired syntax and **agrammatism**. And damage to **Wernicke's area** may result in **Wernicke's aphasia**, in which fluent speakers produce semantically anomalous utterances, or nonsense forms that make their utterance uninterpretable; sometimes patients with aphasia have word-finding difficulties.

Other evidence supports the **lateralization** of language. Children with early brain lesions in the left hemisphere may have the surgical removal of part or all of the left brain; they will show specific linguistic deficits, whereas other cognitive abilities remain intact. If the right brain is damaged or removed, however, language is unimpaired, but other cognitive disorders may result. What we should remember is that there is a kind of **plasticity** of the human brain; children who undergo the removal of the left hemisphere at an early age may acquire language because the normal left hemisphere functions can be taken over by the right hemisphere.

The language faculty is **modular**. It is independent from other cognitive systems with which it interacts. Evidence of modularity can be found in studies of aphasia, of children with **SLI**, of linguistic savants. Children with SLI suffer from language deficits, but are normal in other aspects. **Language savants** are individuals with extraordinary language skills, but with low general intelligence. Their existence suggests that linguistic ability is not derived from some general cognitive ability but exists independently.

Nowadays **biolinguistics** is experiencing a renaissance in the linguistic field (in the 1970s, biolinguistics enjoyed a certain popularity). There are many factors that have led to the return of biolinguistic concerns; among them, the discovery of FOXP2 gene and the publication of Chomsky's Minimalist Program may be the most important factors (Boeckx 2011). Within the biolinguistic perspective, language is studied as a particular object of the biological world, an organ of the body, a mental organ or a language faculty. Language is a recursive generative procedure which constructs discrete infinitive expressions by the application of those computational atoms—the lexical items. The mutation or rewiring of a certain individual's brain caused the appearance of the operation **Merge**, thus making the intelligence of human beings to make a great leap forward. Later the properties were transmitted to the next generations and they externalized their internal thoughts in different ways, which led to the appearance of different languages. In this view, language is firstly used for thinking, and communication is secondary; meaning expression is the primary application, while sound transmission is secondary.

EXERCISES

Exercise I

Lateralization is the term used to refer to any cognitive function that is localized primarily on one side of the brain or the other. Please describe the respective functions of the left hemisphere and the right hemisphere.

Exercise II

The traditional writing system of Chinese languages (e.g. Mandarin, Cantonese) is ideographic (i.e. each concept or word is represented by a distinct character). More recently, the Chinese government has adopted a spelling system called *pinyin*, which is based on the Roman alphabet, and in which each symbol represents a sound. Following are several Chinese words in their character and *pinyin* forms.

木	mù	tree
花	huā	flower
人	rén	man
家	jiā	home
狗	gǒu	dog

Based on the information provided in this chapter, would the location of neural activity be the same or different when Chinese speakers read in these two systems?

Explain the reasons.

Exercise III

If a child has had the diseased left hemisphere surgically removed after language acquisition has begun, can she/he still speak her/his native language? Please explain the reasons for that.

Exercise IV

The following data come from a repetition experiment in which an aphasic subject (S) was asked to produce an exact word-for-word repetition of the experimenter's (E) sentences:
- a. E: No, I do not like fish.
  S: No, fish.
- b. E: One morning the girl was pushed by the man.
  S: One morning the ... the girl is push push boy.
- c. E: The girl is running to the man.
  S: The girl running the ...the girl is running on man.

Analyze the grammatical errors, determine the syndrome and give reasons for your answer.

Exercise V

Agrammatics have problems with sentence comprehension. Experimental studies have shown that they can easily understand *a* and *b*, but that they have trouble understanding *c* and *d*. Explain the comprehension problems of agrammatics and give reasons for the differences in performance between the four sentences below:
- a. The apple that the tiger saw was yellow.
- b. The car was driven by Bill.
- c. The tiger that the lion chased was yellow.
- d. Mary was kissed by Bill.

Exercise VI

1. Some aphasic patients, when asked to read a list of words, substitute other words for those printed. In many cases, the printed words and the substituted words are similar. The following data are from actual aphasic patients. In each case, state what the two words have in common and how they differ.

Printed words	Words spoken by aphasic patients
i. liberty	freedom
abroad	overseas

large	long
short	small
tall	long
ii. decide	decision
conceal	concealment
portray	portrait
bathe	bath
speak	discussion
remember	memory

2. What do the words in groups (i) and (ii) reveal about how words are likely to be stored in the brain?

Exercise VII

The following utterances were made either by Broca's aphasics or Wernicke's aphasics. Write a "**B**" or "**W**" next to each utterance, indicating whether it is uttered by Broca's or Wernicke's aphasics.

    a. Goodnight and in the pansy I can't say but into a flipdoor you can see it.

    b. Well...sunset...uh...horses nine, no, uh, two, tails want swish.

    c. Oh...if I could I would, and a sick old man disflined a sinter, minster.

    d. Words... words...words...two, four, six, eight, ... blaze am he.

Exercise VIII

Chomsky claimed that there is only one human language. Why? If that is true, then how can we explain the fact that there are thousands of different languages in the world?

Suggested Answers

Chapter 1

Exercise I

   a, *c*: acceptable and well-formed;
   b, *d*, *f*, *i*: unacceptable and ill-formed;
   e, *h*, *j*, *k*, *l*, *m*: well-formed but unacceptable.

   We know sentences *a*, *c* are acceptable and well-formed because they accord with the rules of how to combine words together in English, and there is a mentally represented grammar in our minds. We know sentences *b*, *d*, *f*, *i* are ill-formed and unacceptable because they violate the grammatical rules in our minds, while sentences *e*, *h*, *j*, *k*, *l*, *m* are grammatical but they are unacceptable because they are contrary to our common sense of the real world. E. g. *j* appears to be semantically incoherent, in that it expresses a contradiction. It is part of the meaning of the verb KNOW that if we say *I know that* …; we presuppose that the proposition introduced by the word that is true; hence if we then go on to deny the truth of the proposition, we are implying that the proposition is both true and false, and thereby expressing a contradiction.

Exercise II

   Appropriate statements: *b*, *c*, *g*, *h*.
   Inappropriate statements: *a*, *d*, *e*, *f*.

Exercise III

   Model answer for sentence *a*:
   The sentence is ambiguous as the two paraphrases below illustrate:
   (i) He loves me more than he loves you.
   (ii) He loves me more than you love me.

The ambiguity here seems to arise through *ellipsis* (i. e. the omission of one or more words which can be understood from the context): on interpretation (i), *he* and *loves* undergo ellipsis (i. e. are omitted); on interpretation (ii), *love* and *me* undergo ellipsis. Thus in (i), *you* is interpreted as the object of the elliptical sequence, while in (ii), the subject of the clause.

Exercise IV

These sentences are so-called onion-shaped structures. They are grammatical, but it is difficult to interpret them, because too many embedded structures exist in the sentence, and the human parser cannot deal with such embedment. If we change the structure of sentence *b*, then it will be much easier to understand them:

The bird's wing's motion's rapidity is remarkable (left-branching); or,

Remarkable is the rapidity of the motion of the wing of the bird (right-branching).

These onion-shaped sentences can prove that the production and interpretation of the sentence may belong to two isolated parts in the human mind. Grammar and the parsing of the sentence are two different things.

Exercise V

These sentences are called garden-path sentences. They are grammatical and acceptable English sentences if the first verb phrase is interpreted as the modifier of the noun. But when we read them for the first time, we immediately interpret the noun phrase as the logical subject of the verb; as a consequence, the first part of the sentence (that part before the second verb phrase) is interpreted as a complete sentence and the sentence processor doesn't know what to do with the second verb phrase. The sentence processor has been "garden-pathed", i. e. sent down the wrong analysis route.

These sentences show that sentence comprehension must involve something in addition to the grammar.

Sentence *d* can be interpreted as: The soldiers who were driven across the parade ground are a disgrace. The other sentences may be analyzed in the same way.

Exercise VI

Linguists try to study language as a cognitive system internalized within the human brain/mind; our ultimate goal is to characterize the nature of the internalized linguistic system which enables humans to speak and understand their native language. If we say that grammar is the study of grammatical competence, then in devising a grammar of English, we are attempting to describe the grammatical knowledge possessed by a fluent native speaker of English. That is, the fluent native speaker's knowledge of his language (the Competence) will be the focus in linguistic study of linguists. While what people actually say or understand by what someone else says in a given situation (or the actual use of language in concrete situations, i. e. the Performance) is an imperfect reflection of competence: we all make occasional slips of the tongue, or occasionally misinterpret what someone else says to us because of tiredness, boredom, drunkenness, drugs, external distractions, and so forth. However, this does not mean that we don't know our native language, or don't have competence in it. Hence it is clear that grammar is concerned with Competence rather than Performance. Of course, performance can be studied as a field of study, but it is more properly studied within the different — though related—discipline of psycholinguistics, which studies the psychological processes underlying speech production and comprehension.

Exercise VII

Please refer to the text.

Chapter 2

Exercise I

Describe the consonants in the word "skinflint" by using the chart below.

	1. voiced or voiceless	2. place of articulation	3. manner of articulation	4. oral or nasal
[s]	voiceless	alveolar	fricative	oral
[k]	voiceless	velar	stop	oral
[n]	voiced	alveolar	stop	nasal
[f]	voiceless	labiodental	fricative	oral
[l]	voiced	alveolar	liquid (lateral)	oral
[t]	voiceless	alveolar	stop	oral

Exercise II

Studying a new subject often involves learning a large number of technical terms. Phonetics is particularly difficult in this respect. Read over the definitions of the terms in this chapter, and do the exercises below.
1. Circle the words that begin with a bilabial consonant:
   mat   gnat   sat   **bat**   rat   **pat**
2. Circle the words that begin with a velar consonant:
   knot   **got**   lot   cot   hot   pot

3. Circle the words that begin with a labiodental consonant:
   fat　cat　　that　　mat　　chat　　**vat**
4. Circle the words that begin with an alveolar consonant:
   zip　**nip**　lip　　**sip**　**tip**　**dip**
5. Circle the words that end with a fricative:
   race　**wreath**　**bush**　bring　**breathe**　bang　**rave**　**rose**　**rough**
6. Circle the words in which the consonant in the middle is voiced:
   tracking　**mother**　**robber**　**leisure**　massive　**stomach**　**razor**
7. Circle the words that contain a high vowel:
   sat　**suit**　got　**meet**　mud
8. Circle the words that contain a low vowel:
   weed　**wad**　load　**lad**　rude
9. Circle the words that contain a front vowel:
   gate　caught　**cat**　**kit**　put
10. Circle the words that contain a rounded vowel:
    who　me　us　but　him

Exercise III

a—e: [ŋ], [h], [w], [ɔː], [iː]

f. /j/: voiced palatal glide (or semivowel)

g. /ð/: voiced interdental fricative

h. /d/: voiced alveolar plosive (or stop)

i. /r/: voiced alveolar liquid (or retroflex)

j. /æ/: low (open) front spread vowel

Exercise IV

It is possible to transcribe phonetically any utterance, in any language, in several different ways, all of them using the alphabet and conventions of the IPA (the same thing is possible with most other intonational phonetic alphabets). A transcription which is made by using letters of the simplest possible shapes, and in the simplest possible number, is called a simple phonemic transcription.

Exercise V

Transcribe the following phrases as you would say them yourself.

1. pliːz ˈkʌm həum.
2. hi iz gəuiŋ bai trein.
3. ðə ˈæŋgri əˈmerikən.
4. hiz ˈnəulədʒ əv ðə truːθ.

5. ai prə'fə 'ʃugə ənd kriːm.
6. nɔm tʃɔmski iz ə lingwist hu titʃəz ət em ai ti.
7. fə'netiks iz ðə stʌdi əv spiːtʃ saundz.
8. sʌm 'pipəl θiŋk fə'netiks iz veri 'intərestiŋ.

Exercise VI

For each group of sounds listed, state the phonetic feature(s) they all share.
Example: [p] [b] [m] Features: bilabial, stop, consonant.
1. Features: stop, consonant.
2. Features: back, rounded, vowel.
3. Features: front, spread, vowel.
4. Features: voiceless, consonant.
5. Features: voiced, consonant.
6. Features: alveolar, consonant.

Chapter 3

Exercise I

/keit/ cate—/geit/ gate,   /beik/ bake—/meik/ make,
/lais/ lice—/rais/ rice,   /pʌn/ pun—/fʌn/ fun,
/sit/ sit—/ʃit/ shit,   /ritʃ/ rich—/ridʒ/ ridge,
/pet/ pet—/pæt/ pat,   /sin/ sin—/siŋ/ sing,
/θai/ thigh—/ðai/ thy,   /bit/ bit—/biːt/ beat.

Exercise II

a. The sounds that end the words in column **A** are [t, s, p, f, k]; they are all **voiceless** consonants. While the sounds that end the words in column **B** are [d, z, b, z, m]; they are all **voiced** consonants.

b. The words in column **C** end with a vowel; there are no codas in any of these words.

c. [ʌj] and [aj] in these words are in complementary distribution, because they never occur in the same phonological context, or in identical environments. They are allophones of the same phoneme /ai/, and they cannot distinguish one word from another.

d. life [lʌjf],   lives [laivz],   lie [lai],   file [fail],   bike [bʌjk], lice [lʌjs]

e. Change the phoneme /ai/ into /ʌj/ before the voiceless consonants.

Exercise III

a. /əs.ˈtɔ.nəʃ/   /kə.ˈlæps/   /ə.ˈmeiz/
/ˈek.sət/   /əɡ.ˈzist/   /əm.ˈpru:v/
/ə.ˈmæ.dʒən/   /rə.ˈzent/   /sə.ˈpraiz/
/ˈkæn.səl/   /rə.ˈvəult/   /kəm.ˈbain/
/ə.ˈli.sət/   /ə.ˈdɔpt/   /bə.ˈli:v/
/ˈpræk.təs/   /ən.ˈsist/   /ə.ˈtəun/

b. The rule may be like this: Stress the next-to-last syllable if the final syllable ends with a single consonant; if the final syllable ends with a consonant cluster, then stress the final syllable.

c. If the final syllable ends with a single consonant but the vowel is a long vowel or a diphthong, then stress the final syllable.

Exercise IV

From examples *a*, we know that the stops /t, p, k/ after /s/ in the same syllable won't be aspirated. From examples *b*, we know that the stops /t, p, k/ after /s/ are aspirated, because they don't belong to the same syllable, /s/ is the coda of the front syllable; while the stops are the onset of the next syllable. In examples *c*, we know the stops /t, p, k/ are not aspirated; that means /s/ and these stops belong to the same syllable. Thus, the second syllable in the words *disturb* [di.stʰəːb], *despair* [di.spʰeə] and *discard* [di.skʰɑːd] satisfy the demand of the Maximal Onset Principle.

Exercise V

Here we only provide the syllable structure for exercise *a*; for the others, you may do it in the same way. Some of these words may have more than one acceptable pronunciation, so there may be more than one correct answer for a given item.

a. comfortable [ˈkʌmfətəbl; ˈkəmfətəbəl]

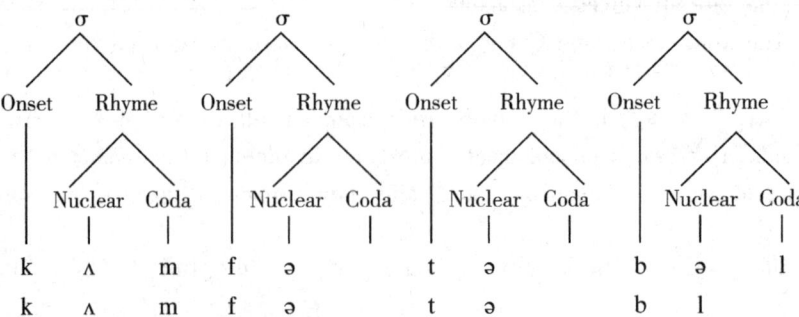

Exercise VI

Delete a /g/ when it occurs in a word initially before a nasal consonant or before a word-final nasal.

Exercise VII

1. Insert a [ə] before the past-tense morpheme when a regular verb ends in a non-nasal alveolar stop, giving [əd].
2. Change the past-tense morpheme to a voiceless [t] when a voiceless sound precedes it.

Exercise VIII

For the features in /p/: [voiceless, labial, stop, unaspirated] and /iː/: [voiced, high, front, spread, nasalized]. The feature [unaspirated] in /p/ and [nasalized] in /iː/ are nondistinctive features; that is, whether you pronounce the word *bean* as [biːn] or [bĩːn], they are the same word. Similarly, you could say *speak* [sp⁼iːk] if you pleased with an aspirated [pʰ], as [spʰiːk], and it would be understood as *speak*. But for the other features, they are distinctive; if you change [voiceless] in /p/ into [voiced], then you get another phoneme /b/. That's the case for all other features in these phonemes.

Chapter 4

Exercise I
   Omitted.

Exercise II
   TTFFF, FTFTF

Exercise III

1. grammatical 2. free 3. derivation 4. compound 5. affix 6. morphemes inflectional 7. allomorphs bound 8. Lexicon 9. coinage 10. interruptible

Exercise IV

a. be + friend + ed   b. en + dear + ment   c. holi + day   d. air + sick + ness   e. psycho + phys + ics

194 语言学

Exercise V

a—3, b—1, c—6, d—5, e—4

Exercise VI

According to the words given in the data, we know the morphemes meaning plurality in this language is *mes*; while *mo* means *your*, *no* means *my* and *i* means *his*. Thus we have the answers for the questions: a— (2), b— (1), c— (2), d— (5), e— (1).

Exercise VII

Write the one proper description from the list under **B** for the italicized part of each word in **A**.

a—3, b—1, c—4, d—2, e—6

Exercise VIII

[d] appears after a vowel or a voiced consonant;

[t] appears after a voiceless consonant;

[id] appears after stop consonants [t] and [d].

Chapter 5

Exercise I

e. g. The prisoners brutally attacked the guard who spotted them.

Two clauses: 1. The prisoners brutally attacked the guard... —main clause
2. —who spotted them. —relative clause

They are both declarative clauses. In clause 1, *the prisoners* (NP) is the subject; *brutally* (Adv.) is an adjunct modifying the VP (*attacked the guard* ...); *attacked* (V) is the predicate; and *the guard who spotted them* (NP) is the complement of the sentence. In the second clause, *who* is the subject; *spotted* is the predicate; and *them* is the complement. The whole clause is used as a relative clause modifying the antecedent NP *the guard*.

Exercise II

Draw the sub-trees for the italicized phrases in the following sentences with the X-bar format.

1. *Angry men in dark glasses* roamed the streets.

Suggested Answers 195

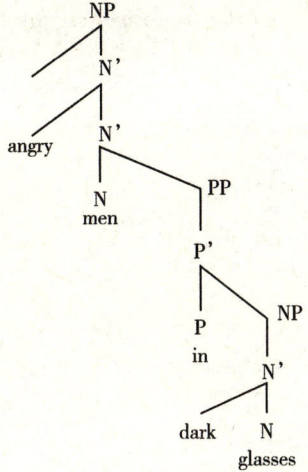

2. *My aunt and uncle's trip* to Alaska was wonderful.

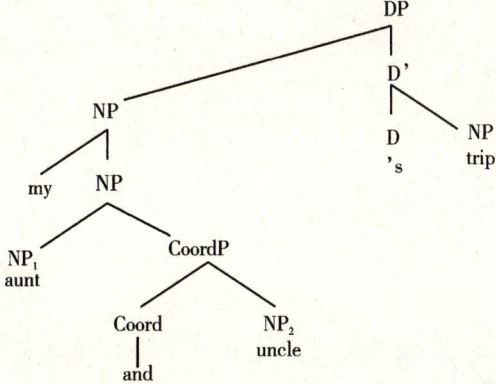

3. The reporter realized *that the senator lied*.

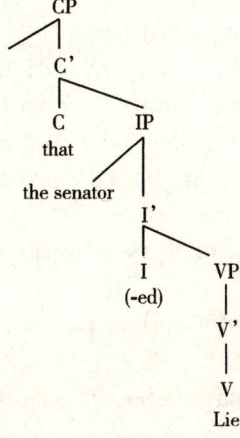

4. *A stranger cleverly observed that a dangerous spy from CIA lurked in the house.*

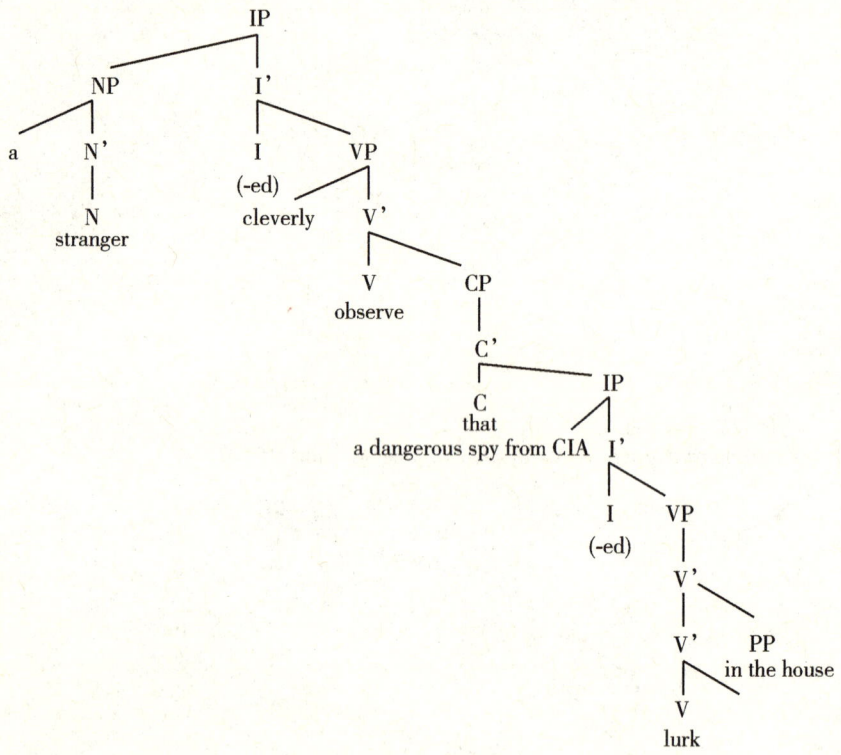

Exercise III

Using one or more of the constituency tests (i. e. stand alone, move as a unit, replacement by a pronoun) discussed in the chapter, determine which boldfaced portions in the sentences are constituents. Provide the grammatical category of the constituents.

1. Tom found **a lovely puppy** in the house.

A lovely puppy is a constituent. It is an NP; it can be moved as a unit to the front of the sentence: it is **a lovely puppy** that Tom found in the house. It can stand alone as the answer to the question: what did Tom find in the house?

2. The **light in this room** is terrible. (not a constituent)

3. **Jack and Jerry** are fighting over the bone. (a constituent)

4. I gave a bone to Jack **and to Jerry** yesterday. (a constituent: I gave a bone to Jack yesterday **and to Jerry**.)

5. I gave a bone to **Jack and** to Jerry today. (not a constituent: *I gave a bone to **Jack and** today to Jerry.)

6. Sam asked **if he could play soccer**. (a constituent)

Exercise IV

In terms of C-selection restrictions, explain why the following sentences are ungrammatical:

1. * Those women located. (*locate* is a verb which must be followed by a complement: those women located a town on a map.)
2. * Robert is fond that his children love animals. (*fond* must be followed by a PP complement: *fond of sth. /doing sth.*)
3. * The children laughed the man. (*laugh* is a verb followed by a PP: *laugh at ...*)
4. * Lisa gave a book. (*give* is a verb with 3 arguments; thus we must provide another argument after give: *Lisa gave a book to him* or *Lisa gave him a book.*)

Exercise V

Paraphrase and draw tree diagrams for each of the following sentences in two ways to show that you understand the ambiguity involved.

1. The student is a dirty street fighter.
    a. a dirty [street fighter].
    b. a [dirty street] fighter.
2. They said she would go yesterday.
    a. Yesterday they said she would go.
    b. She would go yesterday, they said.
3. The magician touched the child with the wand.
    a. The magician touched the child who is with the wand.
    b. With the wand, the magician touched the child.
4. Anna threw the book that Mary had been reading in the study.
    a. The book that Mary had been reading, Anna threw it in the study.
    b. The book that Mary had been reading in the study was thrown by Anna.
5. Who would you like to visit?
    a. Would you like who to visit?
    b. Would you like to visit who?

All these ambiguities could be demonstrated by tree diagrams. You can refer to this chapter to do this.

Exercise VI

Analyze the following sentences, showing their structure is built up in a pairwise fashion by successive merger operations. [Assume that *don't* is a single word which belongs to the same category as words like *must*, *might*, etc., and that infinitival *to* sometimes (but not always) has a specifier/subject of its own.]

1. She is trying to solve the problem.

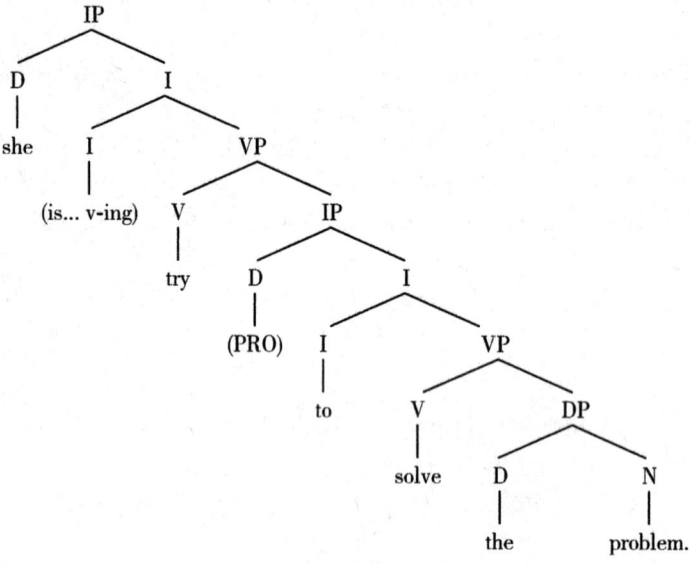

2. I would imagine she has forgotten them.

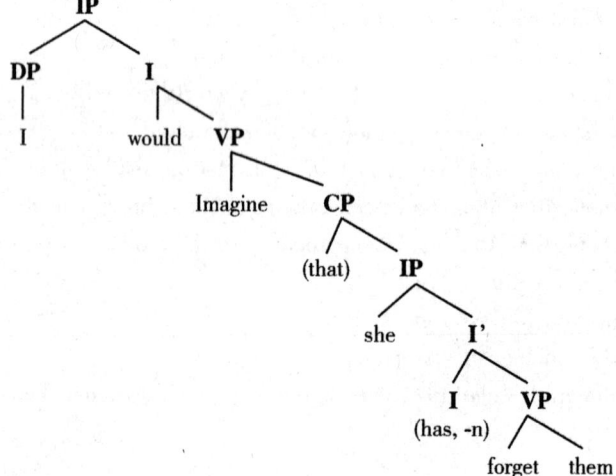

3. They don't seem keen to approve the plan to cut the budget.

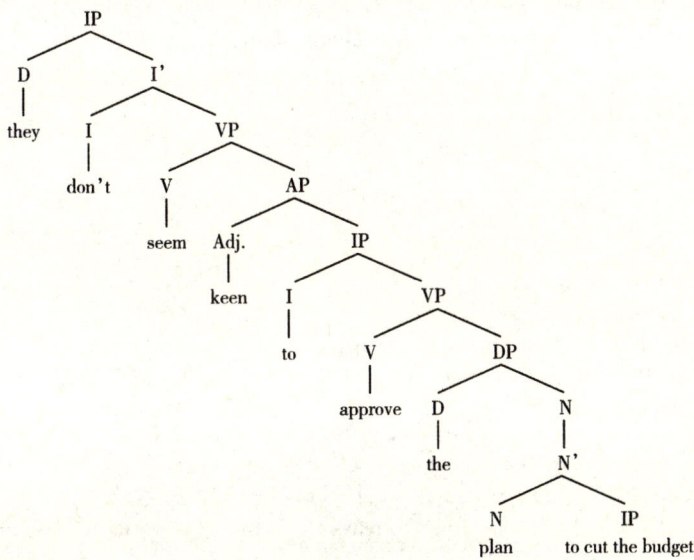

4. They are expecting you to contact them.
5. He wants to try to help others.
   (4 and 5 are omitted)

Exercise VII

The tree diagrams below represent the structures of a variety of different sentences. For each of the five numbered positions in each structure, say what kinds of item (overt or covert) can occupy the position, and what determines the choice of item occupying each position.

a.

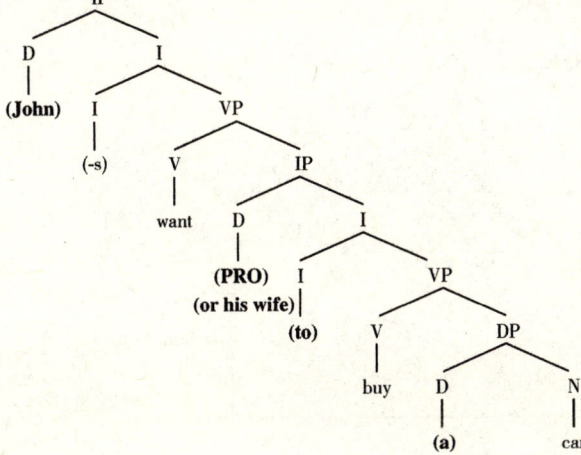

(1) John, he, she, ...
(2) -s, -ed, would, should...
(3) overt or covert: him, his wife, Zhang shan, ... or PRO.
(4) to
(5) a, the, this, that, ...

d.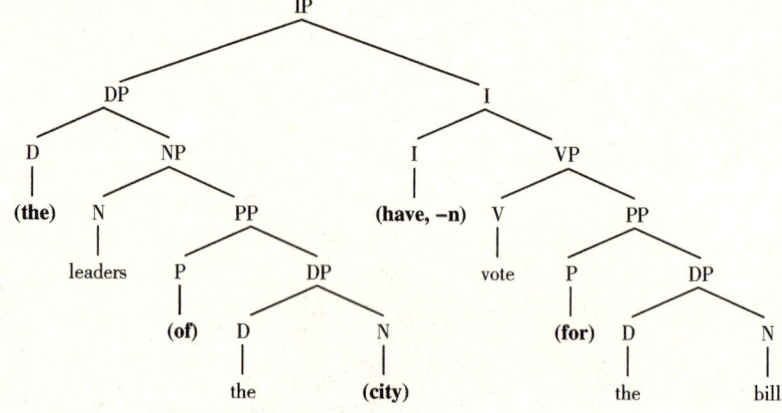

Exercise VIII

Draw a separate tree diagram to represent the structure of each of the following sentences, using arrows to show what has moved from where to where; discuss the role played by traces in accounting for the syntax of these sentences.

1. a. what did you say had happened to who?
   b. *who did you say what had happened to?

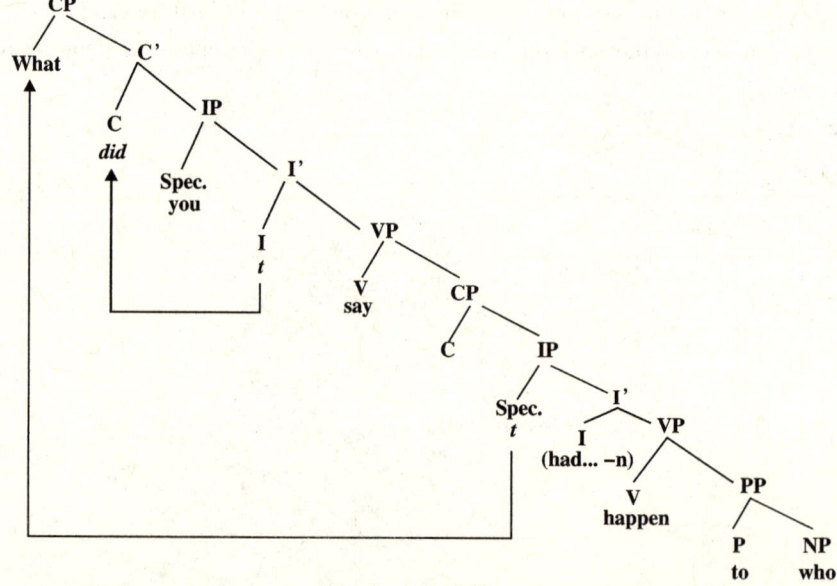

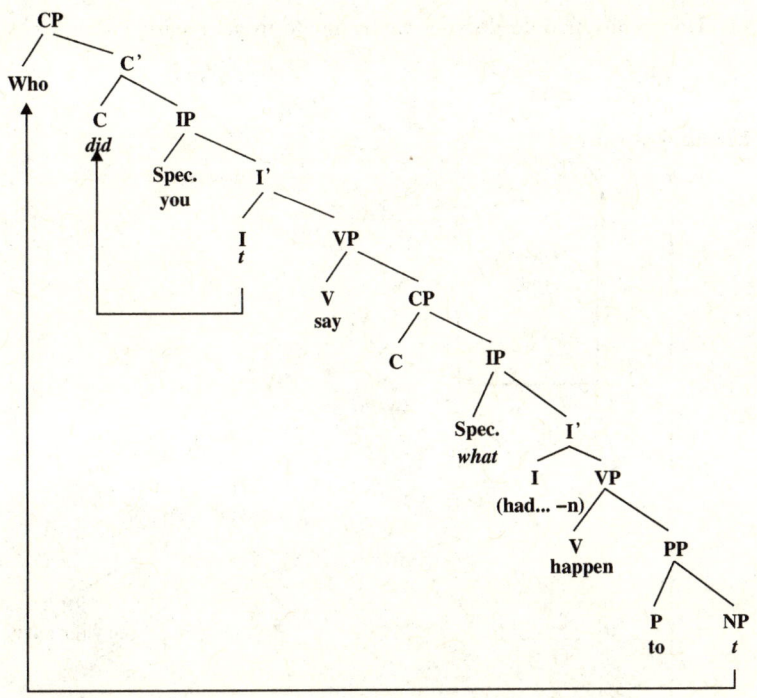

(2) a. The neofascists, I wouldn't want to win the election.
    b. *The neofascists, I wouldn't wanna win the election.

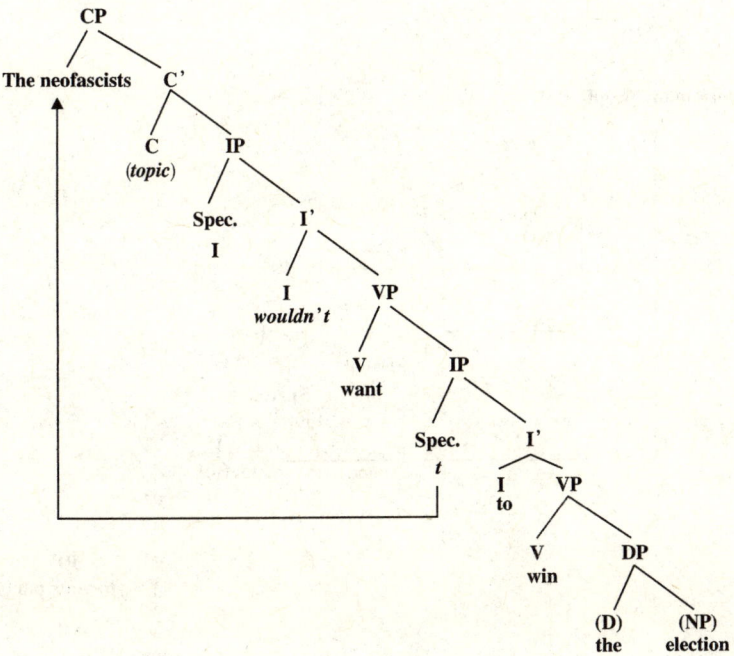

(3) a. How many people do you wanna invite to your party?

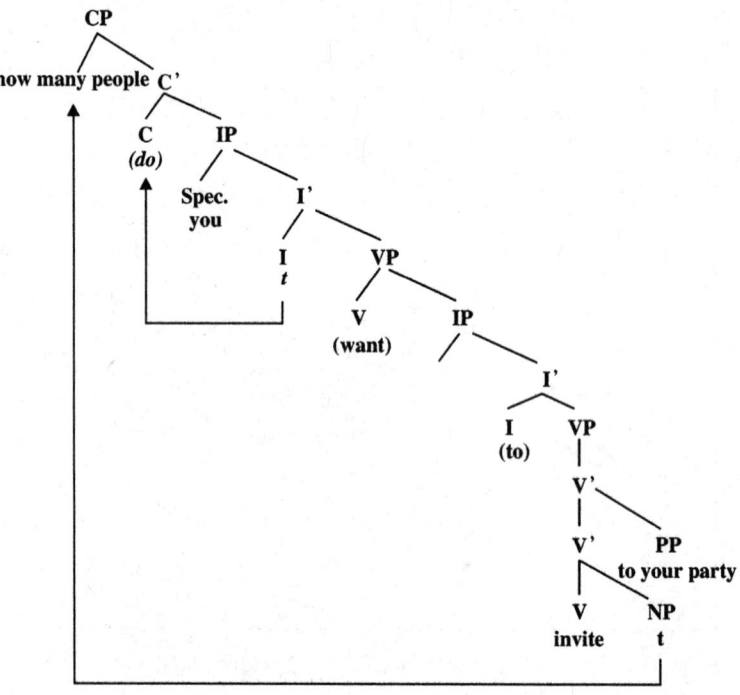

b. *How many people do you wanna come to your party?

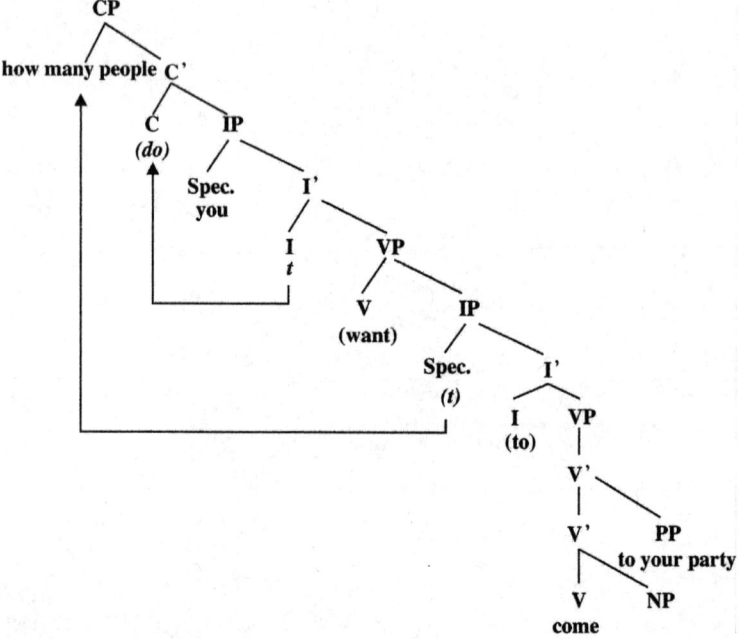

Chapter 6

Exercise I

Which of the following statements are true?
a—e: T F T T T
f—k: T T T T T F

Exercise II

There are several kinds of antonymy. Please indicate whether the pairs in columns A and B are complementary, gradable, or relational opposites.

A	B	C
good	bad	gradable
expensive	cheap	gradable
parent	offspring	relational
beautiful	ugly	gradable
false	true	complementary
pass	fail	complementary
hot	cold	gradable
legal	illegal	complememtary
poor	rich	gradable
fast	slow	gradable
asleep	awake	complementary
husband	wife	relational
rude	polite	gradable

Exercise III

Complete the following diagram by (a) devising a category that distinguishes the word *bus* from the word *car*, and (b) giving the appropriate symbol against each component for the word *motorcycle*.

	Powered	Carries people	Four-wheeled	Public/with fixed stops and routes
bus	+	+	+	+
car	+	+	+	−
van	+	−	+	−
bicycle	−	+	−	−
motorcycle	+	+	−	−

Exercise IV

For each group of words given as follows, state what semantic feature or features distinguish between the classes of (a) words and (b) words. If asked, also indicate a semantic feature that the (a) words and the (b) words share.

Example: (a) widow, mother, sister, aunt, maid.
(b) widower, father, brother, uncle, valet.
The (a) and (b) words are "human".
The (a) words are "female" and the (b) words are "male".

1. (a) bachelor, man, son, paperboy, pope, chief.
   (b) bull, rooster, drake, ram.
   The (a) and (b) words are animate, male.
   The (a) words are human, male.
   The (b) words are animal, male.

2. (a) pine, elm, ash, weeping willow, sycamore.
   (b) rose, dandelion, aster, tulip, daisy.
   The (a) and (b) words are plants.
   The (a) words are trees.
   The (b) words are flowers.

3. (a) walk, run, skip, jump, hop, swim.
   (b) fly, skate, ski, ride, ride, cycle, canoe.
   The (a) and (b) words are move or a change in location.
   The (a) words are move on feet.
   The (b) words are move with an instrument.

4. (a) ask, tell, say, talk, converse.
   (b) shout, whisper, mutter, drawl, holler.
   The (a) and (b) words are manner of speaking.
   The (a) words are say sth. in a Noamal manner.
   The (b) words are say sth, in an abNoamal/unnatural way.

5. (a) absent-present, alive-dead, asleep-awake, married-single.
   (b) big-small, cold-hot, sad-happy, slow-fast
   The (a) and (b) words are antonyms.
   The (a) words are complementary antonyms.
   The (b) words are gradable antonyms.

Exercise V

The following sentences consist of a verb, its noun phrase subject, and various complements and prepositional phrases. Identify the thematic role of each NP by writing *agent*, *theme*, *instrument*, *location*, *source*, *goal*, *experiencer*, *causer*, *patient*, *recipient*, *beneficiary* above the noun.

                agent   *theme*   *source*   *instrument*

Example: [The boy] took [the books] from [the cupboard] with [a handcart].

     experiencer   *theme*
1. [Mary] found [a ball].

       agent   *source*   *goal*
2. [The children] ran from [the playground] to [the swimming pool].

       agent   *theme*   *instrument*
3. [One of the men] unlocked [all the doors] with [a paper clip].

     causer   *patient*   *instrument*
4. [John] melted [the ice] with [a blowtorch].

     agent   *theme*   *goal*   *instrument*
5. [The farmer] loaded [the hay] onto [the truck] with [a pitchfork].

     agent   *patient*   *beneficiary*
6. [Robert] filled in [the form] for [his grandmother].

     experiencer
7. [Kevin] felt ill.

      agent   *location*
8. [The monster] was hiding under [the bed].

Exercise VI

Identify the relationship between the following pairs of sentences:

1. Sentence *a* **presupposes** sentence *b*.
2. Sentence *a* is **inconsistent/contradictory** with sentence *b*.
3. Sentence *b* **entails** sentence *a*.
4. Sentence *a* is **synonymous** with sentence *b*.
5. Sentence *a* **presupposes** sentence *b*.
6. Sentence *b* **entails** sentence *a*.

Exercise VII

The following sentences may be lexically or structurally ambiguous, or both. Provide paraphrases showing that you comprehend all the meanings.

1. I saw him walking by the bank.
    a. I saw him and he was walking by the bank of the river.
    b. I saw him and he was walking by the financial institution.
    c. I was walking by the bank of the river when I saw him.
    d. I was walking by the financial institution when I saw him.
2. The police were ordered to stop drinking about midnight.

a. The police were drinking at midnight, they were ordered to stop.

b. The other people were drinking at midnight, the police were ordered to stop them.

c. At midnight, the police were ordered not to drink.

d. At midnight, the police were ordered to stop the other people drinking.

3. Wanted: Man to take care of cow that does not smoke or drink. (Actual notice)

a. We need man that does not smoke or drink to take care of cow.

b. The cow does not smoke or drink, we need man to take care of the cow.

4. She can't bear children.

a. She can't tolerate children.

b. She can't give birth to children

5. Every man loves a woman.

a. Every man loves a different woman.

b. Every man loves the same woman.

Exercise VIII

In section 6.1.3, figure 6.1, we have given some semantic features to distinguish the subset of English kinship vocabulary including *aunt*, *uncle*, *father*, *mother*, *son*, and *daughter*. Now try to complete the figure by including the other items representing the kinship relations such as *grandfather*, *grandmother*, *grandson*, *grand-daughter*, *sister*, *brother*, *cousin*, *nephew*, and *niece*. If necessary, please add or change some semantic features to distinguish them.

	Male	old/middle/young/younger generation	Related by birth	Related with father
aunt	−	middle	−	−
uncle	+	middle	−	+
mother	−	middle	+	
father	+	middle	+	
son	+	young	+	
daughter	−	young	+	
grandfather	+	old	+	+/−
grandmother	−	old	+	+/−
grandson	+	younger	+	
grand-daughter	−	younger	+	
sister	−	young	+	

brother	+	young	+	
cousin	+/−	young	−	+/−
nephew	+	young	−	+
niece	−	young	−	+

From the description above, we can see that the binary feature may not be applicable in some situations; this is just the case for the semantic feature of the generation.

Chapter 7

Exercise I

There are incomplete passages and utterances in this section. Complete them by filling in each blank with word(s) according to the context.
1. language/word, meanings, context/situation, attention/purposes, communicated, interpreted
2. Syntactics, Semantics, Pragmatics
3. co-operative principle
4. a direct speech act, an indirect speech act
5. Directives
6. Perlocutionary acts
7. conversational implicatures, Politeness Principle (PP)
8. the context

Exercise II

What might the second speaker "mean" in each of the following dialogues? Write a pragmatic paraphrase in each case, and decide which maxim was flouted by the second speaker in each dialogue.
1. I don't like your hat. (Relevance)
2. I won't have some coffee. (Relevance)
3. I haven't done the evaluation forms. (Quantity)
4. I don't think I'm going to Steve's barbecue. (Relevance)
5. No, the dessert was pretty boring. / He has no opinion, either good or bad. (Quantity)

Exercise III

Provide a semantic meaning and a pragmatic meaning for "it's cold here" in the context below.

Semantic meaning: The temperature in this place is very low.
Pragmatic meaning: James, shut the window.

Exercise IV

Draw the implicature from the second speaker's response in the following dialogues.
1. Dave did not buy the eggs.
2. Dave did not fix the leak.
3. Dave invited Chris.
4. The dog did not belong to Dave.
5. Dave did not use all of the printer paper, only some of it.
6. No.
7. I can't talk about it here.
8. There isn't any salad dressing.
9. No.
10. Dave didn't buy the car.

Exercise V

An utterance can simultaneously perform three actions. Analyze the following utterance made by Mike to Annie in terms of locutionary, illocutionary and perlocutionary act.

Locutionary act: Mike uttered the words "*I was rude*", which can be semantically paraphrased as: "*I was ill-mannered*", with *I* referring to *Mike*.

Illocutionary act: Mike performed the act of apologizing to Annie for having interrupted her.

Perlocutionary act: Annie accepted Mike's apology.

Exercise VI

The following two scenes may be humorous and interesting. Can you do a pragmatic analysis and explain why they are interesting?

Situation 1:

It is possible to have humorous effects as a result of one person failing to recognize another person's indirect speech act. The visitor is using an interrogative sentence to make a request, but the passer-by understands it as a direct speech act; that is, asking his ability to do something, and answers it according to this. On the other hand, we can say that the passer-by didn't understand the illocutionary act of the visitor, and of course didn't perform the perlocutionary act.

Situation 2:

In this situation, Mr. Logic is in the post office. It seems that he is making direct speech acts, but the saleswoman understands them as indirect speech acts; that is, making a request by interrogative or declarative sentences. Of course, logically, a statement is stating the facts, and an interrogative sentence is asking a question, but pragmatically the hearer can understand it as indirect speech acts. That's the reason for the misunderstanding or humor.

Exercise VII

In each of the following utterances, decide whether the second speaker's utterance is a representative, a commisive, a directive, an expressive or a declaration.

1. I sentence you to 10 years in prison.   ——Declaration
2. Clean it up!   ——Directive
3. I'll take her to the vet.   ——Commisive
4. It's raining.   ——Representative
5. I'm sorry.   ——Expressive

Chapter 8

Exercise I

    a. childs b. goed c. gooder d. goodest e. bringed f. singed
    g. gooses h. badest i. knifes j. badder k. seed l. haved

Exercise II

According to the SLA researchers, there are differences between errors and mistakes. What are they? Try to give examples to illustrate them.

An **error** takes place when the deviation arises as a result of lack of knowledge; it represents a lack of competence. A **mistake** occurs when learners fail to perform their competence as a result of completing plans, memory limitations, and lack of automaticity. For example, sentences like "*No look my card*", or "*Give you some color see see*" may be errors caused by L1 transfer. But mistakes like slips of the tongue or pen, or the misuse of the pronouns he/she, belong to a performance problem.

Exercise III

Identify all the errors in the following note written by a student to her teacher. For each of the errors, discuss the possible reasons (taken from Ding 2004: 57 – 60).

1. The student may have difficulty distinguishing the "*-n*" sound from the "*-ng*" sound in her Chinese. "*Din*" is definitely misspelled. "*Yin*", "*Lin*" and "*Min*" are

also spelled without "-g". It cannot be decided whether the spelling is correct.

2. The expression "*I feel painful*" should be "*I feel in pain*" or "*It is painful*". "*Painful*" does not mean "full of pains" but "causing pains". We do not usually apply "*painful*" to a person; only situations and injuries can be painful.

3. "*Due to this reason*" can be "*so*". The register is too formal.

4. "*Brought*" should be "*bring*".

5. "*Home work*" should be "*homework*".

6. "*Creat*" should be "*create*".

7. "*Too much problem*" should be either "*too many problems*" or "*any problem*".

Exercise IV

According to research into the order of acquiring interrogation, people found roughly four stages. Please describe the features of each stage for the sentences given below.

Stage 1: Asking intonation questions (with no change in word order).

Stage 2: Asking wh-questions with no subject-verb inversion or with the omission of the auxiliary verb.

Stage 3: Using the subject-verb inversion.

Stage 4: Using embedded questions.

Exercise V

Omitted.

Exercise VI

We all have strongly held beliefs about the ways that foreign or second languages are learned, all these beliefs are based on our own experiences as language learners and as language teachers. According to what we have learned in this chapter, please judge whether these beliefs are right or wrong, and briefly comment on them.

1. You can learn to speak a foreign language quite well without lessons.

The statement is true.

Many people have learned to speak a foreign language quite fluently without any teaching at all: people who travel and work abroad a lot, people who stay in their own country but who mix with speakers of another language. These people are not always totally accurate, but they achieve a level of language ability that is entirely adequate for their needs.

In fact, the three essential conditions for language learning are perfectly met for these people. Firstly, they are usually very motivated — they have a pressing desire to communicate and to get their meaning across. They receive a lot of exposure — they hear the language in use and pick up expressions they need. And they have many opportunities to speak and experiment with the language.

It is quite possible for people to learn a lot without having lessons. Classroom instruction is not a necessary condition for learning.

2. You must use the language freely to learn to speak it even if you make a lot of errors.

True.

This is how you learn to speak when acquiring another language naturally. But in the classroom, many speaking activities involve students in producing a given form or pattern, or expressing a given function, rather than saying what they feel or want to say. We need to change this situation.

Free use involves a far broader range of language and gives learners richer opportunities for acquiring. They need chances to say what they think or feel, and to experiment in a supportive atmosphere with using language they have heard or seen without feeling threatened. They need chances to test the hypotheses they have formed about the way language works, to try things out, to see if they are understood. They are bound to get some things wrong at first, but they will gradually get more accurate in the long run.

In fact, the hypotheses testing hypothesis and the output hypothesis both encourage such kind of practice, and language use is one condition for language learning.

3. Teachers should always correct student errors.

Wrong.

Most teachers disagree with this.

The students say they won't risk speaking in or out of class because they are afraid of making mistakes or being corrected in public; they will become demotivated.

In the case of FLA, the parents often encourage their children to speak in a very positive way. In fact, in the classroom, few teachers correct students when they are doing an activity in pairs or small groups aimed at confidence building and fluency. Ideally, the classroom should be managed so that opportunities exist for both kinds of language use — private and public. Students should know when they can use language freely without worrying about getting things wrong, and when they need to be accurate.

On the other hand, some errors cannot be corrected if the learners are not at the stage to acquire such kinds of rules according to the natural order hypothesis.

4. People of all intellectual abilities can successfully learn another language.

The statement is true.

Everyone is born with an innate ability to learn a language; that's the belief of the innateness hypothesis. It is mainly in formal instruction (where the focus is on learning about the language rather than interacting in the language) that intellectual ability (aptitude) seems to matter.

Some students are less sensitive to grammaticality but better at memorizing; while others use more cognitive strategies. Either way of learning can be successful. If we re-create natural learning conditions in the classroom, all learners will learn.

5. The younger you are the better you will learn another language.

It's true to some extent.

Some experts believe that there is a "critical period" and that children who begin to learn a new language before puberty will learn better; after puberty, it is more difficult to attain native-like fluency and pronunciation. In fact, it depends a lot on the circumstances.

Adults usually learn faster to begin with because they use more cognitive and meta-cognitive strategies. Children have better memories and rely less on cognitive strategies; they are even less likely than adults to benefit from formal grammar teaching. With children, teachers often use more active methods, reflecting their ability to imitate and rote-learn and to speak without being self-conscious. Exposure and involvement are critical for all age groups.

Chapter 9

Exercise I

Lateralization is the term used to refer to any cognitive function that is localized primarily on one side of the brain or the other. Please describe the respective functions of the left hemisphere and the right hemisphere.

The left hemisphere has primary responsibility for analytic tasks such as arithmetic and language; whereas the right hemisphere controls visual and spatial skills; it processes stimuli more holistically. We can briefly summarize the brain lateralization in the following way:

Left hemisphere	**Right hemisphere**
analytic reasoning	holistic reasoning
language and speech	perception of nonlinguistic sounds
temporal ordering judgment	visual and spatial skills
reading and writing	pattern-matching tasks
mathematical thinking	recognition of musical melodies
associative thought	recognition of familiar faces
rhythmic perception.	nonverbal information.

Exercise II

The traditional writing system of Chinese languages (e.g. Mandarin, Cantonese) is ideographic (i.e. each concept or word is represented by a distinct character). More recently, the Chinese government has adopted a spelling system called *pinyin*, which is based on the Roman alphabet, and in which each symbol represents a sound. Following are several Chinese words in their character and *pinyin* forms.

Neuronal activity varies in location within the brain according to whether the stimulus is language or nonlanguage; the patterns of neuronal activity in people reading different kinds of writing are different. According to the description in this chapter, we know that Japanese people with left-hemisphere damage are impaired in their ability to read *kana* (like our Chinese *pinyin*); whereas people with right-hemisphere damage are impaired in their ability to read *kanji* (*Chinese ideographic character*). Also, experiments with normal Japanese speakers show that the right hemisphere is better and faster than the left hemisphere at reading *kanji*, and vice versa. Thus, we can predict that when we are reading Chinese ideographic characters, the location of neural activity will be on the right hemisphere, while in reading *pinyin*, the left hemisphere will be responsible for it. We still need experimental evidence to prove this.

Exercise III

If a child has had the diseased left hemisphere surgically removed after language acquisition has begun, can she/he still speak her/his native language? Please explain the reasons for that.

According to the descriptions in the book, even though that child has had the diseased left hemisphere surgically removed after language acquisition has begun, she/he can still speak her/his native language. She/He may firstly experience an initial period of aphasia, and then reacquire a linguistic system that is virtually indistinguishable from that of normal children; she/he may also show many of the development patterns of normal language acquisition.

The reason for this is: whereas the left hemisphere is innately predisposed to specialize for language, there is also evidence of considerable plasticity (i.e. flexibility) in the system during the early stages of language development. This means that under certain circumstances, the right hemisphere can take over many of the language functions that would normally locate in the left hemisphere.

Exercise IV

The following data come from a repetition experiment in which an aphasic subject (S) was asked to produce an exact word-for-word repetition of the experimenter's (E) sentences:
    a. E: No, I do not like fish.
       S: No, fish.
    b. E: One morning the girl was pushed by the man.

    S: One morning the ... the girl is push push boy.
  c. E: The girl is running to the man.
     S: The girl running the ...the girl is running on man.

Analyze the grammatical errors, determine the syndrome and give reasons for your answer.

In all cases, the realizations of the aphasic patients' sentences are syntactically less complex than the target sentences, and omissions and simplifications typically affect functional projections (DP, IP and CP). They also produce many inflectional errors, e. g. gender errors, number errors, etc. In *a*, the patient just repeats the complement: a content word *fish*, and omits all the other elements; this is a typical telegraphic speech. In *b*, the inflection (-ed) of the verb *push* is omitted and the prepositional phrase *by the man* is replaced by another noun *boy*. In the case of *c*, the patient firstly omits the preposition *to* and the determiner *the*, then uses another preposition *on* to substitute it. All these errors mean that the patient has problems in production of functional words and inflections; maybe they also have problems in understanding the passive sentences. These are the syndromes of the **agrammatism** in Broca's aphasics.

As we know, the sentences Broca's aphasics produce are characterized by their simplicity or reduced syntactic complexity. These sentences are often incomplete, with functional elements (including grammatical inflections) being omitted. The agrammatism patients have a fundamental disorder of the linguistic representational system (i. e. the grammar). They have problems in comprehending functional categories as well as in producing them.

Exercise V

Agrammatics have problems with sentence comprehension. Experimental studies have shown that they can easily understand *a* and *b*, but that they have trouble in understanding *c* and *d*. Explain the comprehension problems of agrammatics and give reasons for the differences in performance between the four sentences below:
  a. The apple that the tiger saw was yellow.
  b. The car was driven by Bill.
  c. The tiger that the lion chased was yellow.
  d. Mary was kissed by Bill.

In sentence *a* and *c*, the attributive sentences modify two different antecedents. In sentence *a*, *the apple* and *the tiger* are two different kinds of things in the world; one is an object, another is animate. While in *c*, *the tiger* and *the lion* belong to the same kind; both are animate. Similarly in *b* and *c*, *the car* and *Bill* are not the same kind of object, while *Mary* and *Bill* are the same kind. The patient can understand *a* and *b*, while he has problems in understanding *c* and *d*. That means they may have difficulty understanding complex sentences in which comprehension depends exclusively on syntactic structure and where they cannot rely on their real-world knowledge. The meaning of the sentence *a* and *b* can be provided by nonlinguistic knowledge. That's also the syndrome of Broca's aphasics.

Exercise VI

1. Some aphasic patients, when asked to read a list of words, substitute other words for those printed. In many cases, the printed words and the substituted words are similar. The following data are from actual aphasic patients. In each case, state what the two words have in common and how they differ.

2. What do the words in groups (i) and (ii) reveal about how words are likely to be stored in the brain?

1. In case (i), the words have similar meaning or word category, even the meanings of the words are not connected; they may be related in some other way. For example, *large* and *long*, *short* and *small* may belong to the positive or negative side of the measurement. In case (ii), they are similar in meaning, but different in the parts of speech or word category; one is a verb, another is a noun.

2. This kind of word substitution that aphasic patients produce tells us about how words are organized in the mental lexicon. Neural connections exist among semantically or categorically related words. Words are not mentally represented in a simple list but rather in an organized network of connections.

Exercise VII

The following utterances were made either by Broca's aphasics or Wernicke's aphasics. Write a "**B**" or "**W**" next to each utterance, indicating whether it is uttered by Broca's or Wernicke's aphasics.

    a. Goodnight and in the pansy I can't say but into a flipdoor you can see it.
    b. Well...sunset...uh...horses nine, no, uh, two, tails want swish.   **B**
    c. Oh...if I could I would, and a sick old man disflined a sinter, minster.   **W**
    d. Words... words...words...two, four, six, eight, ... blaze am he.   **B**

Exercise VIII

Chomsky claimed that there is only one human language. Why? If that is true, then how can we explain the fact that there are thousands of different languages in the world?

Firstly, if we understand human language as an organ of the body, it is the initial state of the human language faculty, it is different from our common sense language, then it is very clear that there is only one human language because the structure of the human brain is the same biologically, and that language is originally used to express our internal thought. Language is in fact a recursive generative procedure which constructs discrete infinitive expressions by the application of those computational atoms—the lexical items.

Then the question why there are so many languages in the world can be answered in the following way: We say the reason might be that the problem of externalization can be solved in many different and independent ways. Chinese chose Mandarin ideographical characters as its computational atoms while English chose another system; they arrange sentences in different ways.

In this sense, when we study a second language, about all we study is externalization. We study the sounds, the particular lexical choices (which are arbitrary), and the inflectional system. We know how to change verb forms in different tenses and aspects, and we know some facts about word order, and so on. We don't have to learn the syntax and the semantics because that's there already.

The linear property (of the language) has to do with externalization and that's where languages differ. German puts the verb here, but English puts it there and so on. It is the kind of thing you have to learn, but there is no evidence that any of that enters into the thought system. Sentences are understood exactly the same way in your internal thought system no matter whether you put the verb at the end or at the beginning or in the middle and so on.

Bibliography

Bauer, L. 1983. *English Word Formation*. Cambridge: Cambridge University Press.
Bauer, L. 1998. *Vocabulary*. London and New York: Routledge.
Bley-Vroman, R. W. 1989. "What Is the Logical Problem of Foreign Language Learning", in S. Gass and J. Schachter (eds.), *Linguistic Perspective on Second Language Acquisition* (41 – 68). Cambridge : Cambridge University Press.
Boeckx, C. 2011. Biolinguistics: A Brief Guide for the Perplexed. 语言科学 (5): 449 – 463.
Brown, P. & S. Levinson. 1987. *Politeness: Some Universals in Language Usage*. Cambridge: CUP.
Carter, R. 1998. *Vocabulary and Language Teaching*. London and New York: Routledge.
Chomsky, N. 1965. *Aspects of the Theory of Syntax*. Cambridge, MA: MIT Press.
— 1980. "On cognitive structures and their development". In M. Piattelli-Palmarini (ed.), *Language and Learning: the Debate between Jean Piaget and Noam Chomsky*. London: Routledge and Kegan Paul.
— 1988. *Language and Problems of Knowledge: The Managua Lectures*. Cambridge, Mass. : MIT Press.
— 1986. *Knowledge of Language: Its Nature, Origin, and Use*. Praeger, New York.
— 1995. *The Minimalist Program*. The MIT Press.
— 2002. Language and Brain. 语言科学 [1].
— 2004. *On Nature and Language*. The MIT Press.
— 2005. Three Factors in Language Design. *Linguistic Inquiry* (36): 1 – 22.
— 2006. *Language and Mind*. Third Edition. Cambridge University Press.
— 2007a. "Approaching UG from below". In Uli Sauerland and Hans-Martin Gartner (eds.), *Interfaces + Recursion = Language? Chomsky's Minimalism and the View from Syntax-semantics*, 1 – 29. Berlin and New York: Mouton de Gruyter.
— 2007b. Of Minds and Language. *Biolinguistics* 1, 009 – 027. http://

www. bioliguistics. eu.

2008. "On Phases". In *Foundational Issues in Linguistic Theory*, eds. Robert Freidin, Carlos Otero and Maria Zubizarreta. Cambridge, MA: MIT Press.

2009. The Bioliguistic Program: Where Does It Stand Today? *Essays on Linguistics* Volume 39, 5 – 29. Beijing: The Commercial Press.

2010. *Poverty of Stimulus: Unfinished Business*. Transcription of the oral presentation (Johannes-Gutenberg University Mainz, March 24, 2010) edited and certified by Noam Chomsky.

Cook, V. J. 1988. *Chomsky's Universal Grammar: An Introduction*. Cambridge: Basil Blackwell Ltd.

Corder, S. P. 1967. The Significance of Learners' Errors. *IRAL* (5/4): 161 – 70.

Corder S. P. 1974. "Error Analysis", Allen. J, & S. P. Corder (eds.), *The Edinburgh Course in Applied Linguistics* (Vol. 3). London: OUP.

Corder, S. P. 1976. "The Study of Interlanguage", in *Proceedings of the Fourth International Conference of Applied Linguistics*. Munich, Hochschulverlag.

Crystal, D. 沈家煊译. 1997. A Dictionary of Linguistics and Phonetics. 现代语言学词典. 北京：商务印书馆.

Ellis, R. 1994. *The Study of Second Language Acquisition*. 上海：上海教育出版社.

Finch, G. 2003. *How to Study Linguistics*. Playgrave Macmillan.

Fromkin, V., Robert Rodman & Nina Hyams. 2007. *An Introduction to Language*. Eighth Edition. 北京：北京大学出版社.

Gopnik, M. and M. B. Crago. 1991. Familial Aggregation of a Developmental Language Disorder. *Cognition* 39/1: 1 – 50.

Gramley, S. & K. M. Patzold. 2004. *A Survey of Modern English*. Second Edition. London: Routledge.

Hatch, E. & J. Wagner-Gough. 1976. Explaining Sequence and Variation in Second Language Acquisition. *Language Learning*, Special Issues 4: 39 – 47.

Hurst, J. A., M. Baitser, E. Auger, E. Graham and S. Norell. 1990. An Extended Family with a Dominantly Inherited Speech Disorder. *Developmental Medicine and Child Neurology* 32/1: 352 – 355.

Krashen, S. 1977. "Some Issues Relating to the Monitor Model", in H. Brown *et al.* (eds.) On TESOL '77, Washington D. C.: TESOL. 1977.

Lado, R. 1957. *Linguistics Across Cultures: Applied Iinguistics for Language Teachers*. Ann Arbor, Michigan: University of Michigan.

Lenneberg, E. 1967. *Biological Foundations of Language*. New York: Wiler and Sons.

Long, M. 1985. "Input and Second Language Acquisition Theory", in Gass and Madden (eds.), *Input in Second Language Acquisition*. Rowley, Mass.: Newbury House.

Ladefoged, P. 1982. *A Course in Phonetics*. Second Edition. New York: Harcourt Brace Jovanovich, Inc.
Leech, G. 1983. *Principles of Pragmatics*. London: Longman.
Leech, G. 1983. *Semantics*. Harmondsworth: Penguin Books.
Levinson, S. 1983. *Pragmatics*. Cambridge: CUP.
Lyons, J. 1995. *Linguistic Semantics: An Introduction*. Cambridge: Cambridge University Press.
Mey, J. L. 2001. *Pragmatics: An Introduction* (2nd ed.). Blackwell, Oxford.
Palmer, F. R. 1981. *Semantics* (2nd ed.). Cambridge: Cambridge University Press.
Peccei, J. S. 2000. *Pragmatics*. Beijing: Foreign Language Teaching and Research Press.
Pinker, S. 2004. 语言本能. 汕头: 汕头大学出版社.
Poole, S. C. 2000. *An Introduction to Linguistics*. Beijing: Foreign Language Teaching and Research Press.
Quirk, R. *et al.* 1972. *A Grammar of Contemporary English*. London: Longman Group Limited.
Radford, A., Martin Atkinson, David Britain, Harald Clahsen & Andrew Spencer. 2000. *Linguistics: An Introduction*. Beijing: Foreign Language Teaching and Research Press.
Radford, A. 2002. *Syntactic Theory and the Structure of English: A Minimalist Approach*. 北京: 北京大学出版社.
Robins, R. H. 2000. *General Linguistics*. 北京: 外语教学与研究出版社.
Saeed, J. I. 2000. *Semantics*. Beijing: Foreign Language Teaching and Reseach Press.
Salkie, R. 1990. *The Chomsky Update: Linguistics and Politics*. Unwin Hyman Ltd.
Selinker, L. 1972. "Interlanguage". *Interlanguage Review of Applied Linguistics* (10): 209-231.
Smith, N. 2008. *Chomsky: Ideas and Ideals* (Second Edition). 北京: 中国人民大学出版社.
Sperber, D. & D. Wilson. 1986/1995. *Relevance: Cognition and Communication*. Oxford: Basil Blackwell.
Stockwell, R. 2001. *English Words: History and Structure*. Cambridge: Cambridge University Press.
Swain, M. 1985. "Communicative Competence: Some Roles of Comprehensible Input and Comprehensible Output in Its Development", in Gass and Madden (eds.) 1985: 249. *Input in Second Language Acquisition*. Rowley, Mass.: Newbury House.
Swain, M. 1995. "Three Functions of Output in Second Language Learning", In G. Cook & B. Seidlhofer (eds.), *Principles and Practice in Applied Linguistics*.

Oxford: Oxford University Press.

Thomas, J. 1995. *Meaning in Interaction: An Introduction to Pragmatics*. London: Longman.

Verschueren, J. 1999. *Understanding Pragmatics*. London: Arnold.

White, L. 1996. "Universal Grammar and Second Language Acquisition: Current Trend and New Directions", William C. Ritchie and Tejk. Bhatia, *Handbook of Second Language Acquisition*. Academic Press Inc.: 85–119.

Willis, J. 1996. *A Framework for Task-based Learning*. Harlow: Longman.

Yule, G. 2000. *Pragmatics*. 上海：上海外语教育出版社.

常（Chang）辉, 马（Ma）炳军. 2006. 中国学生对-s 和 is 的习得研究. 现代外语（3）.

戴（Dai）炜栋, 何（He）兆熊. 2002. *A New Concise Course on Linguistics for Students of English*. 上海：上海外语教育出版社.

丁（Ding）言荣. 2004. 第二语言习得研究与外语学习. 上海：上海外语教育出版社.

何（He）自然. 1997. *Pragmatics and English Learning*. Shanghai: Shanghai Foreign Language Education Press.

何（He）兆熊. 2000. 新编语用学概要, 上海外语教育出版社.

何（He）兆熊, 梅（Mei）德明. 1998. 现代语言学. 北京：外语教学与研究出版社.

胡（Hu）壮麟. 2001. *Linguistics, A Course Book*. Second Edition. 北京：北京大学出版社.

刘（Liu）红艳. 2005. 《语言与人脑》述评. 当代语言学（1）: 74–79.

石（Shi）定栩. 2002. 乔姆斯基的形式句法——历史进程与最新理论. 北京：北京语言大学出版社.

温（Wen）宾利. 2002. 当代句法学导论. 北京：外语教学与研究出版社.

杨（Yang）彩梅, 宁（Ning）春岩. 2002. 人类语言的生物遗传属性. 现代外语（1）: 103–110.

Glossary and Index

A

acceptable 12 可接受的（句子）
acoustic phonetics 17 声学语音学
acquisition 145, 155 习得
acquisition-learning hypothesis 155 习得——学习假设
acronym 62, 64 词首字母缩略词
adjective 69 形容词
adjunct 111 附加语
adjunction 90 附加（操作）
affix 52, 64 词缀
affective filter hypothesis 155 情感过滤假设
affricate 21 塞擦音
agent 111 施事
agglutinative language 49 粘着语
agrammatism 167 语法缺失症
allomorph 54, 64 语素变体
allophone 33, 45 音位变体
alphabetic abbreviation 62, 64 首字母缩写词
alveolar 20 齿龈音
alveolar ridge 17 齿龈
ambiguous, ambiguity 91 歧义的，歧义

antonym 102 反义词
antonymy 102 反义关系
aphasia 166, 183 失语症
approximant 37 近似音
aptitude 158 （语言）学能
arbitrary, arbitrariness 1, 3, 5, 64 任意的，任意性
argument 71, 110 论元
argument structure 109 论元结构
articulator 17 发音器官
articulatory phonetics 17 发音语音学
assimilation rule 38, 46 同化规则
aspect 73 体（范畴）
aspirated, aspiration 31, 32 送气的，送气
auditory phonetics 17 听觉语音学
auxiliary (Aux) 70 助动词

B

baby talk (BT) 141 宝贝儿语
back-formation 61, 64 逆构词法
base 53, 64, 73 词基
behaviorist 140 行为主义者
behavioral psychologist 4 行为主义心理学家
beneficiary 111 受益者

bilabial　20　双唇音
binary feature　36　二分特征
binding theory　143　约束理论
biolinguistics　8，177　生物语言学
blade　18　舌叶
blend　61　截搭式，紧缩法
borrowing　60，64　借用式
bound morpheme　51　粘着词素
bound root　53　粘着词根
broad transcription　32　宽式标音
Broca's aphasia　167，183　布洛卡失语症
Broca's area　167，185　布洛卡区

C

caretaker talk　141　保姆式语言，照看语
case　71　格
causer　111　使动者
cerebral cortex　164　大脑皮层
circumfix　52　外接缀
classroom setting　145　课堂环境
clause　71　小句
clipping　62，64　截短法
cliticization　87　附着法
coda　41　音节尾音，韵尾
coinage　60，64　创新词
collocationally-restricted synonym　102　搭配限制同义词
co-meronym　104　共同-部分义词
commissive　132　承诺类
common noun　70　普通名词
competence　2，9　语言能力
complete homonym　104　完全同音同形异义词
complement　71，76　补语，补足语，补足成分
complementary distribution　33，36，45　互补分布
complementary opposite　102　互补反义词
complementizers（C）　70，75，83　标句词
complex sentence　72　复合句
componential analysis（CA）　106　成分分析
compounding　58，64　复合构词法
comprehensible input hypothesis　155　可理解输入假设
comprehensible output hypothesis　157　可理解输出假设
consistency　7　一致性
consonant　6，20，22　辅音
consonant cluster rule　40　辅音连缀规则
constituent　69，72　（结构）成分
constraint　90　制约
content word　174　实义词
context　124　语境，上下文
contradiction　108　自相矛盾的说法
contrastive analysis（CA）　148，150　对比分析
contrastive analysis hypothesis　152　对比分析假设
conversion　61　类转构词法
conversational implicature　118，126　会话含义
cooperation（cooperative）principle　118，125　合作原则
coordinate structure　80　并列结构
corpus linguistics　12　语料库语言学
correctness　12　（句子）正确性
covert complementizer　89　隐性标句词
cultural transmission　3　文化传递性
creativity　3　创造性
critical period hypothesis　157　关键期

假设
c-select　110　C—选择，范畴选择

D

declarations　132　宣告类
deletion rule　46　省略规则
demonstrative　70　指示代词
(inter) dental　20　齿音
derivation　56, 64　派生
derivational affix　52, 64　派生词缀
derived word　52　派生词
Descartes　142　笛卡尔
designing feature　13　识别性特征
determiner (Det)　70　限定词，限定成分
developmental linguistics　8　发展语言学
diacritics　32　变音符号
dialectal synonym　101　方言同义词
diphthong　23　双元音
directives　132　指令类
direct speech act　133　直接言语行为
discrete infinity　3, 4, 180　离散的无穷性
discreteness　50　离散性
distinctive feature　45, 105　区别性特征
displacement　3　不受时空限制的特征
ditransitive verb　110　双及物动词
duality (of structure/patterning)　3　（结构）二重性

E

entail (ment)　5, 108　衍推，含义
epenthesis　40　增音
epiglottis　18　喉头盖，会厌

error　148　语误
error analysis　146, 151　语误分析
event-related brain potential (ERP)　166　事件相关脑电位实验
exhaustiveness　7　穷尽性
experiencer　111　感事，感受格
explicitness　7　明晰性
expressives　132　表情语，表达类
external argument　110　外论元
externalization　181　（语言）外化

F

feature　5, 36　特征
felicity condition　131　适宜条件，适应性条件
finite　4, 73　限定性的，定式的
finite clause　73　限定性小句，定式小句
first language acquisition (FLA)　139　母语习得
foreign language　145　外语（与第二语言相对）
fossilization　153　语言石化（现象），语言僵化（现象），语言固化（现象）
free morpheme　51　自由词素
free root　53　自由词根
frequency hypothesis　156　频率假设
fricatives　21　摩擦音
function word　174　虚词，功能词
functional categories　70　功能语类
functional magnetic resonance imaging (fMRI)　166　人脑功能磁共振

G

general linguistics　8　普通语言学
generate　11　生成

generative grammar　11　生成语法
glide　21　滑音
global aphasia　167　全应性失语症
glottal　20　声门音
glottis　26　声门
goal　111　目标
gradable opposite　102　等级反义词
grammaticality　94　合语法性
grammatical (or syntactic) category　69, 70　语法（或句法）范畴
grammatical competence　13　语法能力
grammatical function　61, 69　语法功能
grammatical properties　81　语法属性
grammatical relation　69　语法关系
great leap forward　181　（人类智能）大跃进
grey matter　164　（大脑）灰色物质

H

hard palate　17　硬腭
head　76　中心词
head movement　80, 90, 95　中心词移动
hissing sound　21　嘶音
homograph　104　异音同形异义词
homonym　104　同音同形异义词
homonymy　104　同音同形异义关系
homophone　104　同音异形异义词
hyponym　102　下义词
hyponymy　102　下义关系
hypothesis testing　142　假设检验
hypothesis-testing hypothesis　153　假设—检验假设

I

ill-formed　12　（句子）造得不好的
I-language　178　I–语言，内在化语言
illocutionary act　130　言外行为
illocutionary force　131　言外之力
indirect speech act　133　间接言语行为
infinitive　73　不定式
infinite　4　无限的
infix　52　中缀
inflectional affix　52, 64　曲折词缀
inflectional phrase (IP)　78, 83　曲折短语
initial state　180　（大脑）初始状态
innateness hypothesis　141　天赋说
input hypothesis　155　输入假设
instrument　111　工具（格）
interaction hypothesis　156　互动假设
"$i+1$" theory　155　"$i+1$"理论（克拉申的可理解输入假设）
interlanguage　146, 152　中介语
interlanguage hypothesis　152　中介语假设
internal argument　110　内论元
International Phonetic Alphabet (IPA)　19, 26, 32　国际音标
intonation　44, 46　语调
intralingual error　149　语内错误
intransitive verb　110　不及物动词
intuition　14　（语言）直觉

L

labiodentals　20　唇齿音
language acquisition　11　语言习得
language savant　174, 183　语言专家，

语言天才
language acquisition device（LAD）
141 语言习得机制
larynx 17 喉
lateral 21 边音
lateralization 164, 183 侧化，（尤指脑部的）偏侧优势
lax vowel 23, 26 松元音
learning 145, 155 （语言）学习（与"语言习得"相对应）
left hemisphere 165, 183 （大脑）左半球
length 26, 43, 46 音长
lexeme 63, 64 词位
lexical category 70 词汇性语类（与"功能性语类"对应）
lexical semantics 100, 113 词汇语义学
lexicon 49, 64, 95, 100 词库
linguistic politeness 118 语言礼貌
liquid 21 流音
location 112 位置（格）
locutionary act 130 言内行为
loudness 26 （声音的）响度

M

magnetic encephalography（MEG）166 脑磁（波）图
magnetic resonance imaging（MRI）166 磁共振成像
marked 102 标记性的
maximal onset principle 43 最大首音原则
maxim of manner 126 （合作原则中的）方式准则
maxim of quality 126 （合作原则中的）质量准则
maxim of quantity 126 （合作原则中的）数量准则
maxim of relation 126 （合作原则中的）相关准则
maxim of generosity 129 （礼貌原则中的）慷慨准则
maxim of tact 129 （礼貌原则中的）得体准则
maxim of approbation 129 （礼貌原则中的）赞誉准则
maxim of modesty 129 （礼貌原则中的）谦逊准则
maxim of agreement 129 （礼貌原则中的）一致准则
maxim of sympathy 129 （礼貌原则中的）同情准则
meaningfulness 94 有意义
mentalist view 141, 160 心智主义观
merge 4, 74, 81, 180, 183 合并
merging operation 3 合并操作
meronym 103 部分义词
meronymy 103 部分—整体关系
metalanguage 13 元语言
minimal pair 33, 35, 45 最小对
mistake 148 （语用）错误（与error相对应）
modal 70 情态动词
modular 183 模块的
monitor hypothesis 155 监察假设
mora 43 （构成音节的单位）莫拉
morpheme 10, 50, 64 词素，语素
morphology 10, 50, 63 形态学
morphs 54 语子
movement 86 移动（操作）
move α 90 移动α
motherese 141 妈妈语
motivation 90, 159 动机
multi-valued feature 36 多值特征
mutation 180 （基因）突变

N

narrow transcription 32 严式标音
nasal 21 鼻音
nasality 37 鼻音性
nasal tract 17 鼻腔
natural order hypothesis 154 自然顺序假设
natural settings (or naturalistic settings) 145 自然语境
nested square bracket 77 嵌套性的方括号
neurolinguistics 12, 163, 183 神经语言学
neurolinguist 8 神经语言学家
non-distinctive feature 45 非区别性特征
non-finite clause 73 非限定性小句
no-place predication 110 零论元（空位）述谓结构
NP movement 90 名词短语移动
Noam Chomsky 2, 7, 178 诺曼·乔姆斯基
number 71 （名词的）数
nominative case 71 主格
nucleus 41 （音节）核

O

object 71 宾语
objective case 71 宾格
one-place predicate 111 单论元（一位）述谓结构
onset 41 （音节）首音
oral sound 21 口腔音（与鼻音相对）
oral tract 17, 26 口腔
orthography 55 正确拼字，正字法，正字学

P

palatal 20 腭音
paragrammatism 171 语法错乱症
parameter 142 参数
paraphasias 170 乱语症
passivization 90 被动化
patient 111 受事（格）
performance 9 语言行为
perlocutionary act 130 言后行为
person 71 人称
pharynx 17, 26 咽
phone 33, 45 音素
phoneme 33, 45 音位
phonemic contrast 33, 45 音位对照
phonemic representation 46 音位表征
phonetic representation 46 语音表征
Phonetics 10, 16, 31 语音学
phonetician 30 语音学家
phonological process 31 音位过程
phonological rule 34, 46 音位规则
phonology 10, 31, 45 音位学
phrasal category 70 短语语类
phrase structure rule (tree) 64, 75 短语结构规则（树）
pitch 26, 44 音高
plasticity 166 可塑性
Plato's problem 142 柏拉图问题
politeness principle (PP) 128 礼貌原则
polysemy 104 多义性，一词多义
positron emission tomography (PET) 166 计算机辅助正电子发射断层扫描技术
possessor 111 拥有者
poverty of the stimulus 4, 142, 143

刺激贫乏（假设）
pragmatics　11, 99, 113, 118　语用学
predicate　71, 110　谓词
predication　109　谓项，述谓结构
predication analysis　109　述谓分析
prefix　52　前缀
preposition　71　介词
presuppose　108　预设
primary stress　44　基础重音
Principle of Compositionality　109　语意合成性原理
principle of UG　142　普遍语法原则
productivity　3　（语言）能产性
projection　81　投射
projection principle　109　投射原则
proper noun　70　专有名词
proposition　110　命题
psycholinguists　8　心理语言学

R

recipient　111　接受者
recursion（recursiveness）　3, 82　递归
recursive（generative）procedure　4, 180　递归（生成）程序
reduced word　62　缩略词
reference　100, 113　（语义）指称
referent　100　所指
register　101　语域
relational opposite　102　关系反义词
representatives　132　阐述类
retroflex　21　卷舌音
rhyme（rime）　42　韵，韵基，韵核
right hemisphere　165, 183　（大脑）右半球
root　53, 64　词根

S

Saussure's arbitrariness　1　索绪尔任意性
schwa　26　中元音
second language　145　第二语言（与"外语"相对应）
second language acquisition（SLA）　139　二语习得
secondary stress　44　第二重音
segment　26, 45　音段，切分
segment deletion rule　40　音段省略规则
segment insertion　46　音段插入
selection restrictions　109　选择性限制
semantics　11, 99, 112, 118　语意学
semantic component　106　语意成分
semantic feature　105　语意特征
semantic features（componential）analysis　105　语意特征（成分）分析
semiotics　121　符号学
semivowel　21　半元音
sense　100, 113　意义
sense relation　101　意义关系
sensorymotor system　3, 180　感觉运动系统
sentence　68, 123　句子
sentence-meaning　123　句子意义
sequential rule　40, 46　序列规则
sibilant　37　咝音
sign language　2, 3　手势语
simple sentence　72　简单句
soft palate　17　软腭
source　111　来源（格）
Specific Language Impairment（SLI）　167, 171　特殊语言损伤
specifier　76　标志语，指定语

speech act   130   言语行为
speech act theory   118, 130   言语行为理论
speech sound   16   语音
s-select (ion)   85, 95, 111   S-选择，语义选择
stem   53, 64   词干
stop   21   塞音
stress   26, 44, 46   重音
structural ambiguity   91, 92   结构歧义
structure-dependency   143   结构依存（原则）
subcategorization restriction (or C-selection)   85, 95   次范畴化限制
suffix   53   后缀
superordinate   102   上义词，上坐标词
suprasegmental feature   26, 44, 46   超切分特征
syllable   26, 41, 46   音节
syllabic consonant   43   自成音节辅音
sylvian fissure   167   西尔维亚裂沟
synonym   101   同义词
synonymy   101   同义关系
syntax   1, 10, 68   句法
system of thought   180   思维系统

T

target language   145   目标语
tautology   108   同义反复
telegraphic speech   168   电报式言语，电文语言
tense   73   时态
tense vowel   23, 26   紧元音
theme   111   题元，主题
thematic role   111   题元角色
theta-criterion   113   θ-准则，西塔准则

three-place predicate   110   三位述谓结构
tone   43, 45   音调，声调
tone language   26   声调语言
topicalization   90   主题化
trace   87   语迹
Transfer (interference) error   148   迁移（干扰）错误
Transformational-Generative Grammar   12   转换-生成语法
transitive verb   110   及物动词
truth condition   108   真值条件
truth-conditional semantics   107   真值条件语义学
truth value   108   真理值
two-place predicate   110   双位述谓结构

U

unacceptable   12   （句子）不可接受的
unaspirated   32   不送气的
Universal Grammar (UG)   4, 6, 142   普遍语法
unmarked   102   无标记的
utterance   123   话语
utterance-meaning   123   话语意义
uvula   18   小舌

V

velar   20   软腭音
velum   17   软腭
V-movement   90   动词移动
vocal cord   17   声带
vocal tract   17, 26   声道
voiceless   17   轻音的

voiced 17 浊音的
voicing assimilation rule 39 浊音同化规则
vowel 6, 22 元音
vowel nasalization rule 38 元音鼻化规则

W

wanna contraction 88 wanna 式缩略（want to 的缩略形式）
well-formedness 12, 86 （句子）构造得好的, 合语法性
Wernicke's aphasia 167, 170, 183 威尼克失语症
Wernicke's area 170 威尼克区
Wh-movement 90, 95 Wh－移动
windpipe 17 气管
word 54, 64 词

X

X-bar theory 74, 76 X－标杆理论, X－杠理论